A-Z LEEDS

S0-AII-298

CONTENTS

REFERENCE

Motorway	**M1**
Under Construction	
A Road	**A62**
Under Construction	
Proposed	
B Road	**B6126**
Dual Carriageway	
One-way Street Traffic flow on A Roads is indicated by a heavy line on the driver's left.	➡
Large Scale Pages only	⇨
Restricted Access	
Pedestrianized Road	
Leeds City Centre Loop Junction Numbers are shown on Large Scale Pages only	①
Track / Footpath	
Residential Walkway	
Cycleway (selected)	🚲
Railway Station Level Crossing Heritage Sta. Tunnel	
Built-up Area	ALMA ST.
Local Authority Boundary	

Posttown Boundary	
Postcode Boundary within Posttown	
Map Continuation 31 Large Scale City Centre 4	
Car Park (selected)	P
Church or Chapel	†
Fire Station	■
Hospital	H
House Numbers (A & B Roads only)	13 8
Information Centre	🄸
National Grid Reference	4 30
Park & Ride	King Lane P+
Police Station	▲
Post Office	★

Toilet:
  without facilities for the Disabled
  with facilities for the Disabled
  for exclusive use by the Disabled
	▽
	▽
	▽

Educational Establishment	
Hospital or Hospice	
Industrial Building	
Leisure or Recreational Facility	
Place of Interest	
Public Building	
Shopping Centre or Market	
Other Selected Buildings	

SCALE

Map Pages 6-59 1:15,840	Map Pages 4-5 1:7,920
0 ¼ ½ Mile	0 ⅛ ¼ Mile
0 250 500 750 Metres	0 100 200 300 400 Metres
4 inches (10.16cm) to 1 mile 6.31cm to 1km	8 inches (20.32cm) to 1 mile 12.63cm to 1km

Copyright of Geographers' A-Z Map Company Limited

Fairfield Road, Borough Green, Sevenoaks, Kent TN15 8PP
Telephone: 01732 781000 (Enquiries & Trade Sales)
             01732 783422 (Retail Sales)
www.a-zmaps.co.uk
Copyright © Geographers' A-Z Map Co. Ltd.

Ordnance Survey This product includes mapping data licensed from Ordnance Survey® with the permission of the Controller of Her Majesty's Stationery Office.
© Crown Copyright 2006. All rights reserved. Licence number 100017302
Edition 3 2006

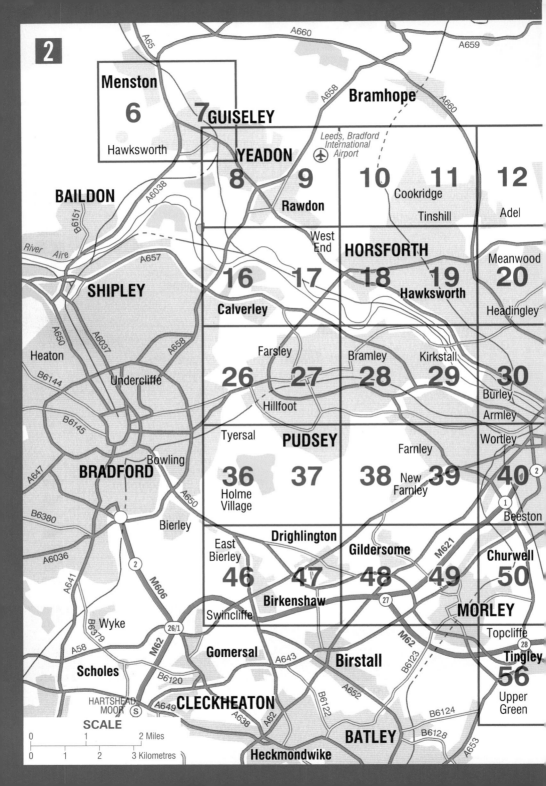

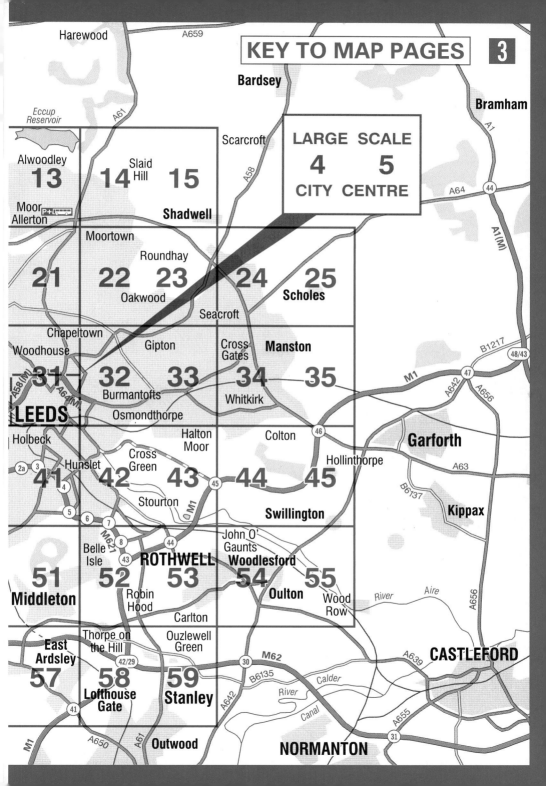

KEY TO MAP PAGES

3

Harewood
A659
Bardsey
Bramham

Eccup Reservoir
Scarcroft

LARGE SCALE
4   **5**
CITY CENTRE

A61
A1
A58
A64   44
A1(M)

Alwoodley
13
Slaid Hill
14   **15**
Moortown

Moor Allerton P+🚃

Shadwell

Roundhay
21   **22**   **23**   **24**   **25**
Oakwood   Scholes
Seacroft

Chapeltown
Woodhouse   Gipton   Cross Gates   Manston
B1217
48/43

31   **32**   **33**   **34**   **35**
Burmantofts   M1   47
A642   A656

LEEDS
Osmondthorpe   Whitkirk

Holbeck   Halton Moor   Colton   46   **Garforth**
2a   3
Hunslet   Cross Green   A63
41   **42**   **43**   45   **44**   **45**
4   Stourton   M1   Hollinthorpe   B6137   **Kippax**

5   6   7   Swillington
M621   8   John O' Gaunts
Belle   44   Woodlesford
Isle   43   **ROTHWELL**
51   **52**   **53**   **54**   **55**
Middleton   Robin Hood   Oulton   River   Aire   A656
Carlton   Wood Row

East Ardsley   Thorpe on the Hill   Ouzlewell Green   A639   **CASTLEFORD**
42/29   M62
57   **58**   **59**   30   B6135   Calder
Lofthouse Gate   **Stanley**   A642   River   A655
41   Canal   31

M1   A650   A61   Outwood   **NORMANTON**

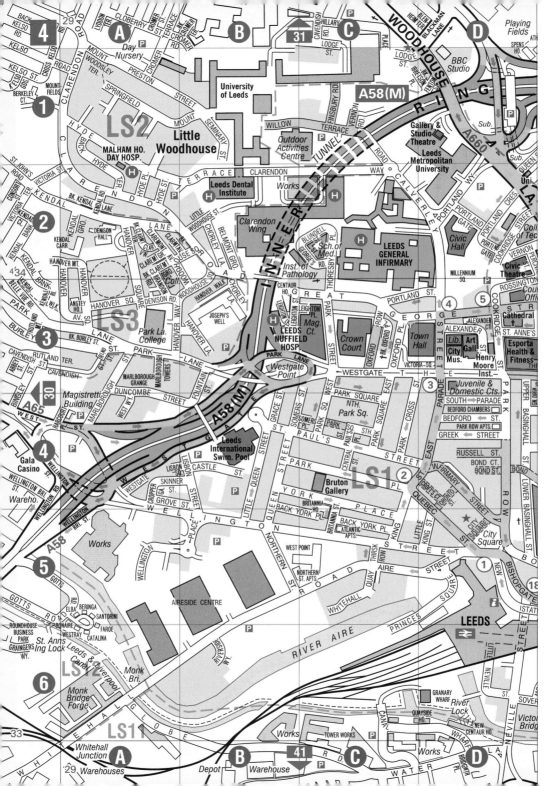

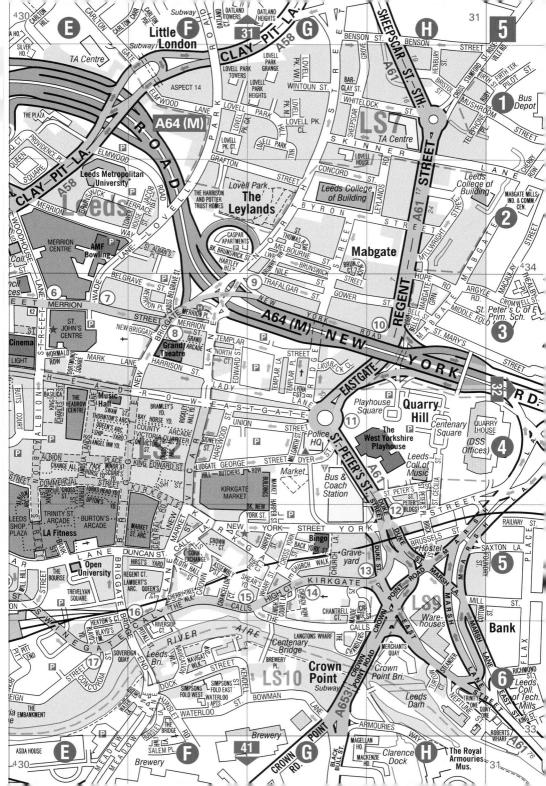

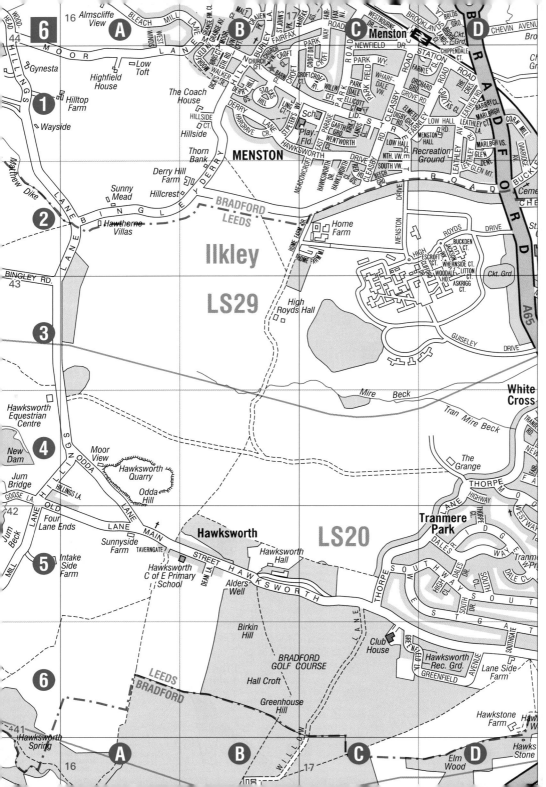

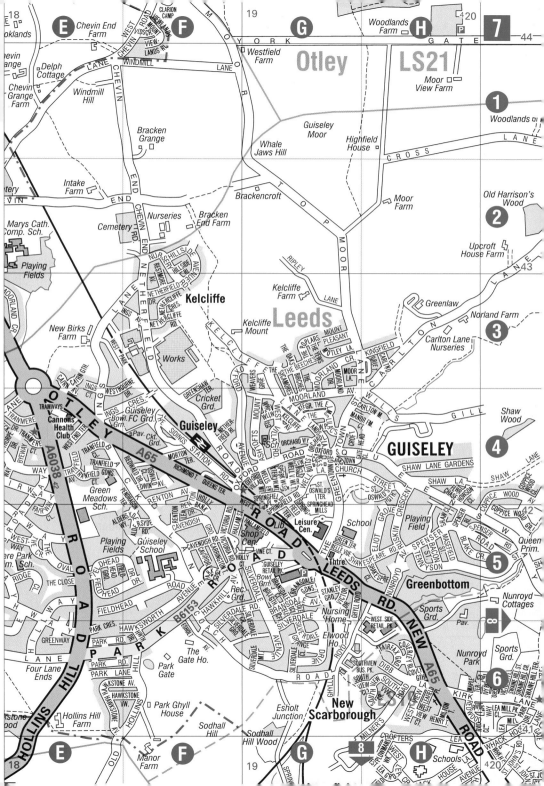

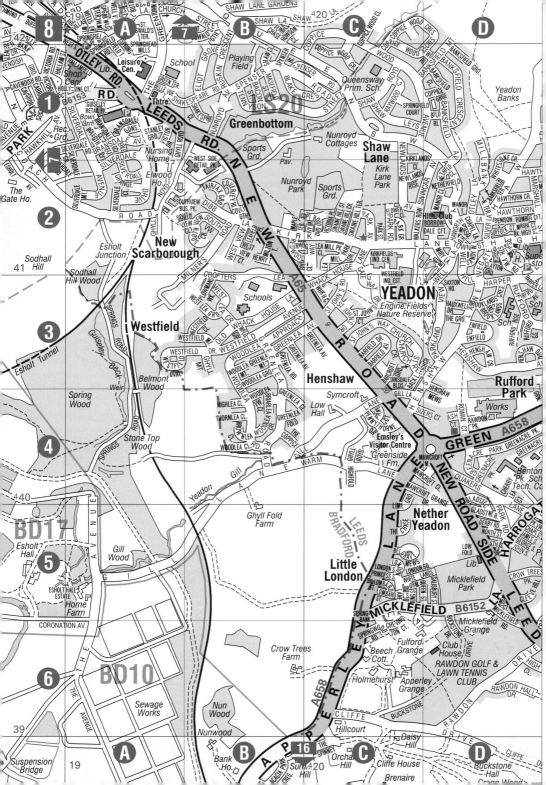

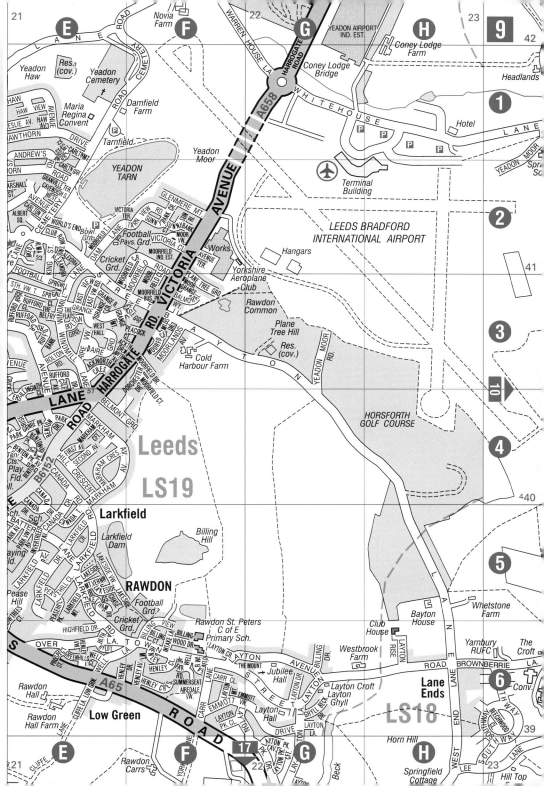

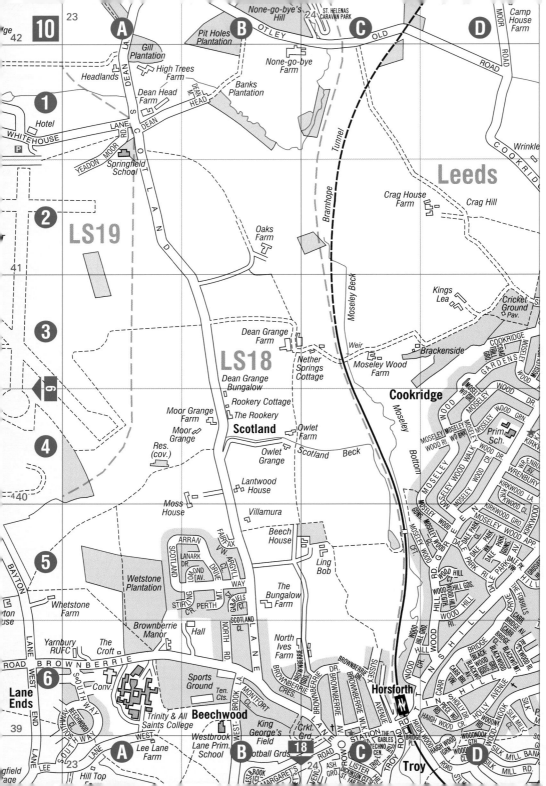

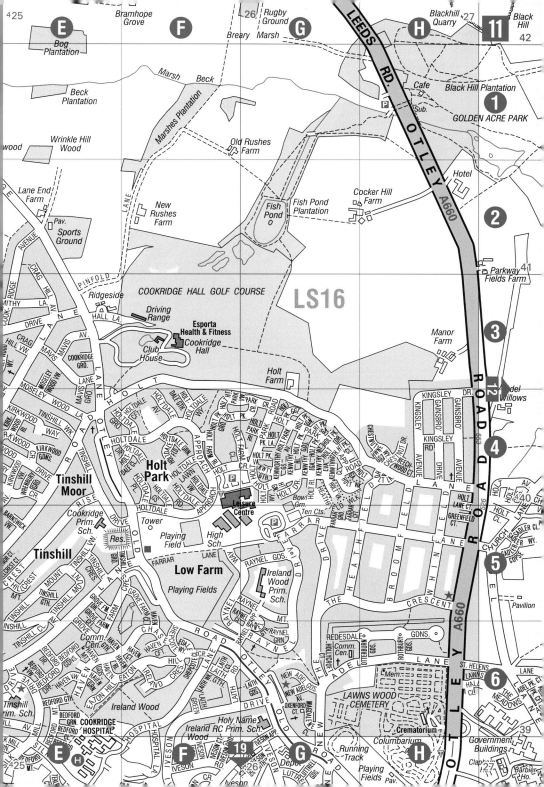

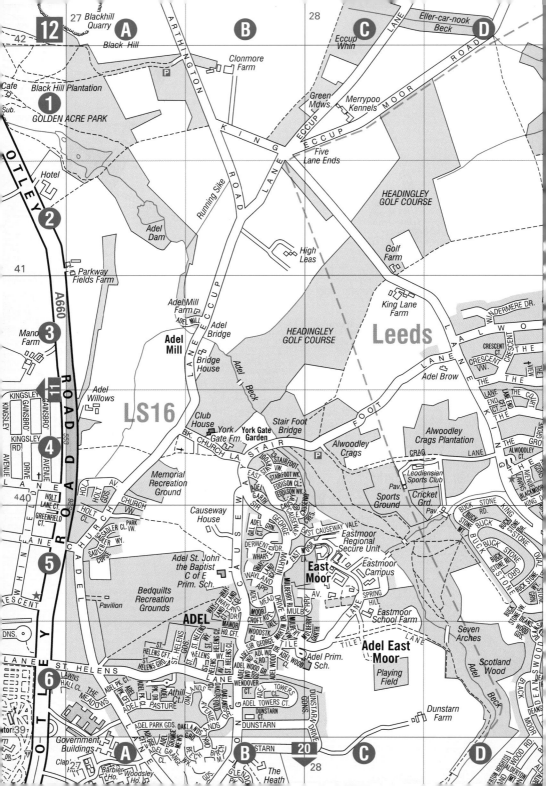

12 27 Blackhill Quarry

A · B · 28 · C · Eller-car-nook Beck · D

42

Black Hill

Eccup Whin

Clonmore Farm

Cafe

1 Black Hill Plantation

GOLDEN ACRE PARK

Sub.

Green Mdws.

Merrypoo Kennels

Five Lane Ends

Hotel

2

HEADINGLEY GOLF COURSE

41

Running Sike

Adel Dam

High Leas

Golf Farm

Parkway Fields Farm

Adel Mill Farm

King Lane Farm

Leeds

Mano Farm **3**

Adel Bridge

Adel Mill

HEADINGLEY GOLF COURSE

Adel Brow

KINGSLEY

GAINSBRO'

11

Adel Willows

Bridge House

Adel Beck

LS16

Alwoodley Crags Plantation

KINGSLEY RD.

4

AVENUE

Club House

York Gate Fm.

York Gate Garden

Stair Foot Bridge

CRESCENT CT.

CRESCENT VW.

Alwoodley Crags

CRAG LANE

CRESCENT

THE VIEW

THE COURT

Leodiensian Sports Club

Memorial Recreation Ground

Stairfoot VW.

Stairfoot WK.

Eddison Cl.

Eddison Wk.

Pav.

Sports Ground

Cricket Grd.

THE GRO.

ALWOODLEY CT.

HOLT

HOLT GDS.

440

CHURCH VW.

Causeway House

EAST GDN.

GEORGE GRN.

EAST CAUSEWAY VALE

Pav.

BLACKMOOR

BUCK STONE RD.

BUCK STONE

HOLT LANE CT.

GREENFIELD CT.

PARK VW.

SADLER CL.

SADLER WY.

SADLER CORPSE

Adel St. John the Baptist C of E Prim. Sch.

DERWENT

WHARFE

WAYLAND

GILL

CAUSEWAY

MARTIN

GEORGE

MULBERRY RI.

Eastmoor Regional Secure Unit

East Moor

Eastmoor Campus

BUCK STONE OVAL

BUCK STONE GRO.

BUCK STONE

WOOD GDS.

5

Bedquilts Recreation Grounds

Pavilion

WAYLAND APP.

WAYLAND

Adel MEAD

CROFT

WOODSTK. CL.

MOOR

MARTIN DRIVE

MULBERRY RD.

GARTH

MULB.

AV.

SPRING HILL

Eastmoor School Farm

Seven Arches

DNS.

ADEL

MANOR HO. CFT.

ST. HELENS

SIR GEORGE

TILE

Adel Prim. Sch.

Adel East Moor

Scotland Wood

Adel Beck

6

ST. HELENS

LAWNS

HALL CL.

THE MEADOWS

ST. HELENS CFT.

ST. HELENS GDS.

ST. HELENS WY.

ST. HELENS GRO.

ADEL PK. CT.

ADEL PK. DR.

ADEL PK. CL.

WENDOVER CT.

ADEL WOOD CL.

ADEL TOWERS CT.

ADEL WO.

ADEL WOOD

DUNSTARN GDNS.

DUNSTARN DRIVE

Playing Field

Government Buildings

Athill Ct.

PASTURE

OAKLANDS

ADEL GRANGE

ADEL PARK GDS.

OAKLANDS GRO.

DUNSTARN CT.

DUNSTARN

Dunstarn Farm

Clap '27

Barbier Ho.

Woodsley Ho.

GLENDOR

The Heath

A · **B** · 28 · **20** · **C** · **D**

39

A 660 ROAD

OTLEY

ARTHINGTON

KING LANE

ECCUP LANE

ECCUP ROAD

MOOR ROAD

FOOT

KING LANE

THE LANE END

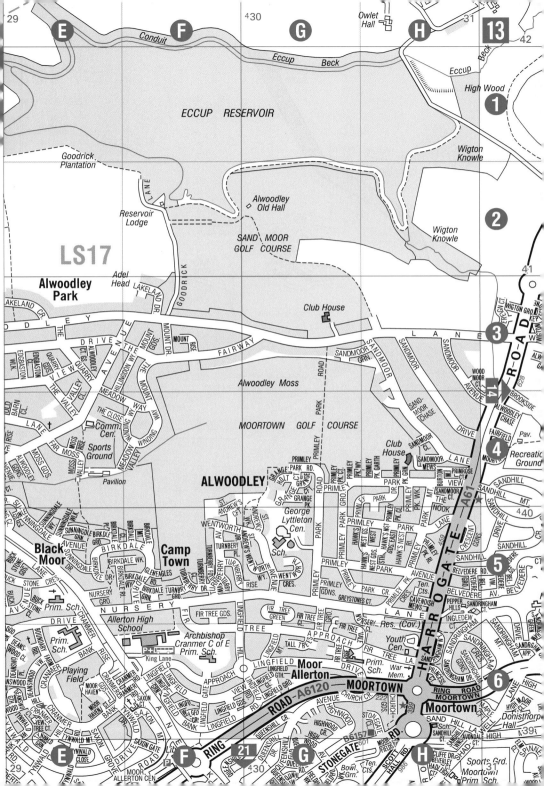

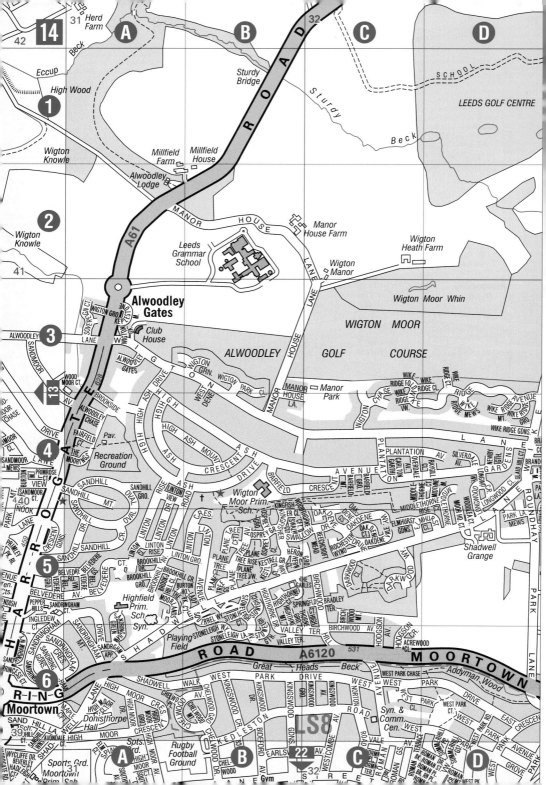

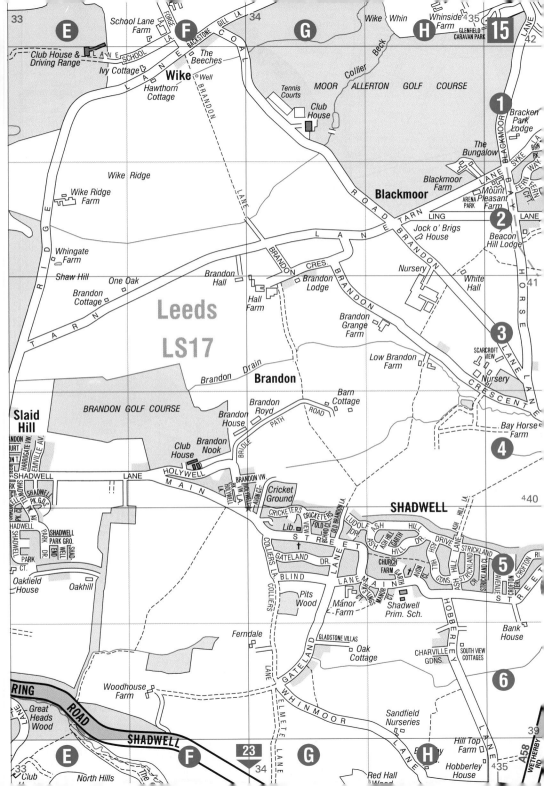

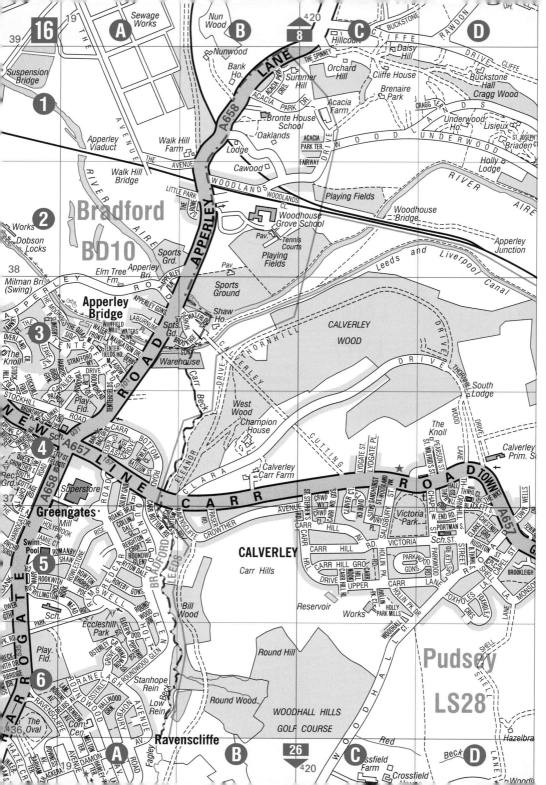

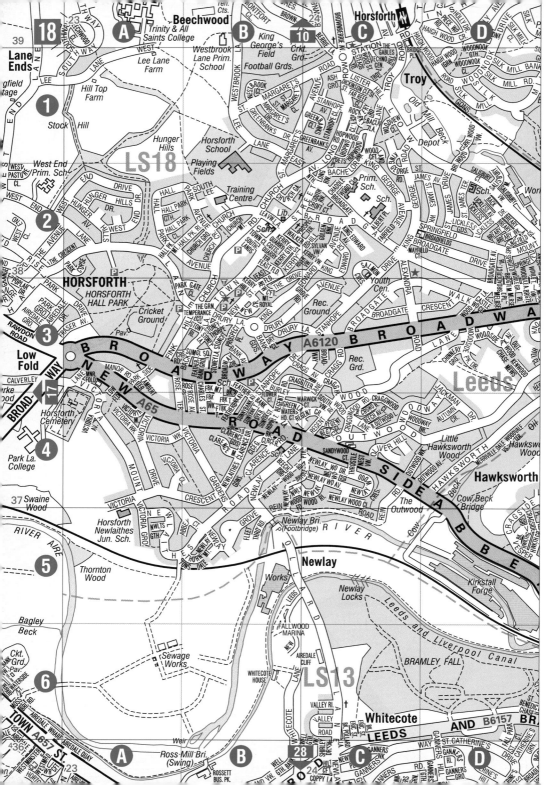

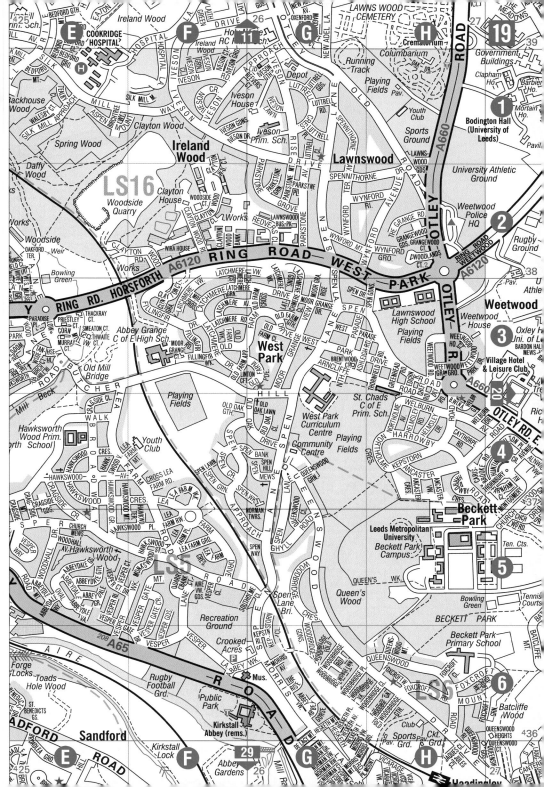

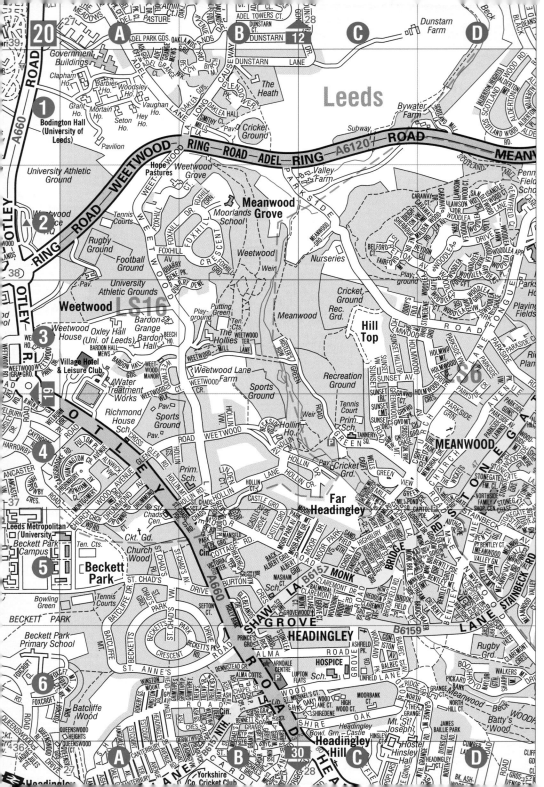

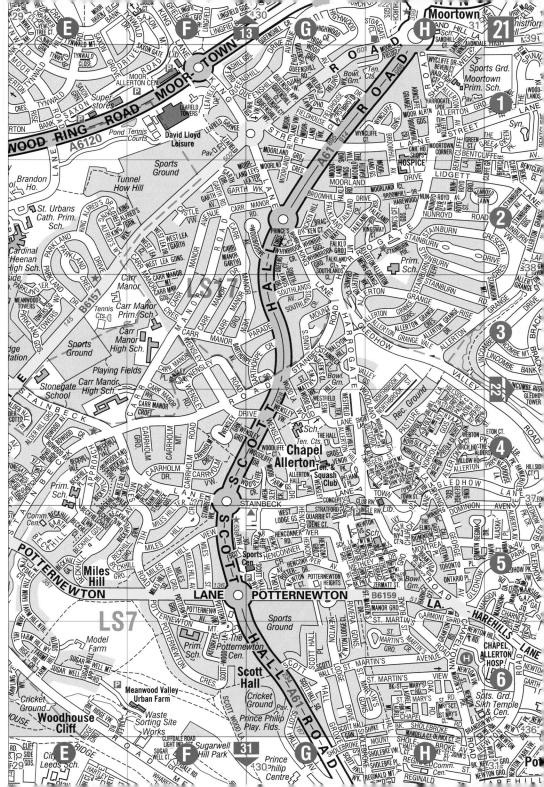

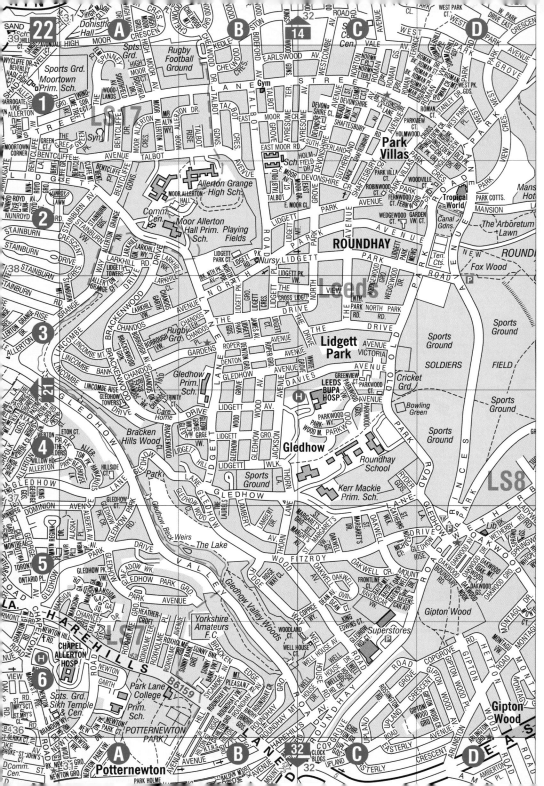

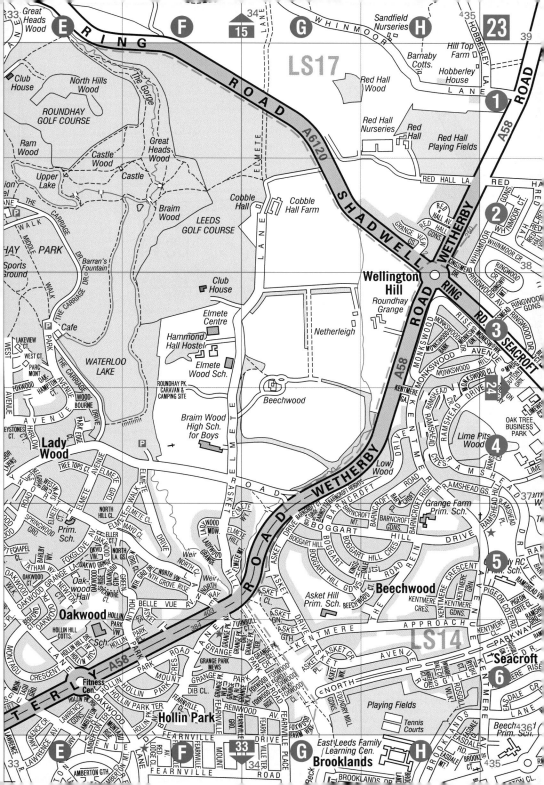

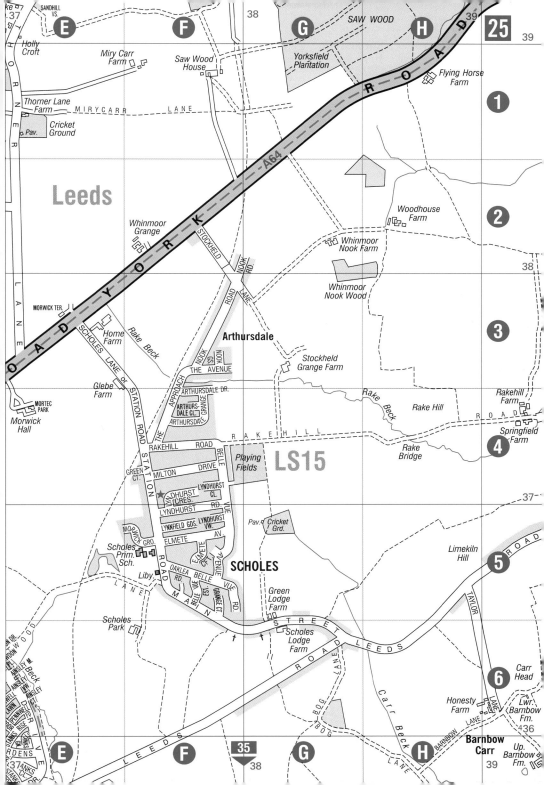

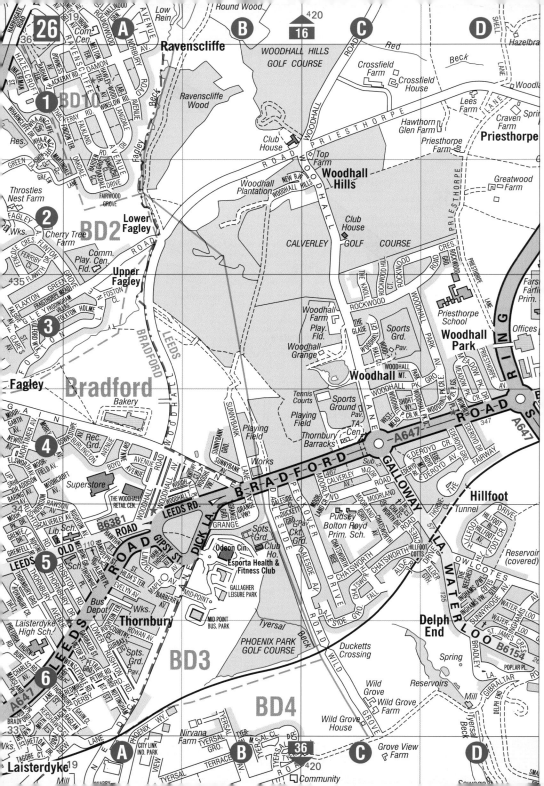

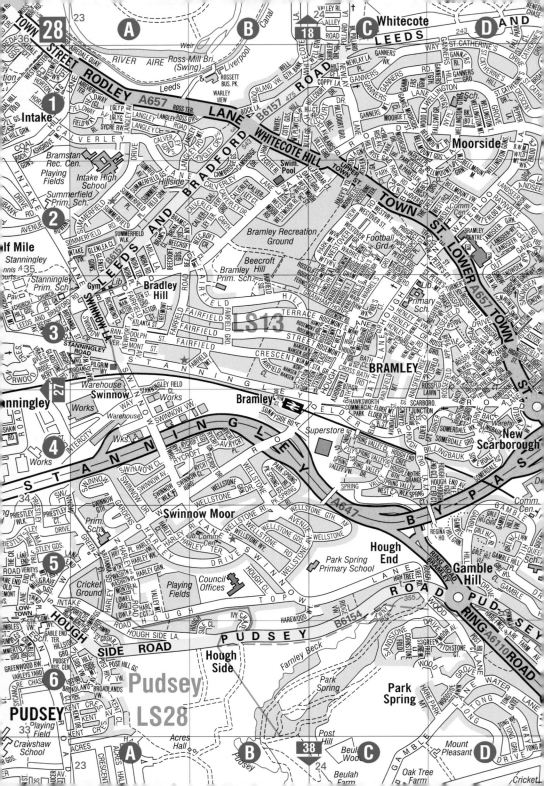

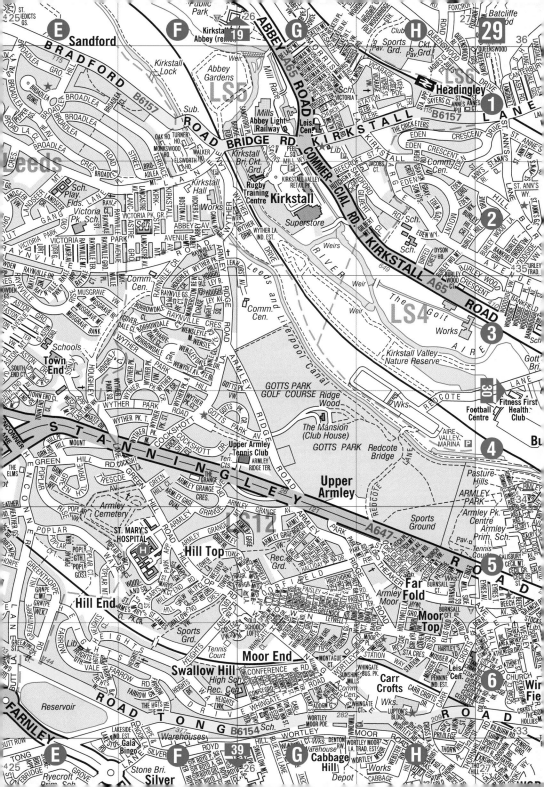

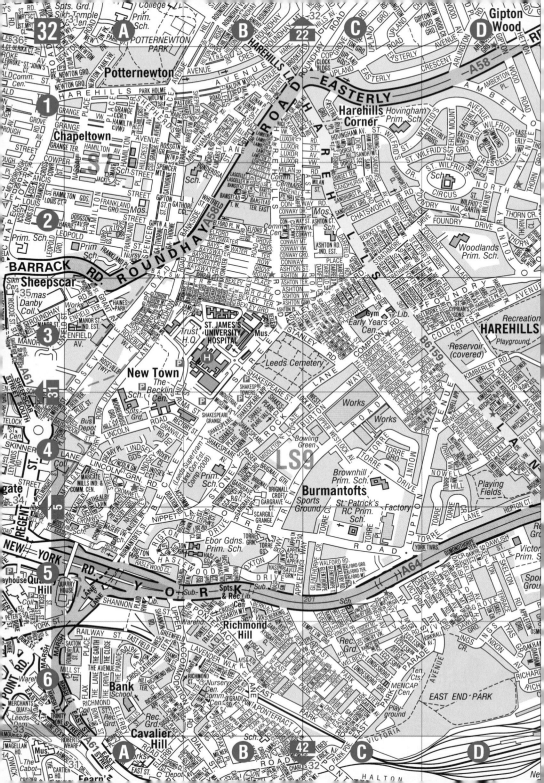

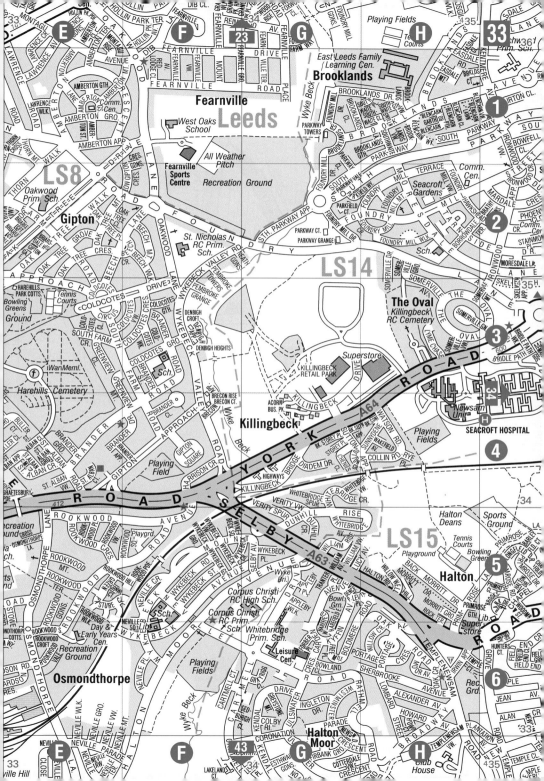

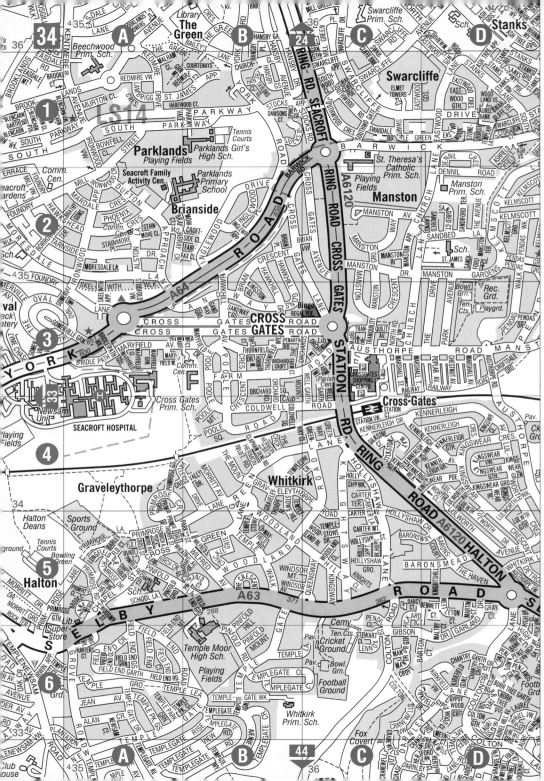

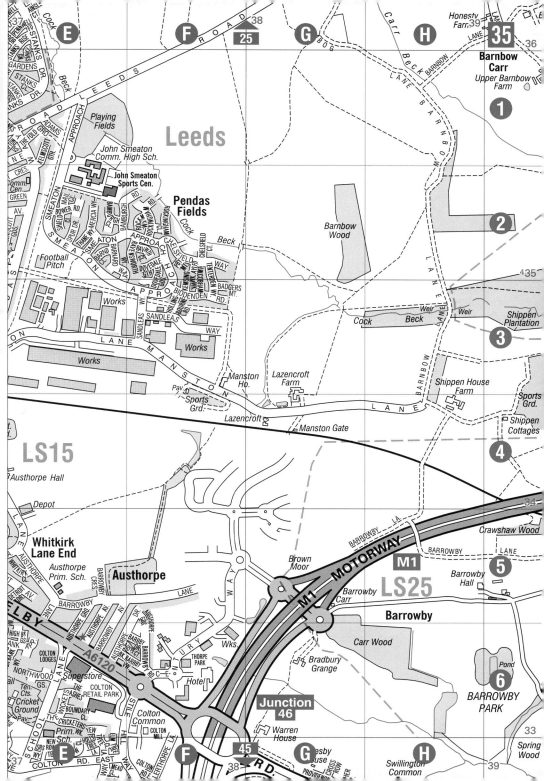

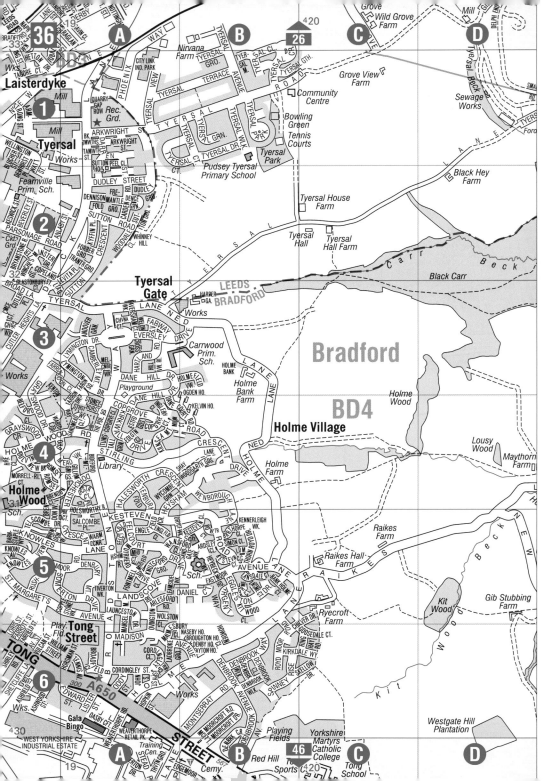

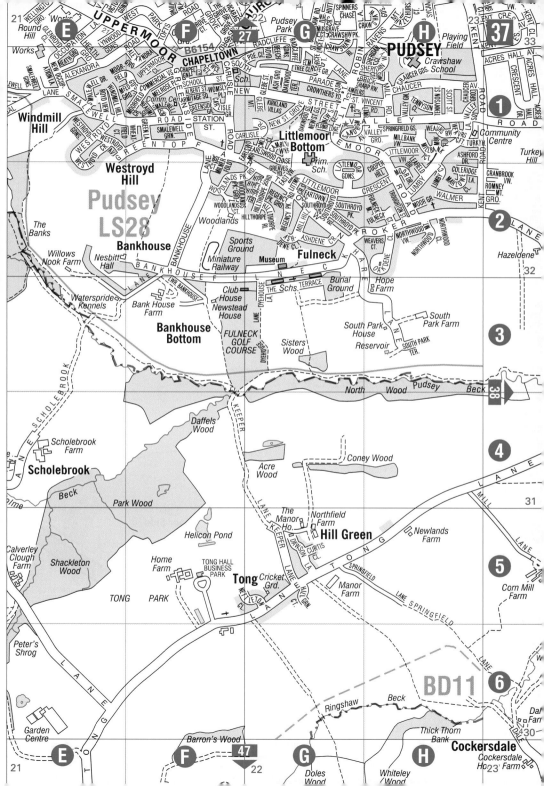

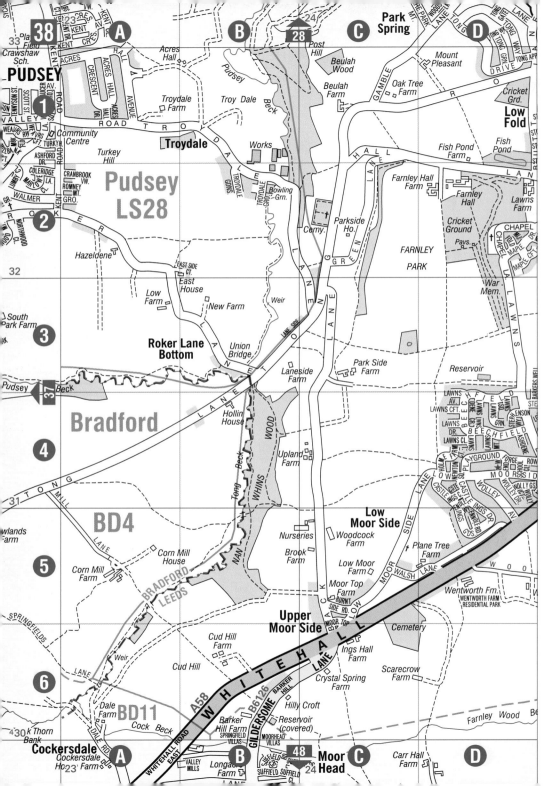

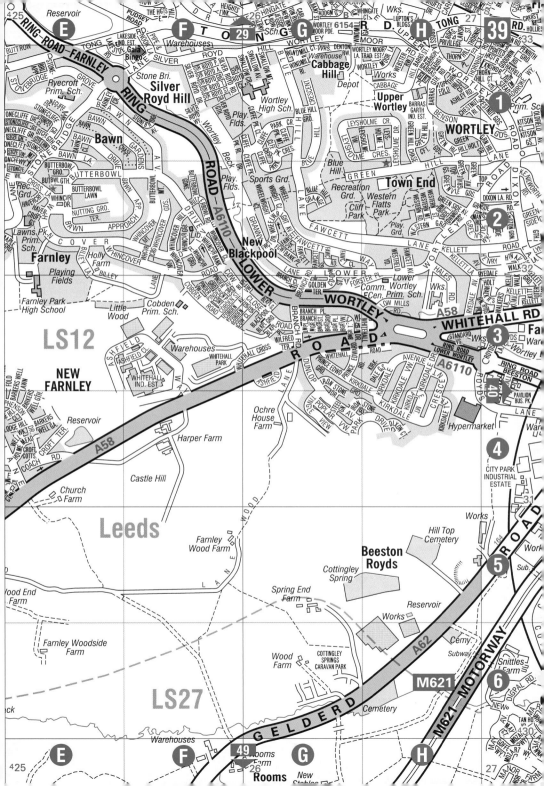

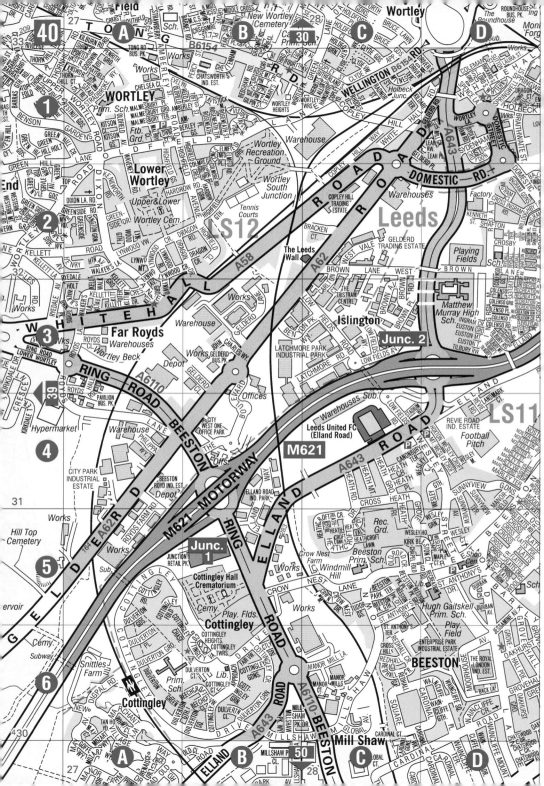

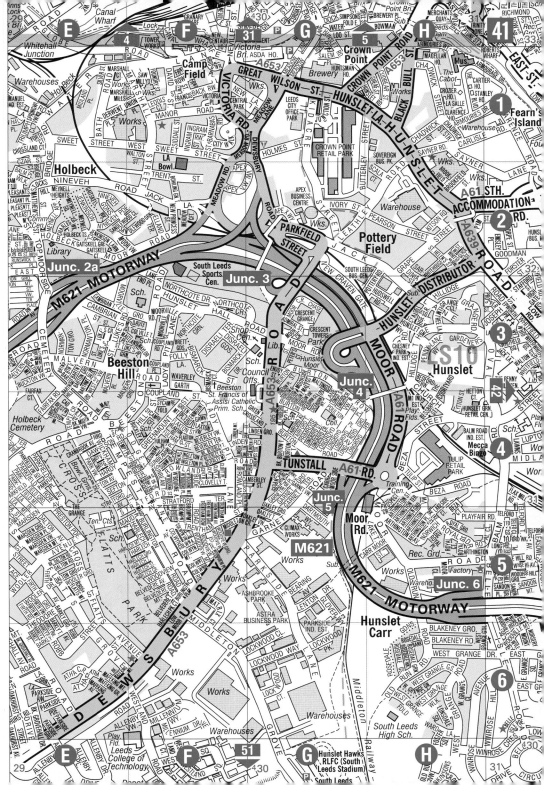

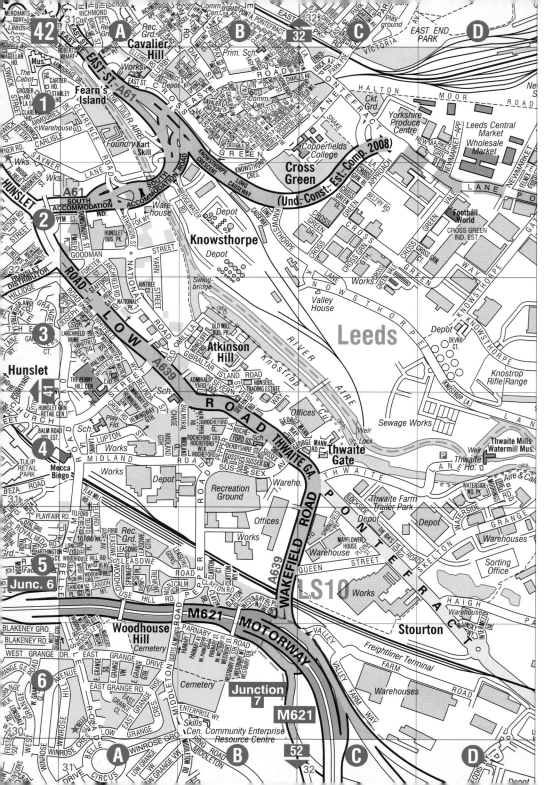

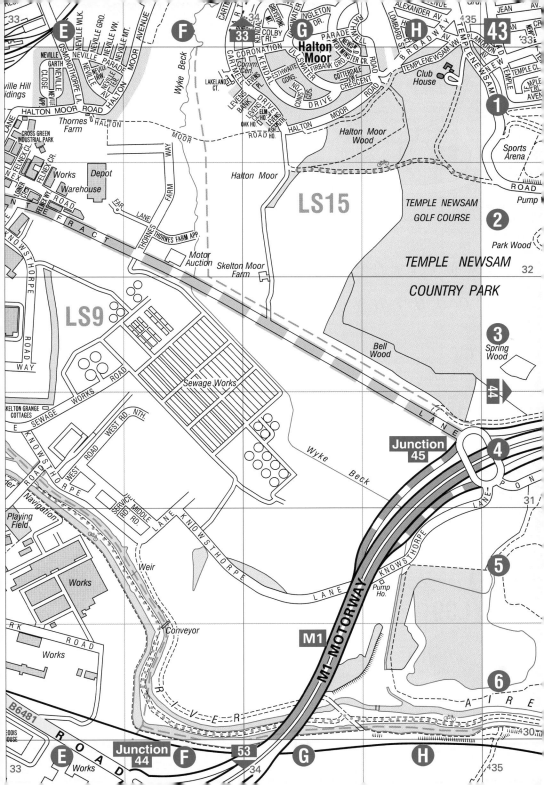

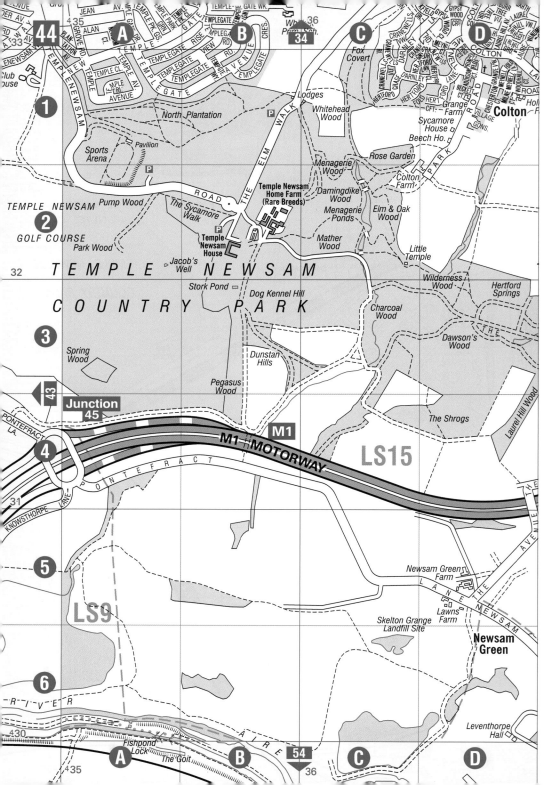

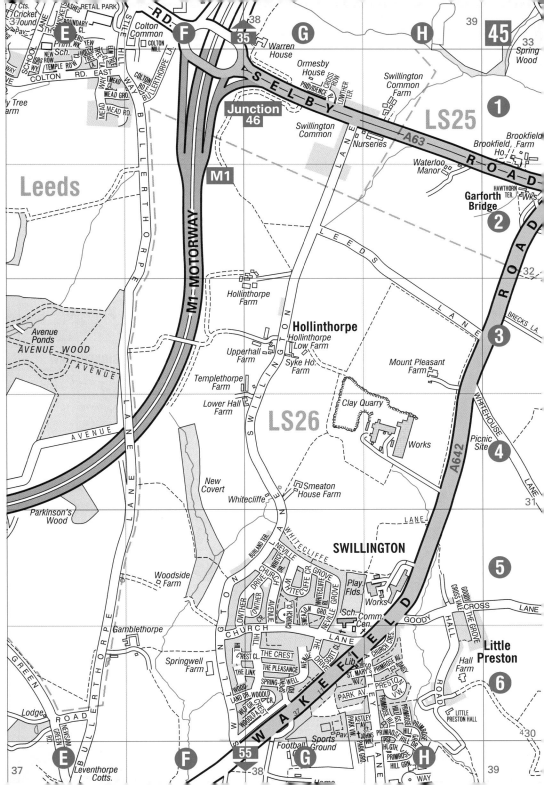

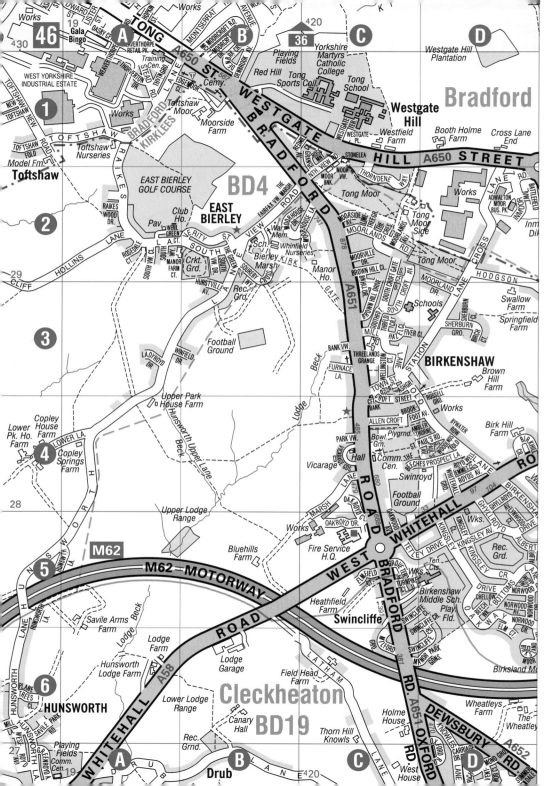

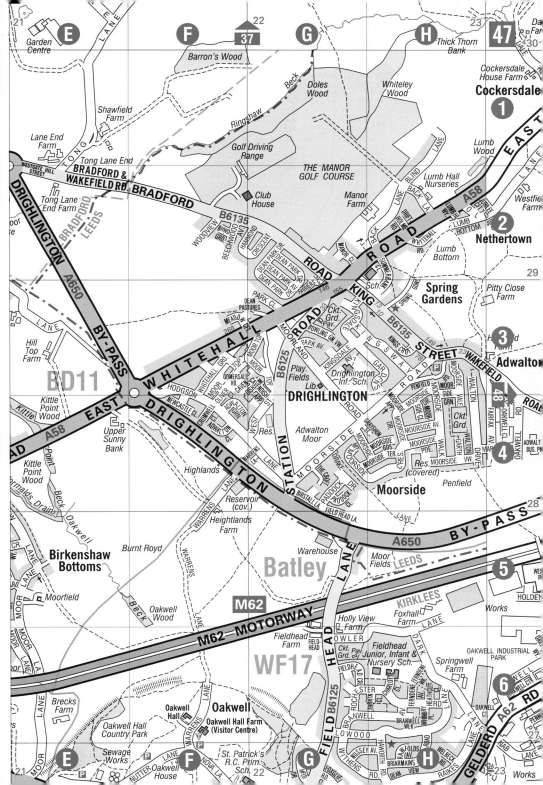

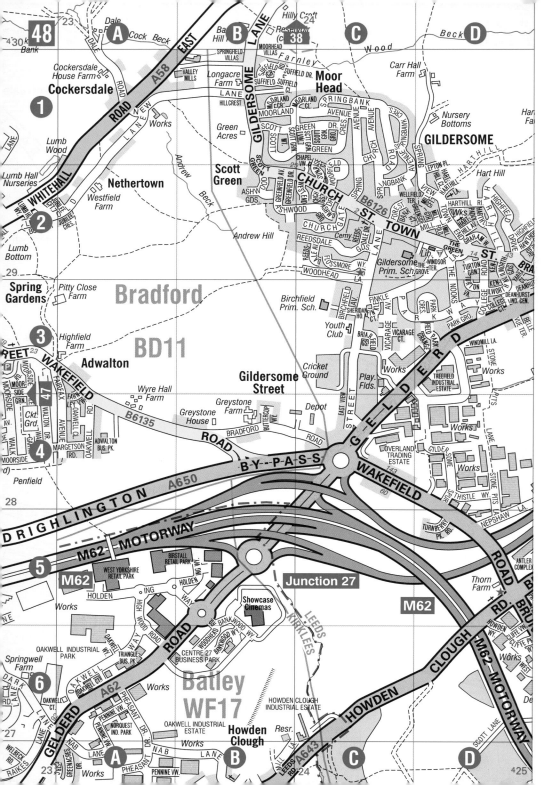

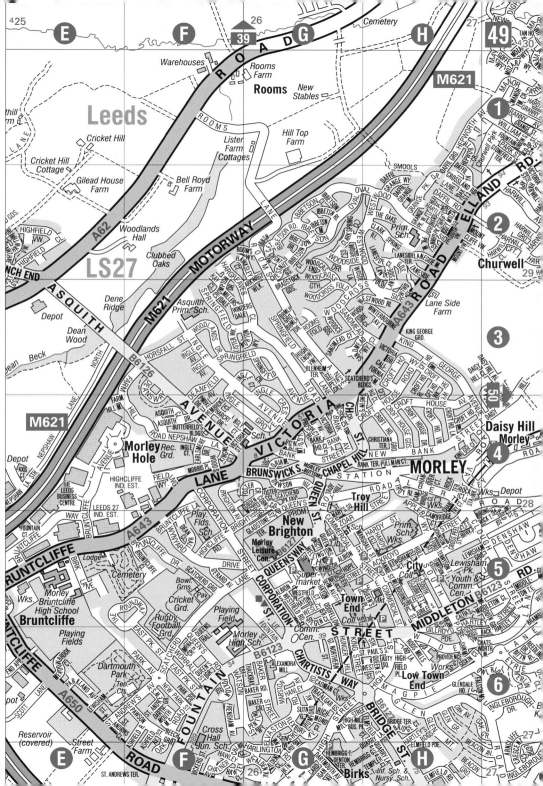

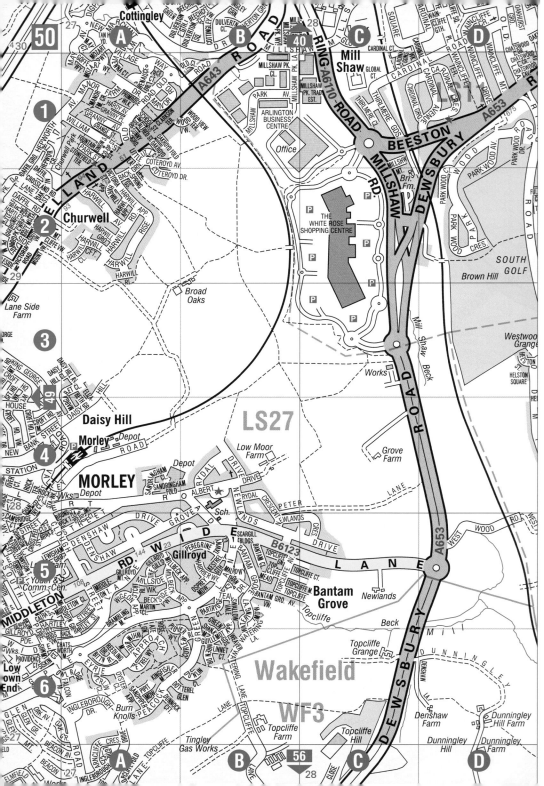

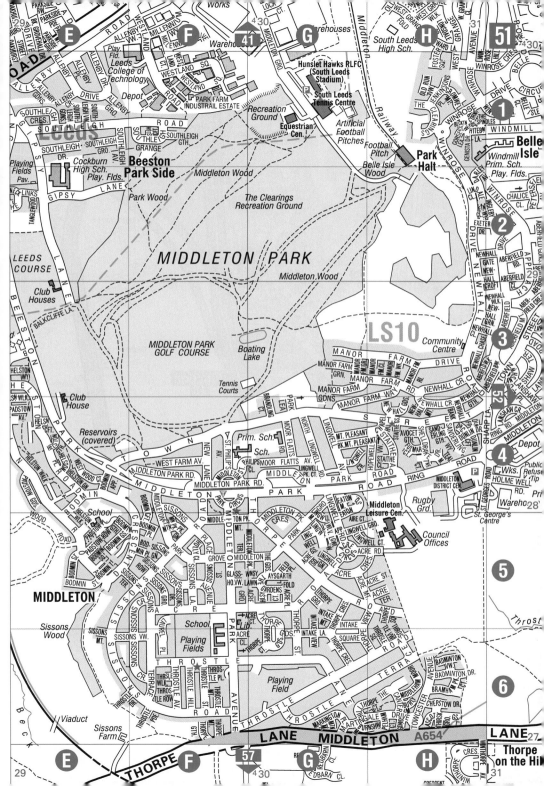

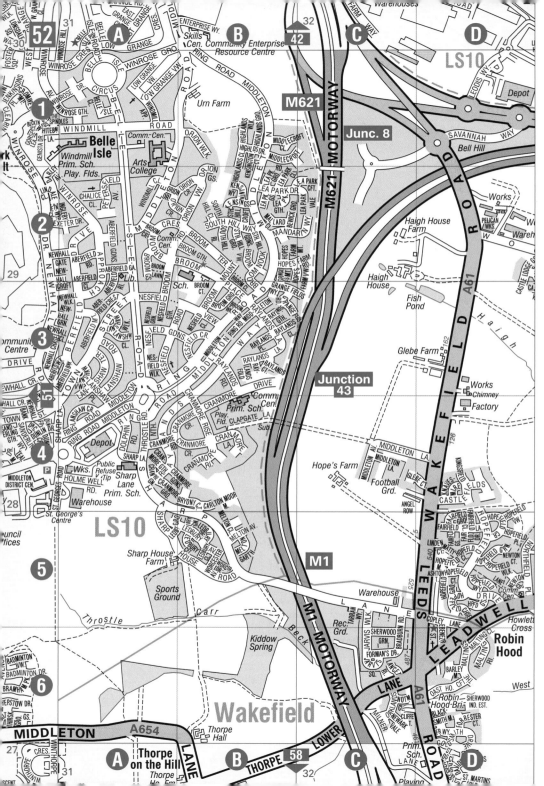

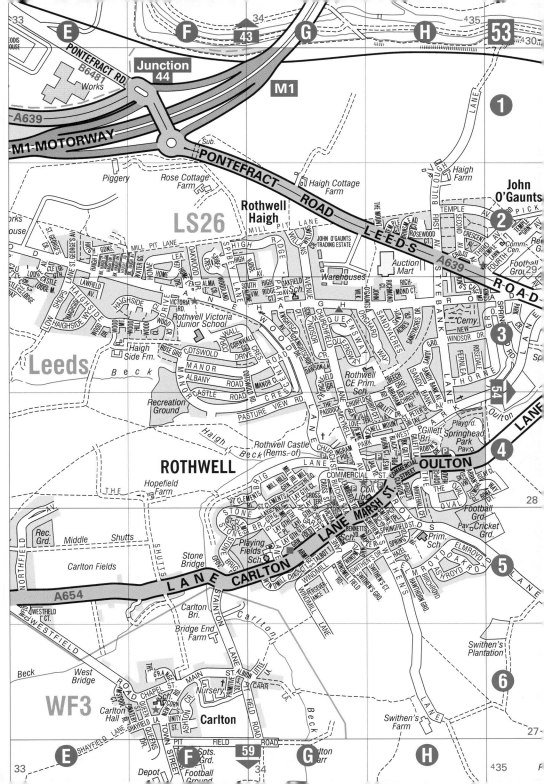

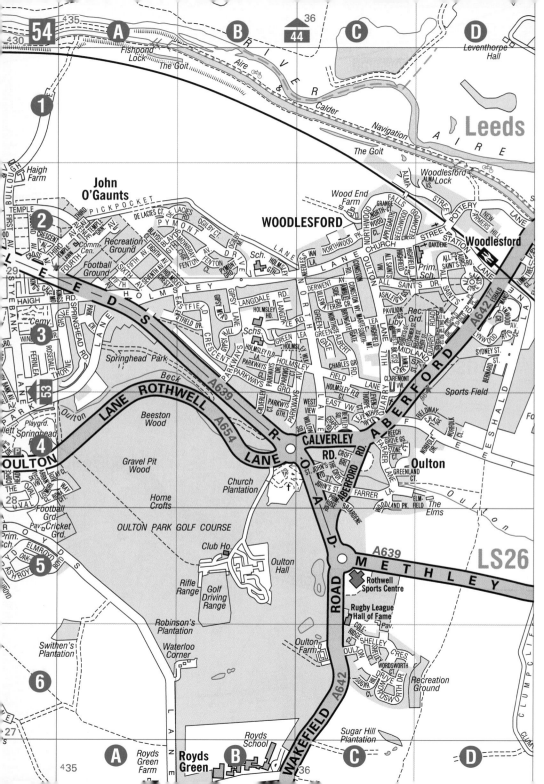

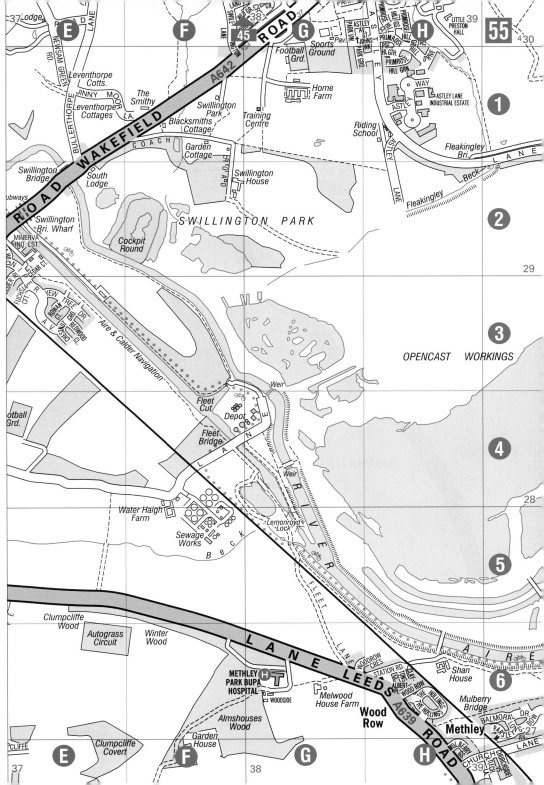

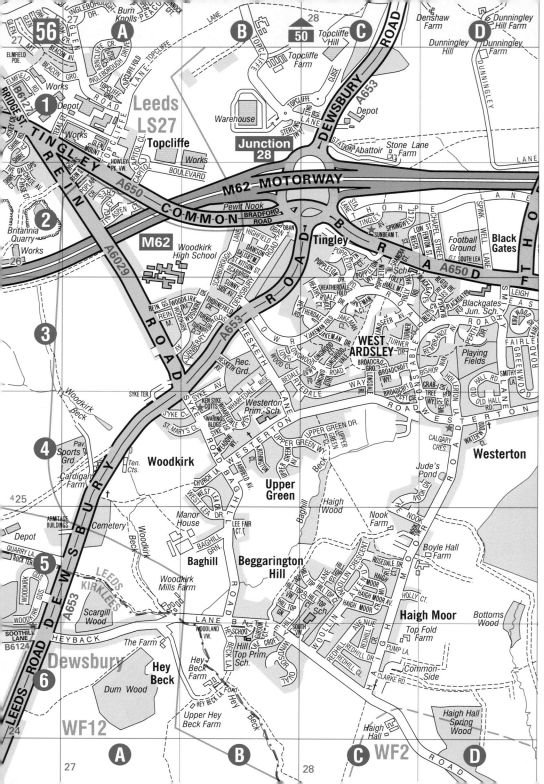

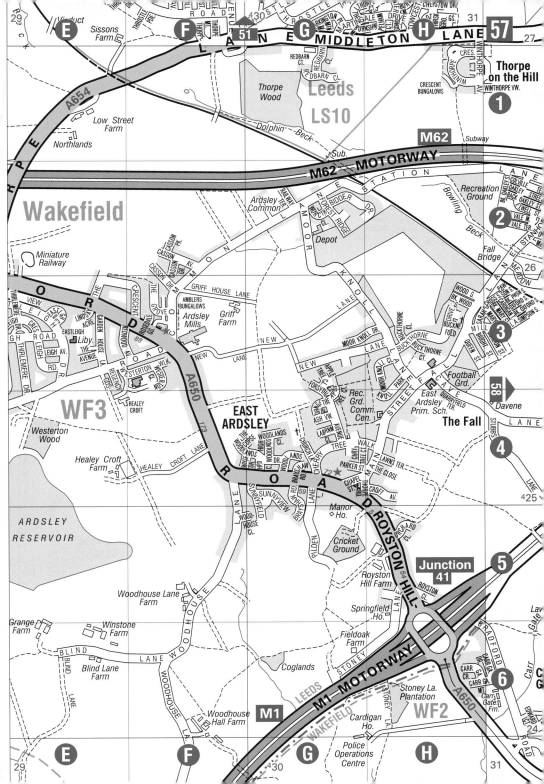

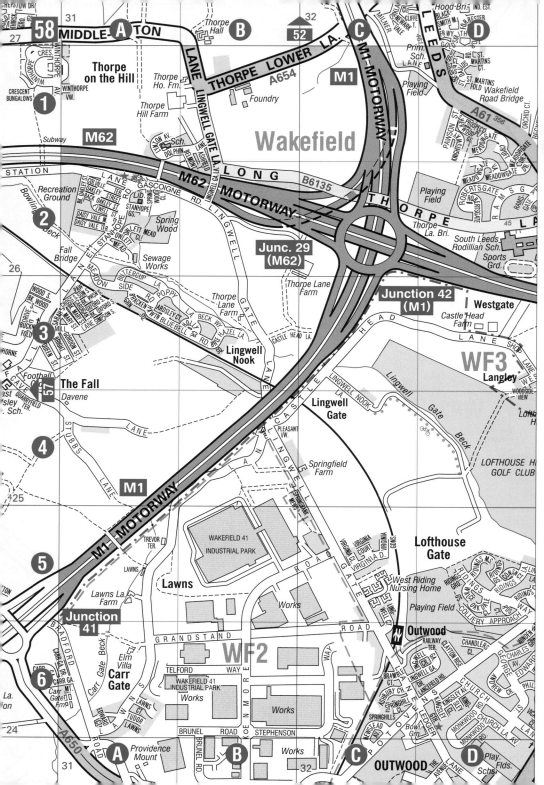

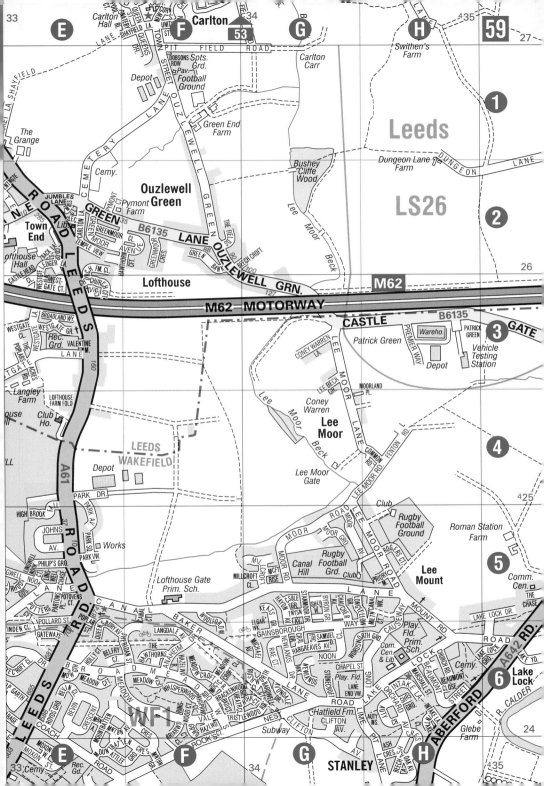

INDEX

Including Streets, Places & Areas, Hospitals & Hospices, Industrial Estates,
Selected Flats & Walkways, Stations and Selected Places of Interest.

HOW TO USE THIS INDEX

1. Each street name is followed by its Postcode District and then by its Locality abbreviation(s) and then by its map reference;
e.g. **Abbey Rd.** LS5: Leeds . . . .5D **18** is in the LS5 Postcode District and the Leeds Locality and is to be found in square 5D on page **18**.
The page number is shown in bold type.

2. A strict alphabetical order is followed in which Av., Rd., St., etc. (though abbreviated) are read in full and as part of the street name;
e.g. **Ashroyd** appears after **Ash Rd.** but before **Ash Ter.**

3. Streets and a selection of flats and walkways too small to be shown on the maps, appear in the index with the thoroughfare to which it is connected shown in
brackets; e.g. **Abbey Gth.** *LS19: Yead* . . . .3D **8** *(off Well Hill)*

4. Addresses that are in more than one part are referred to as not continuous.

5. Places and areas are shown in the index in BLUE TYPE and the map reference is to the actual map square in which the town centre or area is located and not
to the place name shown on the map; e.g. **ADEL** 6B **12**

6. An example of a selected place of interest is **Abbey House Mus.** 6G **19**

7. An example of a station is **Bramley Station (Rail)** . . . .4B **28**. Included are Rail **(Rail)** and Park & Ride **(Park & Ride)**

8. An example of a hospital or hospice is **CHAPEL ALLERTON HOSPITAL** 6H **21**

9. Map references for entries that appear on large scale pages **4-5** are shown first, with small scale map references shown in brackets;
e.g. **Abbey St.** LS3: Leeds . . . .3A **4** (5D **30**).

GENERAL ABBREVIATIONS

All. : Alley	**E.** : East	**Mus.** : Museum
App. : Approach	**Est.** : Estate	**Nth.** : North
Arc. : Arcade	**Fld.** : Field	**Pde.** : Parade
Av. : Avenue	**Flds.** : Fields	**Pk.** : Park
Bk. : Back	**Gdn.** : Garden	**Pas.** : Passage
Blvd. : Boulevard	**Gdns.** : Gardens	**Pl.** : Place
Bri. : Bridge	**Gth.** : Garth	**Prom.** : Promenade
Bldg. : Building	**Ga.** : Gate	**Res.** : Residential
Bldgs. : Buildings	**Gt.** : Great	**Ri.** : Rise
Bungs. : Bungalows	**Grn.** : Green	**Rd.** : Road
Bus. : Business	**Gro.** : Grove	**Shop.** : Shopping
Cvn. : Caravan	**Hgts.** : Heights	**Sth.** : South
C'way. : Causeway	**Ho.** : House	**Sq.** : Square
Cen. : Centre	**Ind.** : Industrial	**St.** : Street
Chu. : Church	**Info.** : Information	**Ter.** : Terrace
Circ. : Circle	**Junc.** : Junction	**Trad.** : Trading
Cir. : Circus	**La.** : Lane	**Up.** : Upper
Cl. : Close	**Lit.** : Little	**Va.** : Vale
Comn. : Common	**Lwr.** : Lower	**Vw.** : View
Cnr. : Corner	**Mnr.** : Manor	**Vs.** : Villas
Cotts. : Cottages	**Mans.** : Mansions	**Vis.** : Visitors
Ct. : Court	**Mkt.** : Market	**Wlk.** : Walk
Cres. : Crescent	**Mdw.** : Meadow	**W.** : West
Cft. : Croft	**M.** : Mews	**Yd.** : Yard
Dr. : Drive	**Mt.** : Mount	

LOCALITY ABBREVIATIONS

Bail : **Baildon**	Gar : **Garforth**	Pud : **Pudsey**
Bard : **Bardsey**	Guis : **Guiseley**	Rothw : **Rothwell**
Bar E : **Barwick in Elmet**	H'fth : **Horsforth**	S'cft : **Scarcroft**
Bat : **Batley**	Kip : **Kippax**	Scho : **Scholes**
B'frd : **Bradford**	Leeds : **Leeds**	Swil : **Swillington**
B'hpe : **Bramhope**	Men : **Menston**	T'ner : **Thorner**
Cleck : **Cleckheaton**	Mick : **Mickletown**	Wake : **Wakefield**
Dew : **Dewsbury**	Morl : **Morley**	Yead : **Yeadon**
E Ard : **East Ardsley**	Otley : **Otley**	

Acres Hall Dr.—Archery Ter.

Acres Hall Dr. LS28: Pud . . . 1A **38**
Acre Sq. LS10: Leeds . . . 5G **51**
Acres Rd. WF3: Wake . . . 3E **59**
Acre St. LS10: Leeds . . . 5H **51**
Acre Ter. LS10: Leeds . . . 5H **51**
Acrewood Cl. LS17: Leeds . . . 6C **14**
Adams Gro. LS15: Leeds . . . 1E **35**
Adams Gym . . . *2D 30*
(off Brudenell Av.)
Adam's Wlk. LS6: Leeds . . . 3D **30**
Ada's Pl. LS28: Pud . . . 3G **27**
Addingham Gdns. LS12: Leeds . . . 6G **29**
Addison Ct. LS15: Leeds . . . 1D **44**
ADEL . . . 6B **12**
ADEL EAST MOOR . . . 6C **12**
Adel Gth. LS16: Leeds . . . 4B **12**
Adel Grange Cl. LS16: Leeds . . . 1A **20**
Adel Grange Cft. LS16: Leeds . . . 1A **20**
Adel Grange M. LS16: Leeds . . . 1A **20**
(not continuous)
Adel Grn. LS16: Leeds . . . 5B **12**
Adel La. LS16: Leeds . . . 5A **12**
Adel Mead LS16: Leeds . . . 5B **12**
ADEL MILL . . . 3B **12**
Adel Mill LS16: Leeds . . . 3B **12**
Adel Pk. Cl. LS16: Leeds . . . 6A **12**
Adel Pk. Ct. LS16: Leeds . . . 6A **12**
Adel Pk. Cft. LS16: Leeds . . . 6A **12**
Adel Pk. Dr. LS16: Leeds . . . 6A **12**
Adel Pk. Gdns. LS16: Leeds . . . 6A **12**
Adel Pasture LS16: Leeds . . . 6A **12**
Adel Towers Cl. LS16: Leeds . . . 6B **12**
Adel Towers Ct. LS16: Leeds . . . 6B **12**
Adel Va. LS16: Leeds . . . 5B **12**
Adel Wood Cl. LS16: Leeds . . . 6B **12**
Adel Wood Dr. LS16: Leeds . . . 6B **12**
Adel Wood Gdns. LS16: Leeds . . . 6B **12**
Adel Wood Gro. LS16: Leeds . . . 6B **12**
Adel Wood Pl. LS16: Leeds . . . 6B **12**
Adel Wood Rd. LS16: Leeds . . . 6B **12**
Admiral St. LS11: Leeds . . . 3G **41**
Admirals Yd. LS10: Leeds . . . 3B **42**
ADWALTON . . . 3A **48**
Adwalton Bus. Pk. BD11: B'frd . . . 4A **48**
Adwalton Cl. BD11: B'frd . . . 4F **47**
Adwalton Grn. BD11: B'frd . . . 4F **47**
Adwalton Moor Bus. Pk. BD4: B'frd . . . 2D **46**
Adwick Pl. LS4: Leeds . . . 3A **30**
Ainsley Ct. LS14: Leeds . . . 6E **25**
Ainsley M. LS15: Leeds . . . 6E **25**
Ainsley Vw. LS15: Leeds . . . 6E **25**
Aintree Ct. LS10: Leeds . . . 3A **42**
Airdale Ter. *LS13: Leeds* . . . *6H 17*
(off Airedale Cft.)
Aireborough Leisure Cen. . . . 5G **7**
Aire Ct. LS10: Leeds . . . 5G **51**
Airedale Cliff LS13: Leeds . . . 6C **18**
Airedale Ct. LS14: Leeds . . . 6H **23**
Airedale Cft. LS13: Leeds . . . 6H **17**
Airedale Dr. LS18: H'fth . . . 3H **17**
Airedale Gdns. LS13: Leeds . . . 1H **27**
Airedale Gro. LS18: H'fth . . . 3H **17**
LS26: Rothw . . . 3D **54**
Airedale Mt. LS13: Pud . . . 6G **17**
Airedale Quay LS13: Leeds . . . 1A **28**
Airedale Rd. LS26: Rothw . . . 3D **54**
Airedale Ter. LS26: Rothw . . . 3D **54**
LS27: Morl . . . *5H 49*
(off South Pde.)
Airedale Vw. *LS13: Leeds* . . . *6H 17*
(off Town St.)
LS19: Yead . . . 6F **9**
LS26: Rothw . . . 3D **54**
Airedale Wharf LS13: Leeds . . . 6H **17**
Aire Gro. LS19: Yead . . . 3E **9**
Aire Pl. LS3: Leeds . . . 4C **30**
Aireside Cen. LS1: Leeds . . . 5A **4** (6E **31**)
Aire St. LS1: Leeds . . . 5C **4** (6F **31**)
Aire Valley Marina
LS4: Leeds . . . 4H **29**
Aire Vw. LS19: Yead . . . 3E **9**
Aire Vw. Gdns. LS5: Leeds . . . 5F **19**
Aireview Ter. LS13: Leeds . . . 1A **28**
Airlie Av. LS8: Leeds . . . 1B **32**
Airlie Pl. LS8: Leeds . . . 1B **32**
Alan Cres. LS15: Leeds . . . 6A **34**
Alaska Pl. LS7: Leeds . . . 5A **22**
Albany Rd. LS26: Rothw . . . 3F **53**
Albany St. LS12: Leeds . . . 6G **29**
Albany Ter. LS12: Leeds . . . 6G **29**
Alberta Av. LS7: Leeds . . . 5A **22**
Albert Cres. BD11: B'frd . . . 5D **46**
Albert Dr. LS27: Morl . . . 4B **50**
Albert Gro. LS6: Leeds . . . 5B **20**
Albert Pl. BD3: B'frd . . . 5A **26**
LS18: H'fth . . . 2C **18**
LS26: Mick . . . 6H **55**
Albert Rd. LS26: Rothw . . . 3C **54**
LS27: Morl . . . 4H **49**
Albert Sq. LS19: Yead . . . 2E **9**
Albert St. LS28: Pud . . . 1F **37**
Albert Ter. *LS19: Yead* . . . *2E 9*
(off Rockfield Ter.)
Albert Way BD11: B'frd . . . 5D **46**
Albion Arc. LS1: Leeds . . . 4E **5**
Albion Av. LS12: Leeds . . . 6B **30**
Albion Pk. LS12: Leeds . . . 5C **30**
Albion Pl. LS1: Leeds . . . 4E **5** (5G **31**)
LS20: Guis . . . 4G **7**
Albion Rd. LS28: Pud . . . 3G **27**
Albion St. LS1: Leeds . . . 4E **5** (5G **31**)
(not continuous)
LS2: Leeds . . . 4E **5** (5G **31**)
LS27: Morl . . . 5G **49**
(not continuous)
WF3: Rothw . . . 6F **53**
Albion Way LS12: Leeds . . . 5C **30**
Alcester Pl. LS8: Leeds . . . 1B **32**
Alcester Rd. LS8: Leeds . . . 1B **32**
Alcester Ter. LS8: Leeds . . . 1B **32**
Alden Av. LS27: Morl . . . 6G **49**
Alden Cl. LS27: Morl . . . 6G **49**
Alder Dr. LS28: Pud . . . 5C **26**
Alder Gth. LS28: Pud . . . 5D **26**
Alder Hill Av. LS6: Leeds . . . 4E **21**
Alder Hill Cotts. LS6: Leeds . . . 4D **20**
Alder Hill Gro. LS7: Leeds . . . 4E **21**
Alders, The LS7: Leeds . . . 4H **21**
Aldersgate *LS12: Leeds* . . . *6A 30*
(off Wesley Rd.)
Aldersyde Rd. LS20: Guis . . . 5F **7**
Aldersyde Way LS20: Guis . . . 5F **7**
Alderton Bank LS17: Leeds . . . 1D **20**
Alderton Cres. LS17: Leeds . . . 1D **20**
Alderton Hgts. LS17: Leeds . . . 1D **20**
Alderton Mt. LS17: Leeds . . . 1D **20**
Alderton Pl. LS17: Leeds . . . 1D **20**
Alderton Ri. LS17: Leeds . . . 1E **21**
Alexander Av. LS15: Leeds . . . 6H **33**
Alexander Ct. LS1: Leeds . . . 3D **4** (5F **31**)
Alexander St. LS1: Leeds . . . 3D **4** (5F **31**)
Alexandra Gro. LS6: Leeds . . . 3C **30**
LS28: Pud . . . 1F **37**
Alexandra Mill LS27: Morl . . . 6G **49**
Alexandra Rd. LS6: Leeds . . . 3C **30**
LS18: H'fth . . . 2C **18**
LS28: Pud . . . 1E **37**
Alexandra Ter. LS19: Yead . . . 2E **9**
(not continuous)
Alfred St. LS27: Morl . . . 1A **50**
Allenby Cres. LS11: Leeds . . . 1E **51**
Allenby Dr. LS11: Leeds . . . 1E **51**
Allenby Gdns. LS11: Leeds . . . 1E **51**
Allenby Gro. LS11: Leeds . . . 1E **51**
Allenby Pl. LS11: Leeds . . . 1E **51**
Allenby Rd. LS11: Leeds . . . 1E **51**
Allenby Vw. LS11: Leeds . . . 6F **41**
Allen Cft. BD11: B'frd . . . 4C **46**
Allerton Av. LS17: Leeds . . . 1H **21**
Allerton Ct. *LS17: Leeds* . . . *1H 21*
(off Harrogate Rd.)
Allerton Cft. *LS7: Leeds* . . . *6A 22*
(off Harehills La.)
Allerton Grange Av. LS17: Leeds . . . 2A **22**
Allerton Grange Cl. LS17: Leeds . . . 3G **21**
Allerton Grange Cres. LS17: Leeds . . . 3H **21**
Allerton Grange Cft. LS8: Leeds . . . 3A **22**
Allerton Grange Dr. LS17: Leeds . . . 3H **21**
Allerton Grange Gdns.
LS17: Leeds . . . 3H **21**
Allerton Grange Ri. LS17: Leeds . . . 3G **21**
Allerton Grange Va. LS17: Leeds . . . 3H **21**
Allerton Grange Wlk. LS17: Leeds . . . 3H **21**
Allerton Grange Way LS17: Leeds . . . 3H **21**
Allerton Gro. LS17: Leeds . . . 1H **21**
Allerton Hall LS7: Leeds . . . 4G **21**
Allerton Hill LS7: Leeds . . . 4G **21**
Allerton M. LS17: Leeds . . . 2H **21**
Allerton Pk. LS7: Leeds . . . 4H **21**
Allerton Pl. LS17: Leeds . . . 1H **21**
Allerton St. LS4: Leeds . . . 3B **30**
Allerton Ter. LS4: Leeds . . . 4B **30**
Alliance St. LS12: Leeds . . . 6G **29**
Allinson St. LS12: Leeds . . . 1C **40**
All Saint's Circ. LS26: Rothw . . . 3D **54**
All Saint's Dr. LS26: Rothw . . . 3C **54**
All Saints Rd. LS9: Leeds . . . 5B **32**
LS26: Rothw . . . 2D **54**
All Saint's Vw. LS26: Rothw . . . 2C **54**
Alma Cl. LS28: Pud . . . 2E **27**
Alma Cotts. LS6: Leeds . . . 6B **20**
Alma Rd. LS6: Leeds . . . 6B **20**
Alma St. LS9: Leeds . . . 4A **32**
LS19: Yead . . . 2E **9**
LS26: Rothw . . . 2C **54**
Alma Ter. LS26: Rothw . . . 3F **53**
Alma Vs. LS26: Rothw . . . 2D **54**
Alnwick Vw. LS16: Leeds . . . 4A **20**
Alpine Ter. LS26: Rothw . . . 3F **53**
Alston La. LS14: Leeds . . . 2A **34**
ALWOODLEY . . . 5G **13**
Alwoodley Chase LS17: Leeds . . . 4A **14**
Alwoodley Ct. LS17: Leeds . . . 4D **12**
Alwoodley Ct. Gdns. LS17: Leeds . . . 3E **13**
Alwoodley Gdns. LS17: Leeds . . . 4E **13**
ALWOODLEY GATES . . . 3A **14**
Alwoodley Gates LS17: Leeds . . . 3A **14**
Alwoodley La. LS17: Leeds . . . 3D **12**
ALWOODLEY PARK . . . 3E **13**
Amberley Gdns. LS12: Leeds . . . 1B **40**
Amberley Rd. LS12: Leeds . . . 1A **40**
Amberley St. LS12: Leeds . . . 1A **40**
Amberton App. LS8: Leeds . . . 1E **33**
Amberton Cl. LS8: Leeds . . . 6E **23**
Amberton Cres. LS8: Leeds . . . 1E **33**
Amberton Gdns. LS8: Leeds . . . 1E **33**
Amberton Gth. LS8: Leeds . . . 1E **33**
Amberton Gro. LS8: Leeds . . . 1E **33**
Amberton La. LS8: Leeds . . . 1E **33**
Amberton Mt. LS8: Leeds . . . 1E **33**
Amberton Pl. LS8: Leeds . . . 1D **32**
Amberton Rd. LS8: Leeds . . . 1D **32**
LS9: Leeds . . . 1D **32**
Amberton St. LS8: Leeds . . . 1E **33**
Amberton Ter. LS8: Leeds . . . 1E **33**
Amblers Bldgs. *LS28: Pud* . . . *1G 37*
(off Amblers Ct.)
Amblers Bungs. WF3: E Ard . . . 3F **57**
Amblers Ct. LS28: Pud . . . 1G **37**
Amblerthorne BD11: B'frd . . . 4D **46**
Ambleside Gdns. LS28: Pud . . . 6E **27**
Ambleside Gro. LS26: Rothw . . . 3C **54**
AMF Bowling
Leeds . . . 2E **5** (4G **31**)
Amspool Ct. WF3: Rothw . . . 6E **53**
Anaheim Dr. WF1: Wake . . . 6F **59**
Ancaster Cres. LS16: Leeds . . . 4H **19**
Ancaster Rd. LS16: Leeds . . . 4H **19**
Ancaster Vw. LS16: Leeds . . . 4H **19**
Anderson Av. LS8: Leeds . . . 3A **32**
Anderson Mt. LS8: Leeds . . . 3A **32**
Andover Grn. BD4: B'frd . . . 3A **36**
Andrew Cres. WF1: Wake . . . 6D **58**
Andrew Ho. *LS28: Pud* . . . *2F 27*
(off Water La.)
Andrews Mnr. *LS19: Yead* . . . *2D 8*
(off Manor Sq.)
Andrew Sq. LS28: Pud . . . 2F **27**
Andrew St. LS28: Pud . . . 3F **27**
Angel Ct. LS3: Leeds . . . 4D **30**
Angel Inn Yd. LS1: Leeds . . . 4E **5**
Angel Row LS26: Rothw . . . 4C **52**
Anlaby St. BD4: B'frd . . . 2A **36**
Annie St. LS27: Morl . . . 5H **49**
Anstey Ho. LS3: Leeds . . . 3A **4**
Antler Complex LS27: Morl . . . 5D **48**
Apex Bus. Cen. LS11: Leeds . . . 2G **41**
Apex Vw. LS11: Leeds . . . 2F **41**
Apex Way LS11: Leeds . . . 2G **41**
APPERLEY BRIDGE . . . 3A **16**
Apperley Gdns. BD10: B'frd . . . 3A **16**
Apperley La. BD10: B'frd, Yead . . . 3A **16**
LS19: Yead . . . 2B **16**
Appleby Pl. LS15: Leeds . . . 5G **33**
Appleby Wlk. LS15: Leeds . . . 5G **33**
Appleby Way LS27: Morl . . . 4H **49**
Applegarth LS26: Rothw . . . 2C **54**
Appleton Cl. LS9: Leeds . . . 5B **32**
Appleton Ct. LS9: Leeds . . . 5B **32**
Appleton Gro. LS9: Leeds . . . 5D **32**
Appleton Sq. LS9: Leeds . . . 5B **32**
Appleton Way LS9: Leeds . . . 5B **32**
Apple Tree Cl. WF3: E Ard . . . 3G **57**
Apple Tree Ct. WF3: E Ard . . . 4G **57**
Approach, The LS15: Scho . . . 4F **25**
Archery Pl. LS2: Leeds . . . 3F **31**
Archery Rd. LS2: Leeds . . . 3F **31**
Archery St. LS2: Leeds . . . 3F **31**
Archery Ter. LS2: Leeds . . . 3F **31**

A-Z Leeds 61

Ardsley Cl.—Avenue Ter.

Ardsley Cl. BD4: B'frd 5B **36**
(not continuous)
Ardsley Ct. WF3: E Ard 3A **58**
Arena Pk. LS17: S'cft 2H **15**
Argent Way BD4: B'frd 5B **36**
Argie Av. LS4: Leeds 2H **29**
Argie Gdns. LS4: Leeds 3A **30**
Argie Rd. LS4: Leeds 3A **30**
Argie Ter. LS4: Leeds 3A **30**
Argyle Rd. LS9: Leeds 3H **5** (5H **31**)
Argyll Cl. LS18: H'fth 5B **10**
Arksey Pl. LS12: Leeds 5A **30**
Arksey Ter. LS12: Leeds 5A **30**
Arkwright St. BD4: B'frd 1A **36**
Arkwright Wlk. LS27: Morl 3G **49**
Arlesford Rd. BD4: B'frd 5A **36**
Arley Gro. LS12: Leeds 5A **30**
Arley Pl. LS12: Leeds 5A **30**
Arley St. LS12: Leeds 5A **30**
Arley Ter. LS12: Leeds 5A **30**
Arlington Bus. Cen. LS11: Leeds 1B **50**
Arlington Gro. LS8: Leeds 6D **22**
Arlington Rd. LS8: Leeds 1D **32**
Armitage Bldgs. WF12: Dew 5A **56**
Armitage Sq. LS28: Pud 1F **37**
Armitage St. LS26: Rothw 5G **53**
ARMLEY 5B **30**
Armley Grange Av. LS12: Leeds 4F **29**
Armley Grange Cres. LS12: Leeds 4F **29**
Armley Grange Dr. LS12: Leeds 5F **29**
Armley Grange Mt. LS12: Leeds 5F **29**
Armley Grange Oval LS12: Leeds 4F **29**
Armley Grange Ri. LS12: Leeds 5F **29**
Armley Grange Vw. LS12: Leeds 5G **29**
Armley Grange Wlk. LS12: Leeds 5G **29**
Armley Gro. Pl. LS12: Leeds 6B **30**
Armley Leisure Cen. 6H **29**
Armley Lodge Rd. LS12: Leeds 4A **30**
Armley Mills Leeds Industrial Mus. 4A **30**
Armley Pk. Ct. *LS12: Leeds* *5A **30***
(off Stanningley Rd.)
Armley Pk. Rd. LS12: Leeds 4A **30**
Armley Ridge Cl. LS12: Leeds 5G **29**
Armley Ridge Rd. LS12: Leeds 2F **29**
(not continuous)
Armley Ridge Ter. LS12: Leeds 4G **29**
Armley Rd. LS12: Leeds 5A **30**
(not continuous)
Armourage Dr. LS10: Leeds 1H **41**
Armouries Dr. LS10: Leeds 1H **41**
Armouries Way LS10: Leeds 6H **5** (6H **31**)
Armstrong St. LS28: Pud 3F **27**
Arncliffe Cres. LS27: Morl 1A **56**
Arncliffe Gth. LS28: Pud 3F **27**
Arncliffe Grange LS17: Leeds 1H **21**
Arncliffe Rd. LS16: Leeds 3G **19**
Arncliffe St. LS28: Pud 3F **27**
Arndale Cen. LS6: Leeds 6B **20**
Arran Dr. LS18: H'fth 5B **10**
Arran Way LS26: Rothw 4H **53**
Arthington Av. LS10: Leeds 5H **41**
Arthington Cl. WF3: E Ard 4B **56**
Arthington Ct. LS10: Leeds 5H **41**
Arthington Gro. LS10: Leeds 5H **41**
Arthington Pl. LS10: Leeds 5H **41**
Arthington Rd. LS16: Leeds 1A **12**
Arthington St. LS10: Leeds 5H **41**
Arthington Ter. LS10: Leeds 5H **41**
Arthington Vw. LS10: Leeds 5H **41**
ARTHURSDALE 3F **25**
Arthursdale Cl. LS15: Scho 4F **25**
Arthursdale Dr. LS15: Scho 4F **25**
Arthursdale Grange LS15: Scho 4F **25**
Arthur St. LS28: Pud 3F **27**
(New St.)
LS28: Pud 3G **27**
(Town St.)
Arthur Ter. *LS28: Pud* *3F **27***
(off Arthur St.)
Artist St. LS12: Leeds 6D **30**
Arundel St. LS28: Pud 6G **27**
Arundel Ter. *LS15: Leeds* *3C **34***
(off Tranquility Av.)
Ascot Gdns. LS10: Leeds 6H **51**
Ascot Ter. LS9: Leeds 6B **32**
Asda Ho. LS11: Leeds 6E **5** (1G **41**)
Ash Av. LS6: Leeds 6B **20**
Ashbrooke Pk. LS11: Leeds 5G **41**
Ashbury Chase WF1: Wake 6C **58**
Ashby Av. LS13: Leeds 3D **28**
Ashby Cres. LS13: Leeds 4D **28**
Ashby Mt. LS13: Leeds 3D **28**
Ashby Sq. LS13: Leeds 3D **28**
Ashby Ter. LS13: Leeds 3D **28**
Ashby Vw. LS13: Leeds 3D **28**
Ash Cres. LS6: Leeds 6B **20**
WF3: Wake 6H **59**
Ashdene LS12: Leeds 4D **38**
Ashdene Cl. LS28: Pud 2G **37**
Ashdene Cres. LS28: Pud 2G **37**
Ashdown St. LS13: Leeds 4C **28**
Ashfield BD4: B'frd 6A **36**
LS12: Leeds 3G **39**
Ashfield Av. LS27: Morl 6F **49**
Ashfield Cl. LS12: Leeds 3F **39**
LS15: Leeds 1D **34**
Ashfield Cres. LS28: Pud 4F **27**
Ashfield Gro. LS28: Pud 4G **27**
Ashfield Pk. LS6: Leeds 6C **20**
Ashfield Rd. LS27: Morl 6F **49**
LS28: Pud 4F **27**
Ashfield Ter. LS15: Leeds 1D **34**
WF3: Leeds 1B **58**
Ashfield Way LS12: Leeds 3E **39**
Ashford Dr. LS28: Pud 1H **37**
Ash Gdns. LS6: Leeds 6B **20**
Ash Gro. BD11: B'frd 3C **46**
LS6: Leeds 2D **30**
LS18: H'fth 1C **18**
LS28: Pud 1G **37**
Ashgrove BD10: B'frd 4A **16**
Ashgrove M. LS13: Leeds 1H **27**
Ash Hill Dr. LS17: Leeds 5H **15**
Ash Hill Gdns. LS17: Leeds 5H **15**
Ash Hill Gth. LS17: Leeds 5H **15**
Ash Hill La. LS17: Leeds 5H **15**
Ash Ho. LS15: Leeds 1G **43**
Ashington Cl. BD2: B'frd 1A **26**
Ashlea Ct. *LS13: Leeds* *1C **28***
(off Ashlea Ga.)
Ashlea Ga. LS13: Leeds 2C **28**
Ashlea Grn. LS13: Leeds 2C **28**
Ashleigh Gdns. LS26: Rothw 3C **54**
Ashleigh Rd. LS16: Leeds 3G **19**
Ashley Av. LS9: Leeds 3C **32**
Ashley Ind. Est. LS7: Leeds 2G **31**
Ashley Rd. LS9: Leeds 3B **32**
LS12: Leeds 1H **39**
Ashley Ter. LS9: Leeds 3C **32**
Ash M. BD10: B'frd 4A **16**
Ash Rd. LS6: Leeds 1A **30**
Ashroyd LS26: Rothw 5H **53**
Ash Ter. LS6: Leeds 6B **20**
Ashtofts Mt. LS20: Guis 4G **7**
Ashton Av. LS8: Leeds 3B **32**
Ashton Ct. *LS8: Leeds* *1B **32***
(off Karnac Rd.)
LS8: Leeds 2C **32**
(Ashton Rd.)
Ashton Cres. WF3: Rothw 6F **53**
Ashton Gro. LS8: Leeds 3B **32**
Ashton Mt. LS8: Leeds 3B **32**
Ashton Pl. LS8: Leeds 3B **32**
Ashton Rd. LS8: Leeds 2C **32**
Ashton Rd. Ind. Est.
LS8: Leeds 2C **32**
Ashton St. LS8: Leeds 2B **32**
Ashton Ter. LS8: Leeds 3B **32**
LS26: Rothw 5D **52**
Ashton Vw. LS8: Leeds 3B **32**
Ash Tree App. LS14: Leeds 1D **34**
Ash Tree Bank LS14: Leeds 6D **24**
Ash Tree Cl. LS14: Leeds 6D **24**
Ash Tree Ct. LS14: Leeds 6D **24**
Ash Tree Gdns. LS14: Leeds 6D **24**
Ash Tree Grange *LS14: Leeds* *6D **24***
(off Ash Tree Bank)
Ash Tree Gro. LS14: Leeds 6D **24**
Ash Tree Vw. *LS14: Leeds* *6D **24***
(off Ash Tree Gdns.)
Ash Tree Wlk. *LS14: Leeds* *6D **24***
(off Ash Tree Cl.)
Ash Vw. LS6: Leeds 6B **20**
WF3: E Ard 4G **57**
Ash Vs. LS15: Leeds 1D **34**
Ashville Av. LS6: Leeds 2B **30**
Ashville Gro. LS6: Leeds 2B **30**
Ashville Rd. LS4: Leeds 2B **30**
Ashville Ter. LS6: Leeds 2B **30**
LS28: Pud *3F **27***
(off New St.)
Ashville Vw. LS6: Leeds 3C **30**
Ashwood LS14: Leeds 2B **24**
Ashwood Dr. LS27: Morl 2B **48**
Ashwood Gdns. LS27: Morl 2B **48**
Ashwood Gro. LS27: Morl 2C **48**
Ashwood Pde. *LS27: Morl* *2B **48***
(off Ashwood Gdns.)
Ashwood St. BD4: B'frd 6A **36**
Ashwood Ter. LS6: Leeds 1D **30**
Ashwood Vs. LS6: Leeds 1D **30**
Asket Av. LS14: Leeds 6G **23**
Asket Cl. LS14: Leeds 5G **23**
Asket Cres. LS14: Leeds 6G **23**
Asket Dr. LS14: Leeds 5G **23**
Asket Gdns. LS8: Leeds 5F **23**
Asket Gth. LS14: Leeds 6G **23**
Asket Grn. LS14: Leeds 5G **23**
Asket Hill LS8: Leeds 4F **23**
Asket Pl. LS14: Leeds 6G **23**
Asket Wlk. LS14: Leeds 6G **23**
Askrigg Ct. LS29: Men 3D **6**
Aspect 14 LS7: Leeds 1F **5** (4G **31**)
Aspect Gdns. LS28: Pud 5E **27**
Aspect Ter. LS28: Pud 5E **27**
Aspen Ct. WF3: Morl 2A **56**
Aspen Mt. LS16: Leeds 1E **19**
Asquith Av. LS27: Morl 3E **49**
Asquith Cl. LS27: Morl 4F **49**
Asquith Dr. LS27: Morl 4F **49**
Assembly St. LS2: Leeds 5F **5** (6G **31**)
Astley Av. LS26: Swil 6G **45**
Astley La. LS26: Swil 6H **45**
Astley La. Ind. Est. LS26: Swil 1H **55**
Astley Way LS26: Swil 1H **55**
Aston Av. LS13: Leeds 3D **28**
Aston Cres. LS13: Leeds 3E **29**
Aston Dr. LS13: Leeds 3E **29**
Aston Gro. LS13: Leeds 3E **29**
Aston Mt. LS13: Leeds 3E **29**
Aston Pl. LS13: Leeds 3E **29**
Aston Rd. LS13: Leeds 3D **28**
Aston St. LS13: Leeds 3D **28**
Aston Ter. LS13: Leeds 3E **29**
Aston Vw. LS13: Leeds 3D **28**
Astor Gro. LS13: Leeds 3A **28**
Astor St. LS13: Leeds 3A **28**
Astra Bus. Pk. LS11: Leeds 5G **41**
Astura Ct. LS7: Leeds 6F **21**
Atha Cl. LS11: Leeds 6E **41**
Atha Cres. LS11: Leeds 6E **41**
Atha Ho. LS2: Leeds 1D **4**
Atha St. LS11: Leeds 6E **41**
Athlone Gro. LS12: Leeds 6A **30**
Athlone St. LS12: Leeds 6A **30**
Athlone Ter. LS12: Leeds 6A **30**
ATKINSON HILL 3B **42**
Atkinson St. LS10: Leeds 2A **42**
Atlanta St. LS13: Leeds 3A **28**
Atlantic Apartments LS1: Leeds 5C **4**
Attlee Gro. WF1: Wake 6E **59**
AUSTHORPE 5E **35**
Austhorpe Av. LS15: Leeds 6E **35**
Austhorpe Ct. *LS15: Leeds* *6E **35***
(off Austhorpe Dr.)
Austhorpe Dr. LS15: Leeds 6E **35**
Austhorpe Gdns. LS15: Leeds 5F **35**
Austhorpe Gro. LS15: Leeds 6E **35**
Austhorpe La. LS15: Leeds 4D **34**
Austhorpe Rd. LS15: Leeds 3C **34**
Austhorpe Vw. LS15: Leeds 5D **34**
Authorpe Rd. LS6: Leeds 5D **20**
Autumn Av. LS6: Leeds 3C **30**
Autumn Cres. LS18: H'fth 4D **18**
Autumn Gro. LS6: Leeds 3C **30**
Autumn Pl. LS6: Leeds 3C **30**
Autumn St. LS6: Leeds 3C **30**
Autumn Ter. LS6: Leeds 3C **30**
Auty Cres. WF3: Wake 6H **59**
Auty M. WF3: Wake 6H **59**
Auty Sq. LS27: Morl 6H **49**
Avenue, The BD10: B'frd 6A **8**
(not continuous)
BD17: B'frd 6A **8**
LS8: Leeds 3C **22**
LS9: Leeds 6A **32**
LS15: Leeds 2D **34**
LS15: Leeds, Swil 5D **44**
LS15: Scho 3F **25**
LS17: Leeds 4D **12**
LS18: H'fth 2H **17**
WF1: Wake 6D **58**
WF3: E Ard 3E **57**
Avenue Cres. LS8: Leeds 1B **32**
Avenue Gdns. LS17: Leeds 4E **13**
Avenue Hill LS8: Leeds 1A **32**
Avenue Lawns LS17: Leeds 4D **12**
Avenue St. BD4: B'frd 6A **36**
Avenue Ter. LS19: Yead 2F **9**

62 A-Z Leeds

Bk. Dorset Ter.—Bk. New York St.

Bk. Dorset Ter. *LS8: Leeds* 2C **32** *(off Dorset Ter.)*
Bk. East Pk. Rd. *LS9: Leeds* 6C **32** *(off E. Park Rd.)*
Bk. Ecclesburn Gro. *LS9: Leeds* 6D **32** *(off Ecclesburn Gro.)*
Bk. Ecclesburn St. *LS9: Leeds* 6C **32** *(off Ecclesburn St.)*
Bk. Edinburgh Rd. *LS12: Leeds* 5G **29** *(off Town St.)*
Bk. Elford Pl. *LS8: Leeds* 2B **32** *(off Elford Gro., not continuous)*
Bk. Ellers Gro. *LS8: Leeds* 1B **32** *(off Ellers Gro.)*
Bk. Ellers Rd. *LS8: Leeds* 1B **32** *(off Ellers Rd.)*
Bk. Elsworth St. LS12: Leeds 6B **30**
Bk. Eric St. LS13: Leeds 6C **18**
Bk. Eshald Pl. LS26: Rothw 3D **54**
Bk. Esmond Ter. LS12: Leeds 6A **30**
Bk. Estcourt Av. *LS6: Leeds* 6A **20** *(off Ash Rd.)*
Bk. Estcourt Ter. *LS6: Leeds* 1A **30** *(off Canterbury Rd.)*
Bk. Fairford Pl. LS11: Leeds 4G **41**
Bk. Featherbank Ter. LS18: H'fth 4B **18**
Bk. Garton Rd. *LS9: Leeds* 6C **32** *(off Garton Rd.)*
Bk. Garton Ter. *LS9: Leeds* 6C **32** *(off Garton Ter.)*
Bk. Gathorne St. *LS7: Leeds* 2A **32** *(off Gathorne St.)*
Bk. Gillett La. LS26: Rothw 4H **53**
Bk. Glebe Ter. *LS16: Leeds* 5B **20** *(off Glebe Ter.)*
Bk. Glenthorpe Ter. *LS9: Leeds* 5C **32** *(off Glenthorpe Ter.)*
Bk. Glossop St. *LS6: Leeds* 1F **31** *(off Glossop St.)*
Bk. Gordon Ter. *LS6: Leeds* 5D **20** *(off Gordon Ter.)*
Bk. Graham Gro. LS4: Leeds 2B **30**
Bk. Granby Gro. *LS6: Leeds* 1B **30** *(off Granby Rd.)*
Bk. Grange Av. *LS7: Leeds* 1H **31** *(off Grange Av.)*
Bk. Grange Cres. *LS7: Leeds* 1A **32** *(off Grange Cres.)*
Bk. Grange Ter. *LS7: Leeds* 1H **31** *(off Grange Ter.)*
Bk. Grange Vw. *LS7: Leeds* 1A **32** *(off Grange Vw.)*
Back Grn. LS27: Morl 2A **50**
Bk. Greenhow Wlk. *LS4: Leeds* 3B **30** *(off Greenhow Rd.)*
Bk. Greenmount Ter. *LS11: Leeds* 4F **41** *(off Greenmount Ter.)*
Bk. Grosvenor Ter. *LS6: Leeds* 1D **30** *(off Grosvenor Ter.)*
Bk. Grove Gdns. *LS6: Leeds* 5C **20** *(off Grove Gdns.)*
Bk. Grovehall Av. LS11: Leeds 6E **41**
Bk. Grovehall Dr. LS11: Leeds 6E **41**
Bk. Haigh Av. LS26: Rothw 2F **53**
Bk. Haigh St. LS26: Rothw 2E **53**
Bk. Haigh Vw. LS26: Rothw 2E **53**
Bk. Halliday Gro. LS12: Leeds 5G **29**
Bk. Halliday Pl. LS12: Leeds 5G **29**
Bk. Hamilton Av. *LS7: Leeds* 1A **32** *(off Hamilton Av.)*
Bk. Hamilton Vw. *LS7: Leeds* 1A **32** *(off Hamilton Vw.)*
Bk. Harehills Av. *LS7: Leeds* 1A **32** *(off Harehills Av.)*
Bk. Harehills La. *LS8: Leeds* 2B **32** *(off Harehills Rd.)*
Bk. Harehills Pk. Vw. *LS9: Leeds* 3D **32** *(off Harehills Pk. Vw.)*
Bk. Harehills Pl. *LS8: Leeds* 2B **32** *(off Harehills Pl.)*
Bk. Hares Av. *LS8: Leeds* 1B **32** *(off Hares Av.)*
Bk. Hares Mt. *LS8: Leeds* 1A **32** *(off Hares Mt.)*
Bk. Hares Ter. *LS8: Leeds* 1B **32** *(off Hares Ter.)*
Bk. Hares Vw. *LS8: Leeds* 1B **32** *(off Hares Vw.)*
Bk. Harold Gro. *LS6: Leeds* 3C **30** *(off Harold Gro.)*
Bk. Hartley Av. *LS6: Leeds* 1F **31** *(off Hartley Av.)*
Bk. Hartley Gro. *LS6: Leeds* 1E **31** *(off Hartley Gro.)*
Bk. Hartley St. LS27: Morl 6A **50**
Bk. Hawksworth Gro. LS5: Leeds 5D **18**
Bk. Headingley Av. *LS6: Leeds* 6A **20** *(off Ash Rd.)*
Bk. Headingley Mt. *LS6: Leeds* 6A **20** *(off Ash Rd.)*
Bk. Heathfield Ter. *LS6: Leeds* 5B **20** *(off Heathfield Ter.)*
Bk. Heddon St. *LS6: Leeds* 5C **20** *(off Heddon St.)*
Bk. Hessle Av. *LS6: Leeds* 2C **30** *(off Hessle Av.)*
Bk. Hessle Mt. *LS6: Leeds* 2C **30** *(off Hessle Mt.)*
Bk. Hessle Ter. *LS6: Leeds* 2C **30** *(off Hessle Ter.)*
Bk. Hessle Vw. *LS6: Leeds* 2C **30** *(off Hessle Vw.)*
Bk. Highbury Ter. *LS6: Leeds* 5C **20** *(off Highbury Ter.)*
Bk. Highfield Rd. LS13: Leeds 3D **28**
Bk. High St. LS19: Yead 2D **8**
Bk. Highthorne Gro. LS12: Leeds 5G **29**
Bk. Highthorne St. *LS12: Leeds* 5G **29** *(off Highthorne St.)*
Bk. Hillcrest Av. *LS7: Leeds* 1A **32** *(off Hillcrest Av.)*
Bk. Hillcrest Vw. *LS7: Leeds* 1A **32** *(off Hillcrest Vw.)*
Bk. Hilltop Av. *LS8: Leeds* 1B **32** *(off Hilltop Av.)*
Bk. Hill Top Mt. *LS8: Leeds* 3A **32** *(off Gledhow Ter.)*
LS8: Leeds 1B **32** *(off Hill Top Mt.)*
Bk. Hilton Pl. *LS8: Leeds* 6B **22** *(off Hilton Pl.)*
Bk. Hilton Rd. *LS8: Leeds* 1B **32** *(off Hilton Rd.)*
Bk. Hollyshaw Ter. LS15: Leeds 5C **34**
Bk. Holywell La. LS17: Leeds 4F **15**
Bk. Hovingham Gro. *LS8: Leeds* 1C **32** *(off Hovingham Gro.)*
Bk. Hovingham Mt. *LS8: Leeds* 1C **32** *(off Hovingham Mt.)*
Bk. Hovingham Ter. *LS8: Leeds* 1C **32** *(off Hovingham Ter.)*
Bk. Hyde Ter. LS2: Leeds 1A **4** (4E **31**)
Bk. Ibbetson Pl. LS1: Leeds 1C **4**
Bk. Ingledew Cres. LS8: Leeds 1D **22**
Bk. Ivy Av. *LS9: Leeds* 5C **32** *(off Ivy Av.)*
Bk. Ivy Gro. *LS9: Leeds* 6D **32** *(off Ivy Gro.)*
Bk. Ivy Mt. *LS9: Leeds* 5C **32** *(off Ivy Mt.)*
Bk. Ivy St. *LS9: Leeds* 5C **32** *(off Ivy St.)*
Bk. Karnac Rd. *LS8: Leeds* 1B **32** *(off Karnac Rd.)*
Bk. Kelso Rd. LS2: Leeds 1A **4** (3D **30**)
Bk. Kendal La. LS2: Leeds 2A **4**
Bk. Kennerleigh Wlk. *LS15: Leeds* 4C **34** *(off Kennerleigh Wlk.)*
Bk. Kensington Ter. LS6: Leeds 2D **30**
Bk. Kings Av. *LS6: Leeds* 3C **30** *(off Kings Av.)*
Bk. Kitson St. *LS9: Leeds* 6B **32** *(off Kitson St.)*
Bk. Knowle Mt. *LS4: Leeds* 2B **30** *(off Stanmore Hill)*
Bk. Lake St. LS10: Leeds 5H **41**
Bk. Lambton Gro. *LS8: Leeds* 1B **32** *(off Lambton Gro.)*
Bk. Landseer Av. *LS13: Leeds* 2E **29** *(off Raynville Rd.)*
Bk. Landseer Gro. *LS13: Leeds* 2E **29** *(off Raynville Rd.)*
Bk. Landseer Ter. *LS13: Leeds* 2E **29** *(off Raynville Rd.)*
Back La. BD11: B'frd 2H **47**
LS11: Leeds 6D **40**
LS12: Leeds 5C **38**
LS13: Leeds 4D **28**
LS18: H'fth 3B **18**
LS19: Yead 3C **8**
LS20: Guis 4E **7**
LS28: Pud 2F **27**
WF3: Rothw 2E **59**
Bk. Langdale Gdns. *LS6: Leeds* 1A **30** *(off Kirkstall La.)*
Bk. Langdale Ter. *LS6: Leeds* 1A **30** *(off Kirkstall La.)*
Bk. Laurel Mt. LS7: Leeds 6H **21**
Bk. Linden Gro. *LS11: Leeds* 4G **41** *(off Linden Gro.)*
Bk. Lodge La. *LS11: Leeds* 5F **41** *(off Lodge La.)*
Bk. Lombard St. LS19: Yead 5C **8**
Bk. Longroyd Ter. *LS11: Leeds* 4G **41** *(off Longroyd Ter.)*
Bk. Low La. *LS18: H'fth* 2D **18** *(off Springfield Mt.)*
Bk. Lucas St. *LS6: Leeds* 1E **31** *(off Lucas St.)*
Bk. Lunan Pl. *LS8: Leeds* 1B **32** *(off Lunan Pl.)*
Bk. Lunan Ter. *LS8: Leeds* 1B **32** *(off Lunan Ter.)*
Bk. Mafeking Av. *LS11: Leeds* 6E **41** *(off Mafeking Av.)*
Bk. Mafeking Mt. LS11: Leeds 6E **41**
Back Mnr. Dr. *LS6: Leeds* 1C **30** *(off Manor Av.)*
Back Mnr. Gro. *LS7: Leeds* 5H **21** *(off Manor Gro.)*
Bk. Markham Av. *LS8: Leeds* 1B **32** *(off Markham Av.)*
Bk. Marshall Av. *LS15: Leeds* 3D **34** *(off Marshall Av.)*
Bk. Marshall St. *LS15: Leeds* 3C **34** *(off Marshall St.)*
Bk. Marshall Ter. *LS15: Leeds* 3C **34** *(off Marshall Ter.)*
Bk. Mary St. WF3: E Ard 3A **58**
Bk. Masham St. *LS12: Leeds* 6B **30** *(off Bk. Middle Cross St.)*
Bk. Maud Av. *LS11: Leeds* 5F **41** *(off Maud Av.)*
Bk. Mayville Av. *LS6: Leeds* 2C **30** *(off Mayville Av.)*
Bk. Mayville Pl. *LS6: Leeds* 2C **30** *(off Mayville Pl.)*
Bk. Mayville St. *LS6: Leeds* 2C **30** *(off Mayville St.)*
Bk. Mayville Ter. *LS6: Leeds* 2C **30** *(off Mayville Ter.)*
Back Mdw. Vw. *LS6: Leeds* 2C **30** *(off Meadow Vw.)*
Bk. Methley Dr. LS7: Leeds 5H **21**
Bk. Mexborough Av. *LS7: Leeds* 1H **31** *(off Mexborough Av.)*
Bk. Mexborough Dr. *LS7: Leeds* 1H **31** *(off Mexborough Dr.)*
Bk. Mexborough Gro. *LS7: Leeds* 1H **31** *(off Mexborough Gro.)*
Bk. Mexborough St. *LS7: Leeds* 1H **31** *(off Mexborough St.)*
Bk. Meynell Av. LS26: Rothw 4G **53**
Bk. Middle Cross St. LS12: Leeds 6B **30**
Bk. Middleton Vw. LS11: Leeds 4E **41**
Bk. Midland Rd. *LS6: Leeds* 2D **30** *(off Midland Rd.)*
Bk. Milan Av. *LS8: Leeds* 2B **32** *(off Karnac Rd.)*
Bk. Milan Rd. *LS8: Leeds* 2B **32** *(off Milan Rd.)*
Bk. Milan St. *LS8: Leeds* 2C **32** *(off Milan St.)*
Bk. Mitford Rd. LS12: Leeds 6B **30**
Bk. Model Rd. LS12: Leeds 6B **30**
Bk. Model Ter. LS12: Leeds 6B **30**
Bk. Model Vw. LS12: Leeds 6B **30**
Bk. Monk Bri. Dr. *LS6: Leeds* 5D **20** *(off Monk Bri. Dr.)*
Bk. Monk Bri. St. *LS6: Leeds* 5D **20** *(off Monk Bri. St.)*
Bk. Montpelier Ter. *LS6: Leeds* 1E **31** *(off Montpelier Ter.)*
Bk. Moorfield Ter. LS12: Leeds 5G **29**
Bk. Morritt Dr. LS15: Leeds 5H **33**
Bk. Mt. Pleasant LS10: Leeds 4G **51**
Back Mt. Vw. *LS6: Leeds* 1D **30** *(off Grosvenor Rd.)*
Bk. Nansen St. LS13: Leeds 3A **28**
Bk. Newport Gdns. *LS6: Leeds* 2B **30** *(off Newport Rd.)*
Bk. Newport Mt. *LS6: Leeds* 2B **30** *(off Newport Rd.)*
Bk. Newport Pl. *LS6: Leeds* 2B **30** *(off Newport Rd.)*
Bk. Newton Gro. LS7: Leeds 1H **31**
Bk. New York St. LS2: Leeds 5G **5** (6H **31**)

64 A-Z Leeds

Bk. Nice Vw.—Baildon Chase

Bk. Nice Vw. LS8: Leeds 1B 32 (off Nice Vw.)
Bk. Norman Mt. LS5: Leeds 1G 29 (off Abbey Rd.)
Bk. Norman Pl. LS8: Leeds 1C 22 (off Norman Pl.)
Bk. Norman Ter. LS8: Leeds 1C 22 (off Norman Ter.)
Bk. Northbrook St. LS7: Leeds 4H 21 (off Northbrook St.)
Back Nth. Pk. Av. LS8: Leeds 3B 22
Bk. Norwood Gro. LS6: Leeds 2C 30 (off Norwood Gro.)
Bk. Norwood Pl. LS6: Leeds 2C 30 (off Norwood Pl.)
Bk. Norwood Rd. LS6: Leeds 2C 30 (off Norwood Rd.)
Bk. Norwood Ter. LS6: Leeds 2C 30
Bk. Nowell Cres. LS9: Leeds 4D 32 (off Nowell Cres.)
Bk. Nowell Mt. LS9: Leeds 4D 32 (off Nowell Mt.)
Bk. Nowell Pl. LS9: Leeds 4D 32 (off Nowell Pl.)
Bk. Nowell Ter. LS9: Leeds 4D 32 (off Nowell Ter.)
Bk. Nunington St. LS12: Leeds 5B 30 (off Armley Pk. Rd.)
Bk. Nunington Vw. LS12: Leeds 4A 30 (off Armley Pk. Rd.)
Bk. Nunroyd Rd. LS17: Leeds 2H 21 (off Nunroyd Rd.)
Bk. Oakfield Ter. LS6: Leeds 5C 20 (off Brookfield Rd.)
Bk. Oakley St. WF3: E Ard 2A 58
Bk. Oakley Ter. LS11: Leeds 5G 41 (off Oakley Ter.)
Bk. Oak Rd. LS7: Leeds 6H 21 (off Chapel Rd.)
Bk. Oakwood Av. LS8: Leeds 5D 22 (off Oakwood Av.)
Bk. Oakwood Dr. LS8: Leeds 5D 22 (off Oakwood Dr.)
Bk. Osmondthorpe La. LS9: Leeds 5E 33 (off Osmondthorpe La.)
Bk. Outwood La. LS18: H'fth 4C 18
Bk. Overdale Ter. LS15: Leeds 5A 34 (off Overdale Ter.)
Bk. Oxford Pl. LS1: Leeds 3C 4
Bk. Oxford St. WF3: E Ard 3A 58
Back Pk. Cres. LS8: Leeds 1D 22
Bk. Parkfield Pl. LS11: Leeds 4E 41 (off Parkfield Pl.)
Bk. Parkfield Rd. LS10: Leeds 3H 41 (off Hunslet Grn. Way)
LS11: Leeds 4E 41 (off Parkfield Rd.)
Back Pk. Vw. LS11: Leeds 4E 41 (off Park Vw.)
Back Pk. Vw. Av. LS4: Leeds 2B 30
Bk. Parkville Rd. LS13: Leeds 2C 28
Bk. Parnaby Av. LS10: Leeds 6B 42 (off Parnaby Av.)
Bk. Parnaby St. LS10: Leeds 6B 42
Bk. Parnaby Ter. LS10: Leeds 6B 42 (off Parnaby Ter.)
Bk. Pasture Gro. LS7: Leeds 4H 21 (off Pasture Gro.)
Bk. Pasture Rd. LS8: Leeds 1B 32 (off Pasture Rd.)
Bk. Pawson St. WF3: E Ard 3A 58
Bk. Pollard La. LS13: Leeds 6C 18
Bk. Poplar Av. LS15: Leeds 3D 34 (off Poplar Av.)
Bk. Potternewton La. LS7: Leeds 5G 21
Bk. Potters St. LS7: Leeds 5H 21 (off Potternewton La.)
Bk. Prospect Ter. LS9: Leeds 6B 32
Bk. Providence Av. LS6: Leeds 1E 31 (off Delph La.)
Bk. Quarry Mt. Ter. LS6: Leeds 1E 31 (off Quarry Mt. Ter.)
Bk. Raglan Rd. LS2: Leeds 2E 31 (off Raglan Rd.)
Bk. Ravenscar Av. LS8: Leeds 5C 22 (off Ravenscar Av.)
Bk. Raynville Mt. LS13: Leeds 2E 29 (off Raynville Rd.)
Bk. Regent Pk. Ter. LS6: Leeds 1D 30 (off Regent Pk. Ter.)
Bk. Regent Ter. LS6: Leeds 3D 30
Bk. Reginald Mt. LS7: Leeds 1H 31 (off Reginald Mt.)
Bk. Reginald Pl. LS7: Leeds 1H 31 (off Reginald Pl.)
Bk. Reginald Ter. LS7: Leeds 1H 31 (off Reginald St.)
Bk. Richmond Mt. LS6: Leeds 1C 30 (off Manor Av.)
Bk. Ridge Mt. Ter. LS6: Leeds 1E 31 (off Cliff Rd.)
Bk. Ridge Vw. LS7: Leeds 6E 21
Bk. Roberts St. LS26: Rothw 3C 54
Bk. Rochester Ter. LS6: Leeds 1B 30 (off Broomfield Rd.)
Bk. Rokeby Gdns. LS6: Leeds 6A 20 (off Ash Rd.)
Bk. Roman Gro. LS8: Leeds 1C 22
Bk. Roman Pl. LS8: Leeds 1D 22
Bk. Roman St. LS8: Leeds 1D 22
Bk. Rose Av. LS18: H'fth 4B 18 (off Rose St.)
Bk. Rosebank Cres. LS3: Leeds 3D 30
Bk. Rosemont Wlk. LS13: Leeds 3C 28
Bk. Rossall Rd. LS8: Leeds 1C 32 (off Rossall Rd.)
Bk. Rossington Rd. LS8: Leeds 1A 32 (off Spencer Pl.)
Bk. Roundhay Cres. LS8: Leeds 6B 22 (off Roundhay Cres.)
Bk. Roundhay Gro. LS8: Leeds 6B 22 (off Roundhay Gro., not continuous)
Bk. Roundhay Pl. LS8: Leeds 6B 22 (off Roundhay Pl.)
Bk. Roundhay Vw. LS8: Leeds 6B 22 (off Roundhay Vw.)
Back Row LS11: Leeds 1F 41
Bk. Rowland Ter. LS11: Leeds 4G 41 (off Rowland Ter.)
Bk. Ruthven Vw. LS8: Leeds 2C 32 (off Ruthven Vw.)
Bk. St Alban Cres. LS9: Leeds 4E 33 (off St Alban Cres.)
Bk. St Elmo Gro. LS9: Leeds 5C 32 (off St Elmo Gro.)
Bk. St Ives Mt. LS12: Leeds 5G 29
Bk. St Mary's Rd. LS7: Leeds 6H 21
Bk. Salisbury Gro. LS12: Leeds 5A 30
Bk. Salisbury Ter. LS12: Leeds 5A 30 (off Armley Lodge Rd.)
Bk. Salisbury Vw. LS12: Leeds 5A 30 (off Cecil Rd.)
Bk. Sandhurst Gro. LS8: Leeds 2C 32 (off Sandhurst Gro.)
Bk. Sandhurst Pl. LS8: Leeds 2C 32 (off Sandhurst Pl.)
Bk. Sandhurst Rd. LS8: Leeds 2C 32 (off Sandhurst Rd.)
Bk. Savile Pl. LS7: Leeds 2H 31 (off Savile Pl.)
Bk. Savile Rd. LS7: Leeds 2H 31 (off Savile Rd.)
Bk. School St. LS27: Morl 5H 49 (off School St.)
Bk. School Vw. LS6: Leeds 2C 30 (off School Vw.)
Bk. Seaforth Av. LS9: Leeds 3D 32 (off Seaforth Av.)
Bk. Seaforth Pl. LS9: Leeds 2C 32 (off Seaforth Pl.)
Bk. Seaforth Ter. LS9: Leeds 2C 32 (off Seaforth Ter.)
Bk. Sefton Av. LS11: Leeds 4E 41 (off Sefton Av.)
Bk. Sefton Ter. LS11: Leeds 4E 41 (off Sefton Ter.)
Bk. Shaftesbury Av. LS8: Leeds 2C 22
Bk. Shepherds LS7: Leeds 1A 32 (off Shepherd's La.)
Bk. Shepherd's Pl. LS8: Leeds 1B 32 (off Shepherd's Pl.)
Bk. Sholebroke Av. LS7: Leeds 6H 21
Bk. Sholebroke Pl. LS7: Leeds 1H 31 (off Sholebroke Pl.)
Bk. Sholebroke Vw. LS7: Leeds 1H 31 (off Sholebroke Vw.)
Bk. Sidlaw Ter. LS8: Leeds 1B 32 (off Markham Av.)
Back Sth. End Gro. LS13: Leeds 3E 29
Bk. Spencer Mt. LS7: Leeds 1A 32 (off Spencer Mt.)
Bk. Springfield Mt. LS12: Leeds 5G 29
Bk. Spring Gro. Wlk. LS6: Leeds 3C 30 (off Spring Gro. Wlk.)
Bk. Stanley St. LS9: Leeds 3B 32 (off Stanley Av.)
Bk. Stanmore Pl. LS4: Leeds 2A 30 (off St Michaels La.)
Bk. Stanmore St. LS4: Leeds 2A 30 (off St Michaels La.)
Bk. Stonegate Rd. LS6: Leeds 4D 20
Backstone Gill La. LS17: Leeds 1F 15
Bk. Storey Pl. LS14: Leeds 4G 33
Bk. Stratford Av. LS11: Leeds 4E 41 (off Stratford Av.)
Bk. Stratford St. LS11: Leeds 4F 41 (off Stratford St.)
Bk. Stratford Ter. LS11: Leeds 4F 41 (off Stratford Ter.)
Bk. Strathmore Dr. LS9: Leeds 2C 32 (off Strathmore Dr.)
Back St Luke's Cres. LS11: Leeds 3E 41 (off St Luke's Cres.)
Bk. Sunnydene LS14: Leeds 4H 33
Bk. Sutton App. LS14: Leeds 4G 33
Bk. Tamworth St. BD4: B'frd 1A 36
Bk. Tempest Rd. LS11: Leeds 4E 41 (off Tempest Rd.)
Bk. Temple Vw. LS11: Leeds 4E 41
Bk. Thornhill St. LS28: Pud 5D 16
Bk. Thornville Row LS6: Leeds 2C 30 (off Thornville Row)
Bk. Tower Gro. LS12: Leeds 5G 29
Bk. Trafford Av. LS9: Leeds 3D 32 (off Trafford Av.)
Bk. Trentham Pl. LS11: Leeds 5F 41 (off Trentham Pl.)
Bk. Vicars Rd. LS8: Leeds 1B 32 (off Vicars Rd.)
Bk. Victoria Av. LS9: Leeds 5C 32 (off Victoria Av.)
Bk. Victoria Gro. LS9: Leeds 5D 32 (off Victoria Gro.)
Bk. Walmsley Rd. LS6: Leeds 2C 30 (off Walmsley Rd.)
Bk. Welburn Av. LS16: Leeds 4H 19
Bk. Welton Av. LS6: Leeds 2C 30 (off Welton Rd.)
Bk. Welton Gro. LS6: Leeds 2C 30 (off Welton Gro.)
Bk. Welton Mt. LS6: Leeds 2C 30 (off Welton Mt.)
Bk. Welton Pl. LS6: Leeds 2C 30 (off Welton Pl.)
Bk. Wesley Rd. LS12: Leeds 6A 30
Bk. Westbury St. LS10: Leeds 6B 42
Bk. Westfield Rd. LS3: Leeds 4D 30 (off Westfield Rd.)
Bk. Westlock Av. LS9: Leeds 4C 32 (off Westlock Av.)
Bk. Westmorland Mt. LS13: Leeds 1D 28
Bk. Westover Rd. LS13: Leeds 2C 28
Bk. Wetherby Gro. LS4: Leeds 3A 30 (off Argie Av.)
Bk. Wetherby Rd. LS8: Leeds 5D 22 (off Wetherby Rd.)
Bk. Wickham St. LS11: Leeds 4E 41 (off Wickham St.)
Bk. William Av. LS15: Leeds 5G 33 (off William Av.)
Bk. Wilton Gro. LS6: Leeds 5C 20 (off Wilton Gro.)
Bk. Winfield Gro. LS2: Leeds 3F 31 (off Winfield Pl.)
Bk. Winston Gdns. LS6: Leeds 6A 20 (off Ash Rd.)
Bk. Woodbine Ter. LS6: Leeds 5C 20
Bk. Woodland Pk. Rd. LS6: Leeds 6C 20 (off Woodland Pk. Rd.)
Bk. Woodstock St. LS2: Leeds 3F 31 (off Bk. Blenheim Ter.)
Bk. Wood St. WF3: E Ard 3H 57
Bk. York Pl. LS1: Leeds 5B 4 (6E 31) (not continuous)
Bk. York St. LS2: Leeds 5G 5 (6H 31)
Bacon St. LS20: Guis 5H 7
Baden Ter. LS13: Leeds 5C 28 (off Pudsey Rd.)
Badgers Mt. LS15: Leeds 3F 35
Badminton Dr. LS10: Leeds 6H 51
Badminton Vw. LS10: Leeds 6H 51
BAGBY FIELDS 2F 31
BAGHILL 5B 56
Baghill Grn. WF3: E Ard 5B 56
Baghill Rd. WF3: E Ard 4B 56
BAGLEY 1G 27
Bagley La. LS13: Pud 1G 27
LS28: Pud 1F 27
Baildon Chase LS14: Leeds 4C 24

A-Z Leeds 65

Baildon Cl.—Bedford Gro.

Baildon Cl. LS14: Leeds ... 5C **24**
Baildon Dr. LS14: Leeds ... 5C **24**
Baildon Grn. LS14: Leeds ... 5C **24**
Baildon Path LS14: Leeds ... 5C **24**
Baildon Pl. LS14: Leeds ... 5C **24**
Baildon Rd. LS14: Leeds ... 4C **24**
Baildon Wlk. LS14: Leeds ... 4C **24**
Bailes Rd. LS7: Leeds ... 6E **21**
Bailey's Cl. LS14: Leeds ... 5A **24**
Bailey's Hill LS14: Leeds ... 6A **24**
Bailey's La. LS14: Leeds ... 6A **24**
Bailey's Lawn LS14: Leeds ... 6A **24**
Bailey Towers LS14: Leeds ... 6A **24**
Bainbrigge Rd. LS6: Leeds ... 1B **30**
Baines St. LS26: Rothw ... 4G **53**
Baker Cres. LS27: Morl ... 6G **49**
Baker La. WF3: Wake ... 5F **59**
Baker Rd. LS27: Morl ... 6G **49**
Baker St. LS27: Morl ... 6G **49**
Balbec Av. LS6: Leeds ... 6C **20**
Balbec St. LS6: Leeds ... 6C **20**
Baldovan Mt. LS8: Leeds ... 1B **32**
Baldovan Pl. LS8: Leeds ... 1B **32**
Baldovan Ter. LS8: Leeds ... 1B **32**
Balkcliffe La. LS10: Leeds ... 3E **51**
Balmoral Chase LS10: Leeds ... 4B **42**
Balmoral Dr. LS26: Mick ... 6H **55**
Balmoral Ter. LS6: Leeds ... 5C **20**
Balmoral Way LS19: Yead ... 3F **9**
Balm Pl. LS11: Leeds ... 2E **41**
Balm Rd. LS10: Leeds ... 5A **42**
Balm Rd. Ind. Est. LS10: Leeds ... 4H **41**
Balm Wlk. LS11: Leeds ... 2D **40**
Bamburgh Cl. LS15: Leeds ... 2E **35**
Bamburgh Rd. LS15: Leeds ... 2E **35**
Bamford Ho. *BD4: B'frd ... 6A **36***
(off Tong St.)
Bangor Gro. LS12: Leeds ... 3G **39**
Bangor Pl. LS12: Leeds ... 3G **39**
Bangor St. LS12: Leeds ... 3G **39**
Bangor Ter. LS12: Leeds ... 3G **39**
Bangor Vw. LS12: Leeds ... 3G **39**
BANK ... 5H 5 (6A 32)
Bank Av. LS18: H'fth ... 3B **18**
LS27: Morl ... 4G **49**
Banker St. LS4: Leeds ... 4B **30**
Bankfield Gdns. LS4: Leeds ... 3A **30**
Bankfield Gro. LS4: Leeds ... 2A **30**
Bankfield Rd. LS4: Leeds ... 3A **30**
Bankfield Ter. LS4: Leeds ... 3A **30**
*LS28: Pud ... 4G **27***
(off Richardshaw Rd.)
Bank Gdns. LS18: H'fth ... 3B **18**
Bank Holme Ct. BD4: B'frd ... 5B **36**
BANKHOUSE ... 2F 37
Bankhouse LS28: Pud ... 2F **37**
BANKHOUSE BOTTOM ... 3F 37
Bank Ho. Cl. LS27: Morl ... 4G **49**
Bankhouse Ct. LS28: Pud ... 2F **37**
Bankhouse La. LS28: Pud ... 2F **37**
Banksfield Av. LS19: Yead ... 1D **8**
Banksfield Cl. LS19: Yead ... 1D **8**
Banksfield Cres. LS19: Yead ... 1D **8**
Banksfield Gro. LS19: Yead ... 1D **8**
Banksfield Mt. LS19: Yead ... 1D **8**
Banksfield Ri. LS19: Yead ... 1D **8**
Banksfield Ter. LS19: Yead ... 2D **8**
Bank Side St. LS8: Leeds ... 2B **32**
(not continuous)
Bank Sq. LS27: Morl ... 4G **49**
Bank St. LS1: Leeds ... 5E **5** (6G **31**)
(Boar La.)
LS1: Leeds ... 4E **5**
(Commercial St.)
LS27: Morl ... 4G **49**
Bank Ter. LS27: Morl ... 4H **49**
LS28: Pud ... 3G **27**
Bank Vw. BD11: B'frd ... 3C **46**
LS7: Leeds ... 4F **21**
Bankwood Way WF17: Bat ... 5B **48**
Banstead St. E. LS8: Leeds ... 2B **32**
Banstead St. W. LS8: Leeds ... 2B **32**
Banstead Ter. E. LS8: Leeds ... 2B **32**
Banstead Ter. W. LS8: Leeds ... 2B **32**
Bantam Cl. LS27: Morl ... 5B **50**
BANTAM GROVE ... 5B 50
Bantam Gro. La. LS27: Morl ... 5B **50**
Bantam Gro. Vw. LS27: Morl ... 5B **50**
Baptist Way LS28: Pud ... 3A **28**
Barberry Av. BD3: B'frd ... 5A **26**
Barclay St. LS7: Leeds ... 1G **5**
Barcroft Gro. LS19: Yead ... 3C **8**
Barden Cl. LS12: Leeds ... 6G **29**
Barden Grn. LS12: Leeds ... 6G **29**
Barden Gro. LS12: Leeds ... 6G **29**
Barden Mt. LS12: Leeds ... 6G **29**
Barden Pl. LS12: Leeds ... 6G **29**
Barden Ter. LS12: Leeds ... 6G **29**
Bardon Hall Gdns. LS16: Leeds ... 3A **20**
Bardon Hall M. LS16: Leeds ... 3A **20**
Bardwell Ct. WF3: Wake ... 6G **59**
Barfield Av. LS19: Yead ... 3C **8**
Barfield Cres. LS17: Leeds ... 4B **14**
Barfield Dr. LS19: Yead ... 3C **8**
Barfield Gro. LS17: Leeds ... 4C **14**
Barfield Mt. LS17: Leeds ... 4C **14**
Barham Ter. BD10: B'frd ... 1A **26**
Barker Hill LS12: Morl ... 6B **38**
Barker Pl. LS13: Leeds ... 4D **28**
Barkers Well Fold LS12: Leeds ... 4D **38**
Barkers Well Gth. LS12: Leeds ... 4E **39**
Barkers Well Ga. LS12: Leeds ... 4E **39**
Barkers Well Lawn LS12: Leeds ... 4E **39**
Barkly Av. LS11: Leeds ... 6E **41**
Barkly Dr. LS11: Leeds ... 6E **41**
Barkly Gro. LS11: Leeds ... 5E **41**
Barkly Pde. LS11: Leeds ... 6E **41**
Barkly Pl. LS11: Leeds ... 6E **41**
Barkly Rd. LS11: Leeds ... 5D **40**
Barkly St. LS11: Leeds ... 6E **41**
Barkly Ter. LS11: Leeds ... 6E **41**
Bar La. LS18: H'fth ... 3G **17**
Barlby Way LS8: Leeds ... 5E **23**
Barleycorn Yd. LS12: Leeds ... 6H **29**
Barley Fld. Ct. LS15: Leeds ... 5A **34**
Barley M. WF3: Rothw ... 6D **52**
Barnard Cl. LS15: Leeds ... 2E **35**
Barnard Way LS15: Leeds ... 2E **35**
BARNBOW CARR ... 6H 25
Barnbow La. LS15: Scho ... 1H **35**
Barnbrough St. LS4: Leeds ... 3A **30**
Barn Cl. LS29: Men ... 1B **6**
Barncroft Cl. LS14: Leeds ... 4H **23**
Barncroft Ct. LS14: Leeds ... 5G **23**
Barncroft Dr. LS14: Leeds ... 5G **23**
Barncroft Gdns. LS14: Leeds ... 5H **23**
Barncroft Grange LS14: Leeds ... 5G **23**
Barncroft Hgts. LS14: Leeds ... 4G **23**
Barncroft Mt. LS14: Leeds ... 5G **23**
Barncroft Ri. LS14: Leeds ... 5H **23**
Barncroft Rd. LS14: Leeds ... 5H **23**
Barncroft Towers LS14: Leeds ... 5G **23**
Barnet Gro. LS27: Morl ... 6G **49**
Barnet Rd. LS12: Leeds ... 6B **30**
Barnswick Vw. LS16: Leeds ... 5E **11**
Baron Cl. LS11: Leeds ... 3E **41**
Baronscourt LS15: Leeds ... 5D **34**
Baronsmead LS15: Leeds ... 5C **34**
Baronsway LS15: Leeds ... 5C **34**
Barrack Rd. LS7: Leeds ... 2H **31**
Barrack St. LS7: Leeds ... 3H **31**
Barraclough Bldgs. BD10: B'frd ... 4A **16**
Barraclough Yd. *LS26: Rothw ... 4G **53***
(off Cross St.)
Barran Ct. LS8: Leeds ... 2B **32**
Barras Gth. Ind. Est. LS12: Leeds ... 1H **39**
Barras Gth. Pl. LS12: Leeds ... 1H **39**
Barras Gth. Rd. LS12: Leeds ... 1H **39**
Barras Pl. LS12: Leeds ... 1H **39**
Barras St. LS12: Leeds ... 1H **39**
Barras Ter. LS12: Leeds ... 1H **39**
BARROWBY ... 5H 35
Barrowby Av. LS15: Leeds ... 6E **35**
Barrowby Cl. LS29: Men ... 1D **6**
Barrowby Cres. LS15: Leeds ... 5E **35**
Barrowby Dr. LS15: Leeds ... 6F **35**
Barrowby La. LS15: Leeds ... 5E **35**
LS25: Gar, Leeds ... 5G **35**
Barrowby Rd. LS15: Leeds ... 6F **35**
Barthorpe Av. LS17: Leeds ... 3F **21**
Barthorpe Cl. BD4: B'frd ... 5B **36**
Barthorpe Cres. LS17: Leeds ... 3G **21**
Barton Ct. LS15: Leeds ... 6C **34**
Barton Gro. LS11: Leeds ... 3E **41**
Barton Hill LS11: Leeds ... 3E **41**
Barton Mt. LS11: Leeds ... 3E **41**
Barton Pl. LS11: Leeds ... 3E **41**
Barton Rd. LS11: Leeds ... 3E **41**
Barton Ter. LS11: Leeds ... 3E **41**
Barton Vw. LS11: Leeds ... 3E **41**
Barwick Rd. LS15: Leeds ... 2B **34**
Basilica LS1: Leeds ... 4E **5**
Batcliffe Dr. LS6: Leeds ... 5A **20**
Batcliffe Mt. LS6: Leeds ... 6A **20**
Bateson St. BD10: B'frd ... 4A **16**
Bath Cl. LS13: Leeds ... 3C **28**
Bath Gro. LS13: Leeds ... 3C **28**
Bath La. LS13: Leeds ... 4C **28**
Bath Rd. LS11: Leeds ... 1E **41**
LS13: Leeds ... 4C **28**
Batley Rd. WF3: E Ard ... 6B **56**
Batter La. LS19: Yead ... 5E **9**
Battlefield BD4: B'frd ... 2D **46**
BAWN ... 2F 39
Bawn App. LS12: Leeds ... 2E **39**
Bawn Av. LS12: Leeds ... 1E **39**
Bawn Chase LS12: Leeds ... 1E **39**
Bawn Dr. LS12: Leeds ... 1E **39**
Bawn Gdns. LS12: Leeds ... 1E **39**
Bawn La. LS12: Leeds ... 1E **39**
Bawn Path *LS12: Leeds ... 1F **39***
(off Bawn Gdns.)
Bawn Va. *LS12: Leeds ... 1E **39***
(off Bawn Gdns.)
Bawn Wlk. *LS12: Leeds ... 1F **39***
(off Bawn Av.)
Bay Horse La. LS17: Leeds, S'cft ... 2H **15**
Bay Horse Yd. LS1: Leeds ... 4F **5**
LS28: Pud ... 2F **27**
Bayswater Cres. LS8: Leeds ... 2B **32**
Bayswater Gro. LS8: Leeds ... 2B **32**
Bayswater Mt. LS8: Leeds ... 2B **32**
Bayswater Pl. LS8: Leeds ... 2B **32**
Bayswater Rd. LS8: Leeds ... 2A **32**
Bayswater Row LS8: Leeds ... 2B **32**
Bayswater Ter. LS8: Leeds ... 2B **32**
Bayswater Vw. LS8: Leeds ... 3B **32**
Bayton La. LS18: H'fth ... 3F **9**
LS19: H'fth, Yead ... 3F **9**
Beacon Av. LS27: Morl ... 6H **49**
Beacon Gro. LS27: Morl ... 6H **49**
Beacon Vw. *LS27: Morl ... 1A **56***
(off Tingley Comn.)
Beamsley Gro. LS6: Leeds ... 3C **30**
Beamsley Mt. LS6: Leeds ... 3C **30**
Beamsley Pl. LS6: Leeds ... 3C **30**
Beamsley Ter. LS6: Leeds ... 3C **30**
Bearing Av. LS11: Leeds ... 5G **41**
Bear Pit Gdns. *LS6: Leeds ... 2B **30***
(off Chapel La.)
Beaumont Av. LS8: Leeds ... 1C **22**
Beaumont Cl. WF3: Wake ... 6H **59**
Beaumont Sq. LS28: Pud ... 1F **37**
Beaumont St. WF3: Wake ... 6H **59**
Beck Bottom LS28: Pud ... 5A **16**
(Carr Rd.)
LS28: Pud ... 2G **27**
(Coal Hill La.)
Beckbury Cl. LS28: Pud ... 3F **27**
Beckbury St. LS28: Pud ... 3F **27**
Becket La. WF3: Rothw ... 1E **59**
Beckett Ct. LS15: Leeds ... 1D **44**
BECKETT PARK ... 5B 20
Beckett's Pk. Cres.
LS6: Leeds ... 6A **20**
Beckett's Pk. Dr. LS6: Leeds ... 6A **20**
Beckett's Pk. Rd. LS6: Leeds ... 6B **20**
Beckett St. LS9: Leeds ... 4A **32**
Beckhill App. LS7: Leeds ... 5E **21**
Beckhill Av. LS7: Leeds ... 5E **21**
Beckhill Chase LS7: Leeds ... 5E **21**
Beckhill Cl. LS7: Leeds ... 5E **21**
Beckhill Dr. LS7: Leeds ... 4E **21**
Beckhill Fold LS7: Leeds ... 4E **21**
Beckhill Gdns. LS7: Leeds ... 5E **21**
Beckhill Gth. LS7: Leeds ... 5E **21**
Beckhill Ga. LS7: Leeds ... 5E **21**
Beckhill Grn. LS7: Leeds ... 5E **21**
Beckhill Gro. LS7: Leeds ... 5E **21**
Beckhill Lawn LS7: Leeds ... 5E **21**
Beckhill Pl. LS7: Leeds ... 4E **21**
Beckhill Row LS7: Leeds ... 4E **21**
Beckhill Va. LS7: Leeds ... 4E **21**
(not continuous)
Beckhill Vw. LS7: Leeds ... 5E **21**
Beckhill Wlk. LS7: Leeds ... 4E **21**
Beck Rd. LS8: Leeds ... 1B **32**
Beckside Gdns. LS16: Leeds ... 4B **20**
Beckside Vw. LS27: Morl ... 5A **50**
Beck Way WF3: E Ard ... 3B **58**
Bedale WF3: E Ard ... 3B **56**
Bedford Chambers LS1: Leeds ... 4D **4**
Bedford Cl. LS16: Leeds ... 6E **11**
Bedford Ct. LS8: Leeds ... 5E **23**
Bedford Dr. LS16: Leeds ... 6E **11**
Bedford Gdns. LS16: Leeds ... 6E **11**
Bedford Gth. LS16: Leeds ... 6E **11**
Bedford Grn. LS16: Leeds ... 6E **11**
Bedford Gro. LS16: Leeds ... 1E **19**

66 A-Z Leeds

Bedford Mt.—Blackmoor La.

Bedford Mt. LS16: Leeds 1E **19**
(not continuous)
Bedford Pl. LS20: Guis 5G **7**
Bedford Row LS10: Leeds 3H **41**
Bedford St. LS1: Leeds 4D **4** (5F **31**)
Bedford Vw. LS16: Leeds 6E **11**
Beech Av. LS12: Leeds 5A **30**
LS18: H'fth 4C **18**
WF3: Wake 6H **59**
Beech Cl. LS9: Leeds 2F **33**
Beech Cres. LS9: Leeds 2F **33**
Beech Cft. WF3: Rothw 2G **59**
Beechcroft Cl. LS11: Leeds 6B **40**
Beechcroft Mead LS17: Leeds 5C **14**
Beechcroft Vw. LS11: Leeds 6B **40**
Beech Dr. LS12: Leeds 5A **30**
LS18: H'fth .4B **18**
Beeches, The BD11: B'frd 4C **46**
LS20: Guis 3G **7**
LS28: Pud 5D **26**
Beechfield LS12: Leeds 4D **38**
Beech Gro. LS6: Leeds 5B **20**
LS26: Rothw 3H **53**
LS27: Morl 6F **49**
LS29: Men 2C **6**
Beech Gro. Gdns. LS26: Rothw 4C **54**
Beech Gro. Ter. LS2: Leeds 3F **31**
Beech Ho. LS16: Leeds 3A **20**
Beech La. LS9: Leeds 2E **33**
Beech Lees LS28: Pud 1E **27**
Beech Mt. LS9: Leeds 2F **33**
Beechroyd LS28: Pud 1G **37**
Beech St. WF3: E Ard 2C **56**
Beech Wlk. BD11: B'frd 5D **46**
LS9: Leeds 2F **33**
LS16: Leeds 1B **20**
BEECHWOOD
LS14 . . . . .5H **23**
LS18 . . . . .6B **10**
Beechwood LS26: Rothw 2C **54**
Beechwood Av. BD11: B'frd 2F **47**
LS4: Leeds 2B **30**
Beechwood Cen. *LS26: Rothw* *2C* ***54***
(off Church St.)
Beechwood Cl. LS17: Leeds 5G **15**
LS18: H'fth .6A **10**
Beechwood Ct. *LS4: Leeds* *2B* ***30***
(off Bk. Beechwood Gro.)
LS14: Leeds 5G **23**
LS16: Leeds 4H **11**
Beechwood Cres. LS4: Leeds 2B **30**
Beechwood Gro. BD11: B'frd 2F **47**
LS4: Leeds 2B **30**
Beechwood Mt. LS4: Leeds 2B **30**
Beechwood Pl. LS4: Leeds 2B **30**
Beechwood Rd. LS4: Leeds 2B **30**
Beechwood Row LS4: Leeds 2B **30**
Beechwood St. LS4: Leeds 2B **30**
LS28: Pud 4E **27**
Beechwood Ter. LS4: Leeds 2B **30**
Beechwood Vw. LS4: Leeds 2B **30**
Beechwood Wlk. LS4: Leeds 2B **30**
Beecroft Cl. LS13: Leeds 2A **28**
Beecroft Cres. LS13: Leeds 2B **28**
Beecroft Gdns. LS13: Leeds 2A **28**
Beecroft Mt. LS13: Leeds 2A **28**
Beecroft St. LS5: Leeds 2G **29**
BEESTON 6D **40**
Beeston LS11: Leeds 1C **50**
BEESTON HILL 3E **41**
Beeston Pk. Cft. LS11: Leeds 5C **40**
Beeston Pk. Gth. LS11: Leeds 5C **40**
Beeston Pk. Gro. LS11: Leeds 5C **40**
Beeston Pk. Pl. LS11: Leeds 5C **40**
BEESTON PARK SIDE 1E **51**
Beeston Pk. Ter. LS11: Leeds 5C **40**
Beeston Rd. LS11: Leeds 5D **40**
Beeston Royd Ind. Est. LS12: Leeds 4A **40**
BEESTON ROYDS 5H **39**
Beevers Ct. LS16: Leeds 1G **19**
BEGGARINGTON HILL 5B **56**
Belford Ct. LS6: Leeds 2C **20**
Belfry, The LS19: Yead 3E **9**
Belfry Ct. WF1: Wake 6E **59**
Belfry Rd. LS9: Leeds 2C **42**
Belgrave M. LS19: Yead 5C **8**
Belgrave St. LS2: Leeds 3E **5** (5G **31**)
Belgravia Gdns. LS8: Leeds 4E **23**
Belinda St. LS10: Leeds 3A **42**
Bellbrooke Av. LS9: Leeds 3D **32**
Bellbrooke Gro. LS9: Leeds 3D **32**
Bellbrooke Pl. LS9: Leeds 3D **32**
Bellbrooke St. LS9: Leeds 3C **32**
BELLE ISLE 1A **52**
Belle Isle Cir. LS10: Leeds 1A **52**
Belle Isle Cl. LS10: Leeds 1A **52**
Belle Isle Pde. LS10: Leeds 6A **42**
Belle Isle Rd. LS10: Leeds 5A **42**
Belle Vue Av. LS8: Leeds 5F **23**
LS15: Scho 4F **25**
Belle Vue Ct. *LS3: Leeds* *4D* ***30***
(off Consort Ter.)
Belle Vue Dr. LS28: Pud 2E **27**
Belle Vue Est. LS15: Scho 5F **25**
Belle Vue Rd. LS3: Leeds 3A **4** (4D **30**)
LS15: Scho 5F **25**
Belle Vue Ter. LS20: Guis 5G **7**
LS27: Morl 3D **48**
Bell Gro. LS13: Leeds 2C **28**
Bell La. LS13: Leeds .2C **28**
Bellmount Cl. LS13: Leeds 2D **28**
Bellmount Gdns. LS13: Leeds 1C **28**
Bellmount Grn. LS13: Leeds 2D **28**
Bellmount Pl. LS13: Leeds 1C **28**
Bellmount Vw. LS13: Leeds 2D **28**
Bell Rd. LS13: Leeds 2C **28**
Bell St. LS9: Leeds 3H **5** (5H **31**)
Belmont Gro. LS2: Leeds 2B **4** (4E **31**)
LS19: Yead 4E **9**
Belmont Ter. WF3: Leeds 1B **58**
Belvedere Av. LS11: Leeds 5F **41**
LS17: Leeds 5H **13**
Belvedere Ct. *LS7: Leeds* *6A* ***22***
(off Harehills La.)
LS17: Leeds 5A **14**
Belvedere Gdns. LS17: Leeds 5A **14**
Belvedere Gro. LS17: Leeds 5H **13**
Belvedere Mt. LS11: Leeds 5F **41**
Belvedere Rd. LS17: Leeds 5H **13**
Belvedere Ter. LS11: Leeds 5F **41**
Belvedere Vw. LS17: Leeds 5A **14**
Benbow Av. BD10: B'frd 6A **16**
Bennett Ct. LS15: Leeds 5D **34**
Bennett Rd. LS6: Leeds 6B **20**
Bennetts Yd. LS26: Rothw 5G **53**
Benson Gdns. LS12: Leeds 1H **39**
Benson St. LS7: Leeds 1G **5** (3H **31**)
Bentcliffe Av. LS17: Leeds 1H **21**
Bentcliffe Cl. LS17: Leeds 2A **22**
Bentcliffe Ct. LS17: Leeds 2A **22**
Bentcliffe Dr. LS17: Leeds 1A **22**
Bentcliffe Gdns. LS17: Leeds 2A **22**
Bentcliffe Gro. LS17: Leeds 2A **22**
Bentcliffe La. LS17: Leeds 2H **21**
Bentcliffe Mt. LS17: Leeds 2A **22**
Bentley Ct. LS7: Leeds 5D **20**
Bentley Gdns. LS7: Leeds 5D **20**
Bentley Gro. LS6: Leeds 5D **20**
Bentley La. LS6: Leeds 5D **20**
Bentley Mt. LS6: Leeds 5D **20**
Bentley Pde. LS6: Leeds 5D **20**
Bentley Sq. LS26: Rothw 4C **54**
Benton Pk. Av. LS19: Yead 4E **9**
Benton Pk. Cres. LS19: Yead 4E **9**
Benton Pk. Dr. LS19: Yead 4E **9**
Benton Pk. Rd. LS19: Yead 4E **9**
Benyon Pk. Way LS12: Leeds 3B **40**
Beringa LS12: Leeds 5A **4** (6E **31**)
Berkeley Av. LS8: Leeds 2C **32**
Berkeley Ct. LS2: Leeds 1A **4** (4D **30**)
Berkeley Cres. LS8: Leeds 2C **32**
Berkeley Gro. LS8: Leeds 2C **32**
Berkeley Ho. *BD4: B'frd* *4A* ***36***
(off Stirling Cres.)
Berkeley Mt. LS8: Leeds 2C **32**
Berkeley Rd. LS8: Leeds 2C **32**
Berkeley St. LS8: Leeds 2C **32**
Berkeley Ter. LS8: Leeds 2C **32**
Berkeley Vw. LS8: Leeds 2C **32**
Berking Av. LS9: Leeds 5B **32**
Berking Row LS9: Leeds 5B **32**
Bernard St. LS26: Rothw 3D **54**
Bertha St. LS28: Pud .3F **27**
Bertrand St. LS11: Leeds 2E **41**
Bessbrook St. LS10: Leeds 4H **41**
Beulah Gro. LS6: Leeds 2F **31**
Beulah Mt. LS6: Leeds 2F **31**
Beulah St. LS6: Leeds 2F **31**
Beulah Ter. *LS6: Leeds* *1F* ***31***
(off Beulah St.)
LS15: Leeds *3C* ***34***
(off Austhorpe Rd.)
Beulah Vw. LS6: Leeds 2F **31**
Beverley Av. LS11: Leeds 4F **41**
Beverley Ct. LS17: Leeds 1H **21**
LS28: Pud 3F **27**
Beverley Mt. LS11: Leeds 4F **41**
Beverley St. BD4: B'frd 2A **36**
Beverley Ter. LS11: Leeds 4F **41**
Beverley Vw. LS11: Leeds 4F **41**
Bevin Cl. WF1: Wake .6E **59**
Bevin Cres. WF1: Wake 6E **59**
Bewick Gro. LS10: Leeds 2B **52**
Bexley Av. LS8: Leeds 3B **32**
Bexley Gro. LS8: Leeds 3B **32**
Bexley Mt. LS8: Leeds 3B **32**
Bexley Pl. LS8: Leeds 3B **32**
Bexley Rd. LS8: Leeds 3B **32**
Bexley Ter. LS8: Leeds 3B **32**
Bexley Vw. LS8: Leeds 3B **32**
Beza Ct. LS10: Leeds 5H **41**
Beza Rd. LS10: Leeds 4H **41**
Beza St. LS10: Leeds 4H **41**
Biddenden Rd. LS15: Leeds 3F **35**
Bidder Dr. WF3: E Ard 2G **57**
Bideford Av. LS8: Leeds 6B **14**
Bideford Mt. BD4: B'frd 4A **36**
Billey La. LS12: Leeds 2E **39**
(not continuous)
Billingbauk Ct. LS13: Leeds 4D **28**
Billingbauk Dr. LS13: Leeds 4D **28**
Billing Ct. LS19: Yead 6F **9**
Billing Dr. LS19: Yead 6G **9**
Billing Vw. LS19: Yead 6F **9**
Billingwood Dr. LS19: Yead 6F **9**
Bingley Rd. LS29: Men 2A **6**
Bingley St. LS3: Leeds 4A **4** (5D **30**)
Birch Av. LS15: Leeds 5A **34**
Birch Ct. BD11: B'frd 3D **46**
Birch Cres. LS15: Leeds 5A **34**
Birches, The LS20: Guis 3G **7**
Birchfield Av. LS27: Morl 3C **48**
Birchfields Av. LS14: Leeds 3C **24**
Birchfields Cl. LS14: Leeds 4C **24**
Birchfields Ct. LS14: Leeds 3C **24**
Birchfields Cres. LS14: Leeds 3C **24**
Birchfields Gth. LS14: Leeds 3C **24**
Birchfields Ri. LS14: Leeds 4C **24**
Birch Hill Ri. LS18: H'fth 3E **19**
Birch Ho. LS7: Leeds .4H **21**
Birch M. LS16: Leeds 1B **20**
Birchroyd LS26: Rothw 5H **53**
Birchtree Way LS16: Leeds 1E **19**
Birchwood Av. LS17: Leeds 6C **14**
Birchwood Hill LS17: Leeds 5C **14**
Birchwood Mt. LS17: Leeds 5C **14**
Birfed Cres. LS4: Leeds 2H **29**
Birkdale Cl. LS17: Leeds 5F **13**
Birkdale Dr. LS17: Leeds 5E **13**
Birkdale Grn. LS17: Leeds 5F **13**
Birkdale Gro. LS17: Leeds 5E **13**
Birkdale Mt. LS17: Leeds 5F **13**
Birkdale Pl. LS17: Leeds 5E **13**
Birkdale Ri. LS17: Leeds 5E **13**
Birkdale Wlk. LS17: Leeds 5E **13**
Birkdale Way LS17: Leeds 5F **13**
BIRKENSHAW 3C **46**
BIRKENSHAW BOTTOMS 5E **47**
Birkenshaw La. BD11: B'frd 4D **46**
Birkhill Cres. BD11: B'frd 4D **46**
Birk La. LS27: Morl 5E **49**
BIRKS 6G **49**
Birksland Moor BD11: B'frd 6D **46**
Birkwith Cl. LS14: Leeds 3B **24**
Birstall La. BD11: B'frd 4G **47**
Birstall Retail Pk. WF17: Bat 5A **48**
Bishopgate St. LS1: Leeds 5D **4** (6F **31**)
Bishop Way WF3: E Ard 3D **56**
Bismarck Ct. LS11: Leeds 3F **41**
Bismarck Dr. LS11: Leeds 3F **41**
Bismarck St. LS11: Leeds 3F **41**
Bittern Ri. LS27: Morl 6A **50**
Black Bull St. LS10: Leeds 6G **5** (1H **41**)
Black Bull Yd. *LS26: Rothw* *4H* ***53***
(off Commercial St.)
Blackburn Ct. LS26: Rothw 4H **53**
Blackett St. LS28: Pud 4D **16**
BLACK GATES 2D **56**
Blackgates Ct. WF3: E Ard 3D **56**
Blackgates Cres. WF3: E Ard 3D **56**
Blackgates Dr. WF3: E Ard 3D **56**
Blackgates Fold WF3: E Ard 3D **56**
Blackgates Ri. WF3: E Ard 3D **56**
Blackman La. LS2: Leeds 1D **4** (3F **31**)
LS7: Leeds 3F **31**
BLACK MOOR 5E **13**
BLACKMOOR 2H **15**
Blackmoor Ct. LS17: Leeds 4D **12**
Blackmoor La. LS17: Bard, S'cft 1H **15**

A-Z Leeds 67

Black Moor Rd.—Bridge Rd.

Black Moor Rd. LS17: Leeds ... 6D **12**
Blackpool Gro. LS12: Leeds ... 3G **39**
Blackpool Pl. LS12: Leeds ... 3G **39**
Blackpool St. LS12: Leeds ... 3G **39**
Blackpool Ter. LS12: Leeds ... 3G **39**
Blackpool Vw. LS12: Leeds ... 3G **39**
Blacksmith M. WF3: Rothw ... 6D **52**
Blackthorn Ct. LS10: Leeds ... 1H **51**
Blackwood Av. LS16: Leeds ... 6D **10**
Blackwood Gdns. LS16: Leeds ... 6D **10**
Blackwood Gro. LS16: Leeds ... 6D **10**
Blackwood Mt. LS16: Leeds ... 6D **10**
Blackwood Ri. LS16: Leeds ... 6D **10**
Blairsville Gdns. LS13: Leeds ... 1B **28**
Blairsville Gro. LS13: Leeds ... 1C **28**
Blake Cres. LS20: Guis ... 5H **7**
Blake Gro. LS7: Leeds ... 5H **21**
Blakeney Gro. LS10: Leeds ... 6H **41**
Blakeney Rd. LS10: Leeds ... 6H **41**
Blandford Gdns. LS2: Leeds ... 3F **31**
Blandford Gro. *LS2: Leeds ... 3F **31***
(off Bk. Blenheim Ter.)
Blayds Gth. LS26: Rothw ... 2A **54**
Blayd's M. LS1: Leeds ... 6E **5** (6G **31**)
Blayds St. LS9: Leeds ... 6B **32**
Blayd's Yd. LS1: Leeds ... 6E **5** (6G **31**)
Bleach Mill La. LS29: Men ... 1A **6**
Blencarn Cl. LS14: Leeds ... 1H **33**
Blencarn Gth. LS14: Leeds ... 1H **33**
Blencarn Lawn LS14: Leeds ... 1H **33**
Blencarn Path LS14: Leeds ... 1H **33**
Blencarn Rd. LS14: Leeds ... 1H **33**
Blencarn Vw. LS14: Leeds ... 1H **33**
Blencarn Wlk. LS14: Leeds ... 1H **33**
Blenheim Av. LS2: Leeds ... 3F **31**
Blenheim Ct. *LS2: Leeds ... 3F **31***
(off Blenheim Wlk.)
Blenheim Cres. *LS2: Leeds ... 3F **31***
(off Blenheim Av.)
Blenheim Gro. LS2: Leeds ... 3F **31**
Blenheim Sq. LS2: Leeds ... 3F **31**
Blenheim Ter. LS2: Leeds ... 1D **4**
LS27: Morl ... 3G **49**
Blenheim Vw. LS2: Leeds ... 3F **31**
Blenheim Wlk. LS2: Leeds ... 3F **31**
Blind La. BD11: B'frd ... 2H **47**
LS17: Leeds ... 5G **15**
WF3: E Ard ... 6E **57**
Bluebell Ct. LS14: Leeds ... 3A **24**
Bluebell Rd. WF3: E Ard ... 3A **58**
Blue Hill Cres. LS12: Leeds ... 1G **39**
Blue Hill Grange LS12: Leeds ... 2G **39**
Blue Hill Gro. LS12: Leeds ... 1G **39**
Blue Hill La. LS12: Leeds ... 1G **39**
Blundell St. LS1: Leeds ... 2C **4** (4F **31**)
Boar La. LS1: Leeds ... 5D **4** (6F **31**)
Bodington Hall (University of Leeds) ... 1H **19**
Bodley Ter. LS4: Leeds ... 4B **30**
Bodmin App. LS10: Leeds ... 4E **51**
Bodmin Cres. LS10: Leeds ... 4E **51**
Bodmin Cft. LS10: Leeds ... 4F **51**
Bodmin Gdns. LS10: Leeds ... 5E **51**
Bodmin Gth. LS10: Leeds ... 5E **51**
Bodmin Pl. LS10: Leeds ... 5F **51**
(not continuous)
Bodmin Rd. LS10: Leeds ... 3D **50**
Bodmin Sq. LS10: Leeds ... 5E **51**
Bodmin St. LS10: Leeds ... 5E **51**
Bodmin Ter. LS10: Leeds ... 5E **51**
Body Balance ... 3A **28**
Bodylines Gym ... *4A **32***
(in Mabgate Mills Industrial & Commercial Cen.)
Body Mania Fitness ... *4H **53***
(off Marsh St.)
Bodytech ... *4H **51***
(in Middleton District Cen.)
Boggart Hill LS14: Leeds ... 5G **23**
Boggart Hill Cres. LS14: Leeds ... 5G **23**
Boggart Hill Dr. LS14: Leeds ... 5G **23**
Boggart Hill Gdns. LS14: Leeds ... 5G **23**
Boggart Hill Rd. LS14: Leeds ... 5G **23**
Bog La. LS15: Scho ... 6G **25**
Boldmere Rd. LS15: Leeds ... 6G **33**
Bolton Grange LS19: Yead ... 3E **9**
Bolton Rd. LS19: Yead ... 3E **9**
Bonaire LS12: Leeds ... 6A **4** (6D **30**)
Bond Ct. LS1: Leeds ... 4D **4**
*LS6: Leeds ... 3C **30***
(off Alexandra Rd.)
Bond St. LS1: Leeds ... 4D **4** (5F **31**)
Bonham Ct. *LS27: Morl ... 5G **49***
(off Queen St.)
Boothroyd Dr. LS6: Leeds ... 6D **20**
Booth's Yd. LS28: Pud ... 5G **27**
Borrough Av. LS8: Leeds ... 3A **22**
Borrough Vw. LS8: Leeds ... 3A **22**
Borrowdale Cl. LS12: Leeds ... 3F **29**
Borrowdale Cres. LS12: Leeds ... 3F **29**
Borrowdale Cft. LS19: Yead ... 2D **8**
Borrowdale Ter. LS14: Leeds ... 2H **33**
Boston Av. LS5: Leeds ... 2F **29**
Boston Towers *LS9: Leeds ... 4A **32***
(off Lindsey Gdns.)
Bottoms La. BD11: B'frd ... 5D **46**
Boulevard, The LS10: Leeds ... 1H **41**
LS12: Leeds ... 4B **40**
LS28: Pud ... 3F **27**
Boundary Cl. LS15: Leeds ... 6E **35**
Boundary Farm Rd. LS17: Leeds ... 6E **13**
Boundary Pl. LS7: Leeds ... 3A **32**
Boundary St. LS7: Leeds ... 3A **32**
Bourse, The LS1: Leeds ... 5E **5**
Bowater Ct. BD4: B'frd ... 5B **36**
Bowcliffe Rd. LS10: Leeds ... 3B **42**
Bower Rd. LS15: Leeds ... 2E **35**
Bowfell Cl. LS14: Leeds ... 1A **34**
Bowland Cl. LS15: Leeds ... 6G **33**
Bowling Grn. Ter. LS11: Leeds ... 2F **41**
Bowling Grn. Vw. BD11: B'frd ... 3G **47**
Bowman La. LS10: Leeds ... 6G **5** (6H **31**)
Bowness Av. BD10: B'frd ... 1A **26**
Bowood Av. LS7: Leeds ... 4E **21**
Bowood Cres. LS7: Leeds ... 4E **21**
Bowood Gro. LS7: Leeds ... 4E **21**
Bow St. LS9: Leeds ... 6A **32**
Boyd Av. BD3: B'frd ... 4A **26**
Bracken Ct. LS12: Leeds ... 2C **40**
LS17: Leeds ... 2G **21**
Bracken Edge LS8: Leeds ... 6B **22**
Bracken Grn. WF3: E Ard ... 3A **58**
Bracken Hill LS17: Leeds ... 2G **21**
Brackenhurst Dr. LS17: Leeds ... 1G **21**
Brackenhurst Pl. LS17: Leeds ... 1G **21**
Brackenwood Cl. LS8: Leeds ... 4A **22**
Brackenwood Ct. WF1: Wake ... 6F **59**
Brackenwood Dr. LS8: Leeds ... 3A **22**
Brackenwood Grn. LS8: Leeds ... 3A **22**
Brackenwood Rd. WF1: Wake ... 6F **59**
Bradburn Rd. WF3: Rothw ... 6C **52**
Bradford & Wakefield Rd. BD4: B'frd ... 2E **47**
Bradford Rd. BD3: Pud ... 4B **26**
BD4: B'frd ... 1B **46**
BD11: B'frd ... 4B **48**
(Buttercup Way)
BD11: B'frd ... 5C **46**
(Whitehall Rd. E.)
BD11: B'frd ... 2F **47**
(Woodview)
BD19: B'frd, Cleck ... 5C **46**
LS20: Guis, Men ... 1D **6**
LS28: Pud ... 4B **26**
LS29: Men ... 1D **6**
WF2: Wake ... 6A **58**
(not continuous)
WF3: E Ard, Morl ... 2B **56**
BRADLEY HILL ... 3A **28**
Bradley Hill Vw. *LS28: Leeds ... 3A **28***
(off Swinnow La.)
Bradley La. LS28: Pud ... 6D **26**
Bradley Ter. LS17: Leeds ... 5C **14**
Bradstock Gdns. LS27: Morl ... 3G **49**
Braithwaite Row LS10: Leeds ... 5A **42**
Braithwaite St. LS11: Leeds ... 1D **40**
Bramble Ct. WF1: Wake ... 6C **58**
Bramble M. LS17: Leeds ... 4E **15**
Bramble Sq. WF3: E Ard ... 3B **58**
Brambling M. LS27: Morl ... 5A **50**
Bramham Pk. Ct. LS10: Leeds ... 6H **51**
Bramleigh Dr. LS27: Morl ... 3G **49**
Bramleigh Gro. LS27: Morl ... 3G **49**
BRAMLEY ... 2D **28**
Bramley Baths (Swimming Pool)
... 2B **28**
Bramley Cen. LS13: Leeds ... 2D **28**
Bramley Gdns. LS14: Leeds ... 2C **24**
Bramley Station (Rail) ... 4B **28**
Bramley's Yd. LS1: Leeds ... 4F **5**
Bramstan Av. LS13: Leeds ... 2A **28**
Bramstan Cl. LS13: Leeds ... 2A **28**
Bramstan Gdns. LS13: Leeds ... 2A **28**
Brancepeth Pl. LS12: Leeds ... 6C **30**
Branch Cl. LS12: Leeds ... 3G **39**
Branch End LS27: Morl ... 2D **48**
Branch Pl. LS12: Leeds ... 3G **39**
Branch Rd. LS12: Leeds ... 3G **39**
(Branch Pl.)
Branch Rd. LS12: Leeds ... 5A **30**
(Stocks Hill)
Branch St. LS12: Leeds ... 3G **39**
Brander App. LS9: Leeds ... 4F **33**
Brander Cl. LS9: Leeds ... 4F **33**
Brander Dr. LS9: Leeds ... 4E **33**
Brander Gro. LS9: Leeds ... 4E **33**
Brander Rd. LS9: Leeds ... 3F **33**
Brander St. LS9: Leeds ... 3F **33**
Brandling Ct. LS10: Leeds ... 4G **51**
BRANDON ... 4G **15**
Brandon Ct. LS17: Leeds ... 4E **15**
Brandon Cres. LS17: S'cft ... 2G **15**
Brandon La. LS17: Leeds ... 1F **15**
LS17: S'cft ... 2H **15**
Brandon Rd. LS3: Leeds ... 3A **4** (5E **31**)
Brandon St. LS12: Leeds ... 6D **30**
Brandon Ter. LS17: Leeds ... 4D **14**
Brandon Vw. LS17: Leeds ... 4F **15**
Brandon Way LS7: Leeds ... 6H **21**
Brandon Way Cres. LS7: Leeds ... 6A **22**
Branksome Pl. LS3: Leeds ... 3A **4**
LS6: Leeds ... 3C **30**
Bransby Cl. LS28: Pud ... 3G **27**
Bransby Ct. LS28: Pud ... 3G **27**
Bransby Ri. LS28: Pud ... 2G **27**
Bransdale Av. LS20: Guis ... 5G **7**
Bransdale Cl. LS20: Guis ... 5G **7**
Bransdale Gdns. LS20: Guis ... 5G **7**
Bransdale Gth. LS20: Guis ... 5G **7**
Brantford St. LS7: Leeds ... 5H **21**
Branwell Av. WF17: Bat ... 6G **47**
Branwell Wlk. WF17: Bat ... 6H **47**
Brathay Gdns. LS14: Leeds ... 2A **34**
Brayshaw Rd. WF3: E Ard ... 5G **57**
Brayton App. LS14: Leeds ... 6C **24**
Brayton Cl. LS14: Leeds ... 6C **24**
Brayton Gth. LS14: Leeds ... 6D **24**
Brayton Grange LS14: Leeds ... 6D **24**
Brayton Grn. LS14: Leeds ... 6D **24**
(not continuous)
Brayton Gro. LS14: Leeds ... 6C **24**
Brayton Pl. LS14: Leeds ... 6D **24**
Brayton Sq. LS14: Leeds ... 6D **24**
Brayton Ter. LS14: Leeds ... 6C **24**
Brayton Wlk. LS14: Leeds ... 6C **24**
Breary Av. LS18: H'fth ... 2D **18**
(not continuous)
Breary Ter. LS18: H'fth ... 2D **18**
Breary Wlk. LS18: H'fth ... 2D **18**
Brecks La. LS26: Kip ... 3H **45**
Brecon App. LS9: Leeds ... 4F **33**
Brecon Ct. LS9: Leeds ... 4F **33**
Brecon Ri. LS9: Leeds ... 4F **33**
Brendon Ct. BD4: B'frd ... 4A **36**
Brendon Ho. *BD4: B'frd ... 5A **36***
(off Landscove Av.)
Brendon Wlk. BD4: B'frd ... 5A **36**
(not continuous)
Brentwood Ct. LS16: Leeds ... 3G **19**
Brentwood Gro. LS12: Leeds ... 6A **30**
Brentwood St. LS12: Leeds ... 6A **30**
Brentwood Ter. LS12: Leeds ... 6A **30**
Brett Gdns. LS11: Leeds ... 3F **41**
Brewery Pl. LS10: Leeds ... 6G **5** (6H **31**)
Brian Cres. LS15: Leeds ... 3B **34**
Brian Pl. LS15: Leeds ... 2B **34**
BRIANSIDE ... 2A **34**
Brian Vw. LS15: Leeds ... 2C **34**
Briar Cl. LS28: Pud ... 3F **27**
Briardene LS26: Rothw ... 5C **54**
Briarfield Gdns. LS27: Morl ... 3C **48**
Briarlea Cl. LS19: Yead ... 4B **8**
Briarmains Rd. WF17: Bat ... 6H **47**
Briarsdale Ct. LS8: Leeds ... 2E **33**
Briarsdale Cft. LS8: Leeds ... 2E **33**
Briarsdale Gth. LS8: Leeds ... 2E **33**
Briarsdale Hgts. LS9: Leeds ... 2E **33**
Briarsdale M. LS9: Leeds ... 2D **32**
Briarwood Cl. WF1: Wake ... 6F **59**
Brick Mill Rd. LS28: Pud ... 1H **37**
Brick St. LS9: Leeds ... 5H **5** (6H **31**)
Bridge, The LS10: Leeds ... 6F **5**
Bridge Ct. LS11: Leeds ... 2E **41**
LS27: Morl ... 6H **49**
Bridge End LS1: Leeds ... 5E **5** (6G **31**)
*LS11: Leeds ... 6G **31***
(off Meadow La.)
Bridge Fold LS5: Leeds ... 1F **29**
Bridge Pl. LS18: H'fth ... 1C **18**
Bridge Rd. LS5: Leeds ... 1F **29**
LS11: Leeds ... 2E **41**
LS13: Leeds ... 6G **17**

68 A-Z Leeds

Bridge St.—Burley Wood Mt.

Bridge St. LS2: Leeds 4G **5** (5H **31**)
LS27: Morl 6H **49** & 1A **56**
Bridge Ter. LS27: Morl 6H **49**
Bridge Vw. LS13: Leeds 6G **17**
Bridgewater Ct. LS6: Leeds 5D **20**
Bridgewater Pl. LS11: Leeds 6D **4** (1F **41**)
Bridgewater Rd. LS9: Leeds 2B **42**
Bri. Wood Cl. LS18: H'fth 2D **18**
Bri. Wood Vw. LS18: H'fth 1D **18**
Bridle Path Rd. LS15: Leeds 3A **34**
LS17: Leeds 4F **15**
Bridle Path Wlk. LS15: Leeds 3A **34**
Briggate LS1: Leeds 5E **5** (6G **31**)
Briggs Bldgs. *LS27: Morl 5H **49***
(off Melbourne St.)
Brighton Av. LS27: Morl 4F **49**
Brighton Cliff LS13: Leeds 3C **28**
Brighton Gro. LS13: Leeds 4D **28**
Bright St. LS27: Morl 5F **49**
LS28: Pud 3H **27**
WF3: E Ard 3H **57**
Brignall Cft. LS9: Leeds 4B **32**
Brignall Gth. LS9: Leeds 4B **32**
Brignall Way LS9: Leeds 4B **32**
Brinsmead Ct. LS26: Rothw 2H **53**
Bristol St. LS7: Leeds 1H **5** (4H **31**)
Britannia Cl. LS28: Pud 3H **27**
Britannia Ct. LS13: Leeds 5A **28**
Britannia Ho. LS1: Leeds 4C **4**
Britannia M. LS28: Pud 5A **28**
Britannia St. LS1: Leeds 5C **4** (6F **31**)
LS28: Pud 3H **27**
Broadcroft Chase WF3: E Ard 4C **56**
Broadcroft Dr. WF3: E Ard 4C **56**
Broadcroft Gro. WF3: E Ard 3C **56**
Broadcroft Way WF3: E Ard 3C **56**
Broadfield Cl. BD4: B'frd 6A **36**
Broadfields LS18: H'fth 2D **18**
Broadgate Av. LS18: H'fth 2D **18**
Broadgate Ct. LS18: H'fth 3D **18**
Broadgate Cres. LS18: H'fth 3C **18**
Broadgate Dr. LS18: H'fth 2D **18**
Broadgate La. LS18: H'fth 2C **18**
Broadgate M. LS18: H'fth 3D **18**
Broadgate Ri. LS18: H'fth 3D **18**
Broadgate Wlk. LS18: H'fth 3C **18**
Broadlands Av. LS28: Pud 6H **27**
Broadlands Ct. LS28: Pud 6H **27**
Broadlands Gdns. LS28: Pud 6A **28**
Broadlands Pl. LS28: Pud 6H **27**
Broadlands Vw. LS28: Pud 6A **28**
Broadland Way WF3: Wake 3E **59**
Broad La. LS5: Leeds 1C **28**
LS13: Leeds 3A **28**
Broad La. Cl. LS13: Leeds 1E **29**
Broadlea Av. LS13: Leeds 1E **29**
Broadlea Cl. LS13: Leeds 1E **29**
Broadlea Cres. LS13: Leeds 1E **29**
Broadlea Gdns. LS13: Leeds 1E **29**
Broadlea Gro. LS13: Leeds 1E **29**
Broadlea Hill LS13: Leeds 1E **29**
Broadlea Mt. LS13: Leeds 2F **29**
Broadlea Oval LS13: Leeds 1E **29**
Broadlea Pl. LS13: Leeds 2E **29**
Broadlea Rd. LS13: Leeds 1E **29**
Broadlea St. LS13: Leeds 1E **29**
Broadlea Ter. LS13: Leeds 1E **29**
Broadlea Vw. LS13: Leeds 1D **28**
Broadmeadows WF1: Wake 6E **59**
Broadstone Way BD4: B'frd 6A **36**
Broad St. LS28: Pud 2E **27**
Broad Wlk. LS2: Leeds 2E **31**
Broadway LS5: Leeds 4E **19**
LS15: Leeds 1H **43**
LS18: H'fth 4H **17**
LS20: Guis 5E **7**
Broadway Av. LS6: Leeds 3C **30**
Broadway Dr. LS18: H'fth 3B **18**
Brodrick Ct. LS6: Leeds 6B **20**
Brodwell Grange
LS18: H'fth 3E **19**
Brompton Gro. LS11: Leeds 5F **41**
Brompton Mt. LS11: Leeds 5F **41**
Brompton Row LS11: Leeds 5F **41**
Brompton Ter. LS11: Leeds 5F **41**
Brompton Vw. LS11: Leeds 5F **41**
Bronte Ho. *BD4: B'frd 3A **36***
(off Eversley Dr.)
LS7: Leeds 2G **31**
Brookfield Av. LS8: Leeds 1B **32**
LS13: Leeds 5F **17**
Brookfield Ct. LS13: Leeds 5F **17**
Brookfield Gdns. LS13: Leeds 6F **17**
Brookfield Pl. LS6: Leeds 5C **20**
(not continuous)
Brookfield Rd. LS6: Leeds 5C **20**
Brookfield St. LS10: Leeds 2H **41**
Brookfield Ter. *LS6: Leeds 5C **20***
(off Brookfield Rd.)
LS10: Leeds 2H **41**
Brookfoot Av. BD11: B'frd 4C **46**
Brookhill Av. LS17: Leeds 5A **14**
Brookhill Cl. LS17: Leeds 5A **14**
Brookhill Cres. LS17: Leeds 5A **14**
Brookhill Dr. LS17: Leeds 5A **14**
Brookhill Gro. LS17: Leeds 5A **14**
Brookhouse Gdns. BD10: B'frd 3B **16**
BROOKLANDS 1H **33**
Brooklands Av. LS14: Leeds 1H **33**
Brooklands Cl. LS14: Leeds 1G **33**
LS29: Men 1D **6**
Brooklands Ct. LS14: Leeds 1H **33**
Brooklands Cres. LS14: Leeds 1G **33**
LS19: Yead 3D **8**
Brooklands Dr. LS14: Leeds 1G **33**
LS19: Yead 3D **8**
Brooklands Gth. LS14: Leeds 1H **33**
Brooklands Gro. LS29: Men 1D **6**
Brooklands La. LS14: Leeds 1H **33**
LS29: Men 1C **6**
Brooklands Towers LS14: Leeds 6A **24**
Brooklands Vw. LS14: Leeds 1H **33**
(not continuous)
Brookleigh LS28: Pud 5D **16**
Brooklyn Av. LS12: Leeds 6A **30**
Brooklyn Pl. LS12: Leeds 6A **30**
Brooklyn St. LS12: Leeds 6A **30**
Brooklyn Ter. LS12: Leeds 6A **30**
Brooksbank Dr. LS15: Leeds 5A **34**
Brookside LS17: Leeds 4A **14**
Broom Cl. LS10: Leeds 2B **52**
Broom Ct. LS10: Leeds 3B **52**
Broom Cres. LS10: Leeds 2A **52**
Broom Cross LS10: Leeds 2A **52**
Broomfield LS16: Leeds 5H **11**
Broomfield Cres. LS6: Leeds 1B **30**
Broomfield Pl. LS6: Leeds 2B **30**
Broomfield Rd. LS6: Leeds 1B **30**
Broomfield St. LS6: Leeds 2B **30**
Broomfield Ter. LS6: Leeds 2B **30**
Broomfield Vw. LS6: Leeds 2B **30**
Broom Gdns. LS10: Leeds 2A **52**
Broom Gth. LS10: Leeds 2B **52**
Broom Gro. LS10: Leeds 3B **52**
Broomhill Av. LS17: Leeds 1H **21**
Broomhill Cres. LS17: Leeds 1H **21**
Broomhill Dr. LS17: Leeds 2G **21**
Broom Hill Rd. LS9: Leeds 4D **32**
Broom Lawn LS10: Leeds 2A **52**
Broom Mills Rd. LS28: Pud 1G **27**
Broom Mt. LS10: Leeds 3B **52**
Broom Nook LS10: Leeds 2B **52**
Broom Pl. LS10: Leeds 2B **52**
Broom Rd. LS10: Leeds 3A **52**
Broom Ter. LS10: Leeds 2B **52**
Broom Vw. LS10: Leeds 2B **52**
Broom Wlk. LS10: Leeds 3B **52**
Broughton Av. LS9: Leeds 3C **32**
Broughton Ho. BD4: B'frd 6B **36**
Broughton Ter. LS9: Leeds 3C **32**
LS28: Pud 5G **27**
Brown Av. LS11: Leeds 3C **40**
Brownberrie Av. LS18: H'fth 6C **10**
Brownberrie Cres. LS18: H'fth 6B **10**
Brownberrie Dr. LS18: H'fth 6C **10**
(not continuous)
Brownberrie Gdns. LS18: H'fth 6B **10**
Brownberrie La. LS18: H'fth 6H **9**
Brownberrie Wlk. LS18: H'fth 6C **10**
Brown Hill Av. LS9: Leeds 3C **32**
Brown Hill Cl. BD11: B'frd 2C **46**
Brown Hill Cres. LS9: Leeds 3C **32**
Brown Hill Dr. BD11: B'frd 3C **46**
Brown Hill Ter. LS9: Leeds 3C **32**
Brown La. E. LS11: Leeds 2D **40**
Brown La. W. LS12: Leeds 2C **40**
Brownlea Cl. LS19: Yead 4B **8**
Brown Pl. LS11: Leeds 3C **40**
Brown Rd. LS11: Leeds 3C **40**
Bruce Gdns. LS12: Leeds 6C **30**
Bruce Lawn LS12: Leeds 6C **30**
Brudenell Av. LS6: Leeds 2D **30**
Brudenell Gro. LS6: Leeds 2D **30**
Brudenell Mt. LS6: Leeds 2C **30**
Brudenell Rd. LS6: Leeds 2C **30**
Brudenell St. LS6: Leeds 2D **30**
Brudenell Vw. LS6: Leeds 2D **30**
Brunel Rd. WF2: Wake 6B **58**
Brunswick Ct. LS2: Leeds 2G **5** (4H **31**)
Brunswick Pl. BD10: B'frd 4A **16**
LS27: Morl 5H **49**
Brunswick Rd. LS28: Pud 5G **27**
Brunswick Row LS2: Leeds 2G **5** (4H **31**)
Brunswick St. LS27: Morl 4G **49**
Brunswick Ter. LS2: Leeds 2E **5** (4G **31**)
(not continuous)
LS27: Morl 5A **50**
BRUNTCLIFFE 5D **48**
Bruntcliffe Av. LS27: Morl 5E **49**
Bruntcliffe Cl. LS27: Morl 5F **49**
Bruntcliffe Dr. LS27: Morl 5F **49**
Bruntcliffe La. LS27: Morl 5E **49**
Bruntcliffe Rd. LS27: Morl 5D **48**
Bruntcliffe Way LS27: Morl 5E **49**
Brussels St. LS9: Leeds 5H **5** (6H **31**)
Bruton Gallery 4C **4** (5F **31**)
Bryan St. LS28: Pud 1F **27**
Bryan St. Nth. LS28: Pud 1F **27**
Bryngate LS26: Rothw 3C **54**
Bryony Ct. LS10: Leeds 4B **52**
Buckden Ct. LS29: Men 2D **6**
Buckingham Av. LS6: Leeds 1C **30**
Buckingham Dr. LS6: Leeds 1C **30**
Buckingham Gro. LS6: Leeds 1C **30**
Buckingham Ho. *LS6: Leeds 1C **30***
(off Headingley La.)
Buckingham Mt. LS6: Leeds 2C **30**
Buckingham Rd. LS6: Leeds 1C **30**
Buckle La. LS29: Men 2D **6**
Buckley Av. LS11: Leeds 4F **41**
Buck Stone Av. LS17: Leeds 5D **12**
Buck Stone Cl. LS17: Leeds 5E **13**
Buck Stone Cres. LS17: Leeds 5E **13**
Buck Stone Dr. LS17: Leeds 5D **12**
Buckstone Dr. LS19: Yead 6C **8**
(not continuous)
Buck Stone Gdns. LS17: Leeds 5E **13**
Buck Stone Grn. LS17: Leeds 5D **12**
Buck Stone Gro. LS17: Leeds 5D **12**
Buck Stone Mt. LS17: Leeds 5D **12**
Buck Stone Oval LS17: Leeds 5D **12**
Buck Stone Ri. LS17: Leeds 5D **12**
Buck Stone Rd. LS17: Leeds 5D **12**
Buck Stone Vw. LS17: Leeds 5D **12**
Buck Stone Way LS17: Leeds 5D **12**
Buckthorne Cl. WF3: E Ard 3H **57**
Buckthorne Ct. WF3: E Ard 3H **57**
Buckthorne Dr. WF3: E Ard 3H **57**
Buckthorne Fold WF3: E Ard 3H **57**
Buckton Cl. LS11: Leeds 3E **41**
Buckton Mt. LS11: Leeds 3E **41**
Buckton Vw. LS11: Leeds 3E **41**
Bude Rd. LS11: Leeds 4F **41**
Buller Cl. LS9: Leeds 4E **33**
Buller Ct. LS9: Leeds 4E **33**
Buller Gro. LS9: Leeds 4D **32**
Buller St. LS26: Rothw 3C **54**
Bullerthorpe La. LS15: Leeds 1F **45**
LS26: Swil 1E **55**
Bullough La. LS26: Rothw 2H **53**
Bungalows, The *LS15: Leeds 2D **34***
(off Church La.)
Burchett Gro. LS6: Leeds 1E **31**
Burchett Pl. LS6: Leeds 1E **31**
Burchett Ter. LS6: Leeds 1F **31**
Burdett Ter. LS4: Leeds 3A **30**
Burghley M. LS10: Leeds 6H **51**
Burland Ter. LS26: Swil 5G **45**
BURLEY 3B **30**
Burley Grange Rd. LS4: Leeds 3A **30**
Burley Hill Cres. LS4: Leeds 2H **29**
Burley Hill Dr. LS4: Leeds 2H **29**
Burley Hill Trad. Est. LS4: Leeds 2A **30**
Burley La. LS18: H'fth 3B **18**
LS29: Men 1B **6**
Burley Lodge Pl. *LS6: Leeds 4C **30***
(off Burley Lodge Rd.)
Burley Lodge Rd. LS6: Leeds 3C **30**
Burley Lodge St. LS6: Leeds 4C **30**
Burley Lodge Ter. LS6: Leeds 4C **30**
Burley Park Station (Rail) 2B **30**
Burley Pl. LS4: Leeds 4B **30**
Burley Rd. LS3: Leeds 3C **30**
LS4: Leeds 2A **30**
Burley St. LS3: Leeds 3A **4** (5D **30**)
Burley Wood Ct. LS4: Leeds 2H **29**
Burley Wood Cres. LS4: Leeds 2H **29**
Burley Wood La. LS4: Leeds 2A **30**
Burley Wood Mt. LS4: Leeds 2H **29**

A-Z Leeds 69

Castle Head La.—Churchfield Gro.

Castle Head La. WF3: E Ard 3B **58**
WF3: Wake 4B **58**
Castle Ings Cl. LS12: Leeds 4D **38**
Castle Ings Dr. LS12: Leeds 4D **38**
Castle Ings Gdns. LS12: Leeds 4D **38**
Castle Lodge Av. LS26: Rothw 2E **53**
Castle Lodge Ct. LS26: Rothw 3E **53**
Castle Lodge Gdns. LS26: Rothw 3D **52**
Castle Lodge Garth LS26: Rothw 2E **53**
Castle Lodge M. LS26: Rothw 3E **53**
Castle Lodge Way LS26: Rothw 3E **53**
Castle Rd. LS26: Rothw 4F **53**
Castle St. LS1: Leeds 4B **4** (5E **31**)
Castleton Cl. LS12: Leeds 6D **30**
Castleton Rd. LS12: Leeds 5C **30**
Castle Vw. LS17: Leeds 2F **21**
Castle Wood Cl. LS18: H'fth 3D **18**
Catalina LS12: Leeds 6A **4** (6E **31**)
Cathcart St. LS6: Leeds 2E **31**
Catherine Gro. LS11: Leeds 4F **41**
Cautley Rd. LS9: Leeds 1B **42**
Cavalier App. LS9: Leeds 1B **42**
Cavalier Cl. LS9: Leeds 1B **42**
Cavalier Ct. LS9: Leeds 1B **42**
Cavalier Dr. BD10: B'frd 3A **16**
Cavalier Gdns. LS9: Leeds 1B **42**
Cavalier Ga. LS9: Leeds 1B **42**
Cavalier Grn. LS9: Leeds 1B **42**
CAVALIER HILL 6A **32**
Cavalier M. LS9: Leeds 1B **42**
Cavalier Vw. LS9: Leeds 1B **42**
Cave La. WF3: E Ard 3H **57**
Cavendish App. BD11: B'frd 3G **47**
Cavendish Ct. *BD11: B'frd 3G* ***47***
(off Cavendish App.)
Cavendish Dr. LS20: Guis 5F **7**
Cavendish Gro. LS20: Guis 5F **7**
Cavendish M. BD11: B'frd 3G **47**
LS17: Leeds 5H **13**
Cavendish Pl. LS28: Pud 4F **27**
Cavendish Ri. LS28: Pud 6A **28**
Cavendish Rd. LS2: Leeds 1C **4** (3F **31**)
LS20: Guis 5F **7**
Cavendish Sq. LS28: Pud 4G **27**
Cavendish St. LS3: Leeds 3A **4** (5D **30**)
LS19: Yead 2E **9**
LS28: Pud 6A **28**
Caythorpe Rd. LS16: Leeds 4H **19**
Cecil Gro. LS12: Leeds 5A **30**
Cecil Mt. LS12: Leeds 5A **30**
Cecil Rd. LS12: Leeds 5A **30**
Cecil St. LS12: Leeds 5A **30**
Cedar Av. LS12: Leeds 6H **29**
Cedar Cl. LS12: Leeds 6A **30**
Cedar Ct. *LS17: Leeds 1H* ***21***
(off Harrogate Rd.)
LS26: Rothw 3E **55**
Cedar Mt. LS12: Leeds 6H **29**
Cedar Pl. LS12: Leeds 6H **29**
Cedar Rd. LS12: Leeds 6H **29**
Cedar St. LS12: Leeds 6H **29**
Cedar Ter. LS12: Leeds 6H **29**
Cemetery La. WF3: Rothw 2E **59**
Cemetery Rd. LS11: Leeds 3E **41**
LS19: Yead 2E **9**
LS28: Pud 5E **27**
Centaur Ho. LS1: Leeds 3B **4** (5E **31**)
Central Pk. LS11: Leeds 1F **41**
Central Rd. LS1: Leeds 5F **5** (6G **31**)
Central St. LS1: Leeds 4C **4** (5F **31**)
Centre 27 Bus. Pk. WF17: Bat 6B **48**
Century Way LS15: Leeds 6F **35**
Chaddle Wood Cl. LS18: H'fth 2C **18**
Chadwick St. LS10: Leeds 1H **41**
(not continuous)
Chadwick St. Sth. LS10: Leeds 1H **41**
Chalfont Rd. LS16: Leeds 3H **19**
Chalice Cl. LS10: Leeds 2A **52**
Chalner Av. LS27: Morl 6F **49**
Chalner Cl. LS27: Morl 6F **49**
Chancellor Ct. LS2: Leeds 5F **5** (6G **31**)
Chancellor St. LS6: Leeds 2F **31**
Chandlers, The LS2: Leeds 6G **5**
Chandlers Cl. WF1: Wake 6D **58**
Chandlers Wharf LS13: Leeds 5G **17**
Chandos Av. LS8: Leeds 3A **22**
Chandos Fold LS8: Leeds 4A **22**
Chandos Gdns. LS8: Leeds 3A **22**
Chandos Gth. LS8: Leeds 3A **22**
Chandos Grn. LS8: Leeds 3A **22**
Chandos Pl. LS8: Leeds 3B **22**
Chandos Ter. LS8: Leeds 3B **22**
Chandos Wlk. LS8: Leeds 3A **22**
Change All. LS1: Leeds 4E **5**
Chantrell Ct. LS2: Leeds 5G **5** (6H **31**)
Chantry Ct. LS27: Morl 4H **49**
Chantry Cft. LS15: Leeds 6D **34**
Chantry Gth. LS15: Leeds 6D **34**
CHAPEL ALLERTON 5F **21**
CHAPEL ALLERTON HOSPITAL 6H **21**
Chapel Allerton Lawn Tennis & Squash Club 4G **21**
Chapel Ct. LS15: Leeds 5A **34**
Chapel Fold LS6: Leeds 2B **30**
LS11: Leeds 5C **40**
LS12: Leeds 6A ***30***
(off Wesley Rd.)
LS15: Leeds 5A **34**
LS28: Pud 1G ***37***
(off Littlemoor Rd.)
Chapel Grn. LS28: Pud 1F **37**
Chapel Hill LS10: Leeds 4H **51**
LS19: Yead 2D **8**
LS27: Morl 4G **49**
Chapel La. LS6: Leeds 1B **30**
(not continuous)
LS12: Leeds 2D **38**
(Maple Dr.)
LS12: Leeds 6A **30**
(Stocks Hill)
LS19: Yead 2D **8**
Chapel Pl. LS6: Leeds 6B **20**
Chapel Rd. LS7: Leeds 6H **21**
Chapel Sq. *LS6: Leeds 6B* ***20***
(off Chapel St.)
LS6: Leeds 6B **20**
LS13: Leeds 6G **17**
LS15: Leeds 5A **34**
LS19: Yead 5D **8**
LS28: Pud 4G **27**
(Richardshaw La.)
Chapel St. LS28: Pud 4D **16**
(Thornhill Gro.)
WF3: E Ard 2D **56**
(Fenton St.)
WF3: E Ard 4G **57**
(Thorpe Rd.)
WF3: Rothw 6F **53**
WF3: Wake 6G **59**
Chapel Ter. *LS6: Leeds 6B* ***20***
(off Chapel St.)
CHAPELTOWN 1H **31**
Chapeltown LS28: Pud 1F **37**
Chapeltown Bus. Cen. *LS7: Leeds 1H* ***31***
(off Chapeltown Rd.)
Chapeltown Rd. LS7: Leeds 2H **31**
Chapel Vw. LS27: Morl 1C **48**
Chapel Yd. *LS15: Leeds 1D* ***44***
(off Meynell Rd.)
LS26: Rothw 4C **54**
Charles Av. LS9: Leeds 1B **42**
WF1: Wake 6D **58**
Charles Gdns. LS11: Leeds 2E **41**
Charles Gro. LS26: Rothw 3C **54**
Charles St. LS18: H'fth 3B **18**
LS27: Morl 5H **49**
LS28: Pud 2F **27**
Charlotte Cl. WF17: Bat 6H **47**
Charlotte Gro. LS15: Leeds 5B **34**
Charlton Gro. LS9: Leeds 6C **32**
Charlton Pl. LS9: Leeds 6C **32**
Charlton Rd. LS9: Leeds 6C **32**
Charlton St. LS9: Leeds 6C **32**
Charnley Dr. LS7: Leeds 5A **22**
Chartist's Ct. *LS27: Morl 6G* ***49***
(off Gt. Northern St.)
Chartists Way LS27: Morl 6G **49**
Chartwell Ct. LS17: Leeds 4D **14**
Charville Gdns. LS17: Leeds 6H **15**
Chase, The LS19: Yead 5C **8**
Chase Av. LS27: Morl 2A **56**
Chatswood Av. LS11: Leeds 1D **50**
Chatswood Cres. LS11: Leeds 1D **50**
Chatswood Dr. LS11: Leeds 6D **40**
Chatsworth Av. LS28: Pud 5C **26**
Chatsworth Cl. LS8: Leeds 2C **32**
Chatsworth Cres. LS28: Pud 5C **26**
Chatsworth Dr. LS28: Pud 5C **26**
Chatsworth Fall LS28: Pud 5C **26**
Chatsworth Ind. Est. LS12: Leeds 1B **40**
Chatsworth M. LS27: Morl 6A **50**
Chatsworth Ri. LS28: Pud 5C **26**
Chatsworth Rd. LS8: Leeds 2C **32**
LS28: Pud 5C **26**
Chaucer Av. LS28: Pud 1H **37**
WF3: Wake 5G **59**
Chaucer Gdns. LS28: Pud 1H **37**
Chaucer Gro. LS28: Pud 1H **37**
Cheapside *LS27: Morl 4G* ***49***
(off Chapel Hill)
Chellow Ter. BD11: B'frd 5D **46**
Chelsea Cl. LS12: Leeds 1A **40**
Chelsfield Ct. LS15: Leeds 2F **35**
Chelsfield Way LS15: Leeds 2F **35**
Cheltenham St. LS12: Leeds 1B **40**
Chelwood Av. LS8: Leeds 6B **14**
Chelwood Cres. LS8: Leeds 1B **22**
Chelwood Dr. LS8: Leeds 6B **14**
Chelwood Gro. LS8: Leeds 6B **14**
Chelwood Mt. LS8: Leeds 6B **14**
Chelwood Pl. LS8: Leeds 6A **14**
Chenies Cl. LS14: Leeds 4G **33**
Chepstow Dr. LS10: Leeds 6H **51**
Cherry Ct. LS6: Leeds 5D **20**
LS9: Leeds 4A ***32***
(off Cherry Pl.)
Cherry Gro. LS6: Leeds 6D **20**
Cherry Lea Ct. LS19: Yead 4D **8**
Cherry Pl. LS9: Leeds 4A **32**
Cherry Ri. LS14: Leeds 3C **24**
Cherry Row LS9: Leeds 2H **5** (4A **32**)
Cherry Tree Av. BD10: B'frd 4A **16**
Cherry Tree Ct. WF3: E Ard 4G **57**
Cherry Tree Cres. LS28: Pud 2F **27**
Cherry Tree Dr. LS28: Pud 2F **27**
Cherry Tree Wlk. LS2: Leeds 5F **5**
WF3: E Ard 4G **57**
Cherrywood Cl. LS14: Leeds 2B **24**
Cherrywood Gdns. LS14: Leeds 2B **24**
Chervana Ct. BD4: B'frd 3A **36**
Chesney Av. LS10: Leeds 3H **41**
Chesney Pk. Ind. Est. LS10: Leeds 3H **41**
Chester St. LS12: Leeds 5A **30**
Chesterton Ct. LS15: Leeds 1D **44**
Chestnut Av. LS6: Leeds 2C **30**
LS15: Leeds 3D **34**
Chestnut Cl. *LS7: Leeds 6A* ***22***
(off Harehills La.)
Chestnut Dr. LS16: Leeds 4H **11**
Chestnut Gdns. LS12: Leeds 1A **40**
LS27: Morl 2G **49**
Chestnut Gro. LS6: Leeds 2C **30**
LS26: Rothw 3E **55**
LS28: Pud 5D **16**
Chestnut Pl. LS6: Leeds 2C **30**
Chestnut Ri. LS12: Leeds 1H **39**
Chestnut St. LS6: Leeds 2C **30**
Chestnut Vw. LS27: Morl 2G **49**
Chestnut Way LS16: Leeds 4H **11**
Chevin Av. LS29: Men 1D **6**
Chevin End LS29: Guis, Men 2D **6**
Chevin End Rd. LS29: Guis 2F **7**
Chevington Ct. LS19: Yead 6C **8**
Chichester St. LS12: Leeds 5A **30**
Chiltern Ct. LS13: Leeds 6G **17**
Chilver Dr. BD4: B'frd 5C **36**
Chippendale Ct. LS29: Men 1D **6**
Chirton Gro. LS8: Leeds 6C **22**
Chiswick St. LS6: Leeds 4C **30**
Chiswick Ter. *LS6: Leeds 3C* ***30***
(off Chiswick Vw.)
Chorley La. LS2: Leeds 2B **4** (4E **31**)
LS3: Leeds 3B **4** (5E **31**)
Christ Chu. Av. LS12: Leeds 5H **29**
Christ Chu. Mt. LS12: Leeds 5H **29**
Christ Chu. Pde. LS12: Leeds 5H **29**
Christ Chu. Pl. LS12: Leeds 5H **29**
Christ Chu. Rd. LS12: Leeds 5H **29**
Christ Chu. Ter. LS12: Leeds 5H **29**
Christ Chu. Vw. LS12: Leeds 5H **29**
Christiana Ter. LS27: Morl 4H **49**
Christopher Rd. LS6: Leeds 2F **31**
Church Av. LS6: Leeds 4D **20**
LS18: H'fth 2B **18**
LS26: Swil 5G **45**
LS27: Morl 1C **48**
Church Cl. LS14: Leeds 1B **34**
(not continuous)
LS26: Swil 5G **45**
Church Ct. LS19: Yead 3D **8**
Church Cres. LS17: Leeds 6G **13**
LS18: H'fth 2B **18**
LS19: Yead 3C **8**
LS26: Swil 6H **45**
Church Cft. LS29: Men 1B **6**
Church Farm Cl. WF3: Rothw 3E **59**
Church Farm Gth. LS17: Leeds 5H **15**
Churchfield Cft. LS26: Rothw 4H **53**
Churchfield Gro. LS26: Rothw 3G **53**

A-Z Leeds 71

Churchfield La.—Colenso Ter.

Churchfield La. LS26: Rothw 3G **53**
Churchfield Rd. LS26: Rothw 4G **53**
Church Gdns. LS17: Leeds 6H **13**
LS27: Morl 2C **48**
Church Ga. LS18: H'fth 2B **18**
Churchgate LS27: Morl 2C **48**
Church Gro. LS6: Leeds 4C **20**
LS18: H'fth 2B **18**
Church Hill Gdns. LS28: Pud 3H **27**
Church Hill Grn. LS28: Pud 3H **27**
Church Hill Mt. LS28: Pud 3H **27**
Churchill Gdns. *LS2: Leeds 3F **31***
(off Bk. Blenheim Ter.)
Church La. LS2: Leeds 5G **5** (6H **31**)
LS6: Leeds 4D **20**
LS7: Leeds 5H **21**
LS15: Leeds 3C **34**
LS16: Leeds 5A **12**
LS18: H'fth 2B **18**
LS26: Mick 6H **55**
LS26: Swil 6F **45**
LS28: Pud 6G **27**
WF1: Wake 6D **58**
WF3: E Ard 4G **57**
(Cherry Tree Wlk.)
WF3: E Ard 4B **56**
(W. Lea Dr.)
Church La. Av. WF1: Wake 6D **58**
Church M. LS5: Leeds 5E **19**
Church Mt. LS18: H'fth 2B **18**
Church Rd. LS12: Leeds 6A **30**
LS18: H'fth 3B **18**
WF3: Wake 6H **59**
Church Row LS2: Leeds 5G **5** (6H **31**)
Churchside Vs. LS26: Mick 6H **55**
Church St. LS5: Leeds 1G **29**
LS10: Leeds 4H **41**
LS19: Yead 3C **8**
LS20: Guis 4G **7**
LS26: Rothw 4G **53**
(Ingram Pde.)
LS26: Rothw 2C **54**
(Northwood Falls)
LS27: Morl 4G **49**
(Bank Sq.)
LS27: Morl 2C **48**
(West End)
Church Vw. LS16: Leeds 4A **12**
LS29: Men 1B **6**
Church Wlk. LS2: Leeds 5G **5** (6H **31**)
Church Way LS27: Morl 4G **49**
Church Wood Av. LS16: Leeds 5A **20**
Church Wood Mt. LS16: Leeds 4A **20**
Church Wood Rd. LS16: Leeds 5A **20**
CHURWELL 1A **50**
CITY 5H **49**
City Ga. LS3: Leeds 5D **30**
City Link Ind. Pk. BD4: Pud 1A **36**
City Mills *LS27: Morl 5H **49***
(off Peel St.)
City Mus. 3D **4** (5F **31**)
City Pk. Ind. Est. LS12: Leeds 4A **40**
City Sq. LS1: Leeds 5D **4** (6F **31**)
City Varieties Music Hall 4E **5** (5G **31**)
City Wlk. LS11: Leeds 1F **41**
City W. One Office Pk. LS12: Leeds 4B **40**
Clapgate La. LS10: Leeds 4B **52**
Clapham Dene Rd. LS15: Leeds 4B **34**
Clara Dr. LS28: Pud 4B **16**
Clara St. LS28: Pud 3F **27**
Claremont LS28: Pud 6H **27**
Claremont Av. LS3: Leeds 2A **4** (4E **31**)
Claremont Ct. LS6: Leeds 5C **20**
Claremont Cres. LS6: Leeds 6D **20**
Claremont Dr. LS6: Leeds 5C **20**
Claremont Gdns. LS28: Pud 3F **27**
Claremont Gro. LS3: Leeds 2A **4** (4E **31**)
LS28: Pud 6G **27**
Claremont Pl. LS12: Leeds 6G **29**
Claremont Rd. LS6: Leeds 5C **20**
Claremont St. LS12: Leeds 6G **29**
LS26: Rothw 3C **54**
Claremont Ter. LS12: Leeds 6G **29**
Claremont Vw. LS3: Leeds 2A **4** (4E **31**)
LS26: Rothw 3C **54**
Claremont Vs. *LS3: Leeds 2B **4***
(off Claremont Av.)
Claremount LS6: Leeds 5C **20**
Clarence Dr. LS18: H'fth 4B **18**
Clarence Gdns. LS18: H'fth 4B **18**
Clarence Gro. LS18: H'fth 4B **18**
Clarence Ho. LS10: Leeds 1H **41**
Clarence M. LS18: H'fth 4B **18**
Clarence Rd. LS10: Leeds 1A **42**
LS18: H'fth 4B **18**
Clarence St. LS13: Leeds 4C **28**
Clarence Ter. LS28: Pud 5G **27**
Clarendon Pl. LS2: Leeds 3E **31**
Clarendon Rd. LS2: Leeds 1A **4** (3E **31**)
Clarendon Ter. *LS27: Morl 1A **50***
(off Park St.)
LS28: Pud 1G **37**
Clarendon Way LS2: Leeds 2B **4** (4E **31**)
Clarion Camp LS29: Men 1F **7**
Clark Av. LS9: Leeds 6B **32**
Clark Cres. LS9: Leeds 6B **32**
Clarke Rd. WF3: E Ard 6C **56**
Clarke St. LS28: Pud 5D **16**
Clark Gro. LS9: Leeds 1B **42**
Clark La. LS9: Leeds 6B **32**
(not continuous)
Clark Mt. LS9: Leeds 6B **32**
Clark Rd. LS9: Leeds 6B **32**
Clark Row LS9: Leeds 1B **42**
Clarkson Ter. LS27: Morl 1A **50**
Clarkson Vw. LS6: Leeds 1E **31**
Clark Spring Cl. LS27: Morl 2G **49**
Clark Spring Ri. LS27: Morl 2H **49**
Clark Ter. LS9: Leeds 6B **32**
Clark Vw. LS9: Leeds 1B **42**
Clay Pit La. LS2: Leeds 2E **5** (4G **31**)
LS7: Leeds 1F **5** (4G **31**)
Clayton Cl. LS10: Leeds 5B **42**
Clayton Ct. LS10: Leeds 5B **42**
LS16: Leeds 3F **19**
Clayton Dr. LS10: Leeds 5B **42**
Clayton Grange LS16: Leeds 3F **19**
Clayton Gro. LS19: Yead 2D **8**
Clayton Ri. WF1: Wake 6D **58**
Clayton Rd. LS10: Leeds 5B **42**
Claytons Cl. LS26: Mick 6H **55**
Clayton St. LS26: Rothw 4H **53**
Clayton Way LS10: Leeds 5B **42**
Clayton Wood Bank LS16: Leeds 2F **19**
Clayton Wood Cl. LS16: Leeds 2F **19**
Clayton Wood Ct. LS16: Leeds 2F **19**
Clayton Wood Ri. LS16: Leeds 2F **19**
Clayton Wood Rd. LS16: Leeds 2E **19**
Clearings, The LS10: Leeds 1H **51**
Cleasby Rd. LS29: Men 2C **6**
Cleeve Hill LS19: Yead 5D **8**
Clement Ter. LS26: Rothw 5G **53**
*LS27: Morl 5H **49***
(off Ackroyd St.)
Cleveleys Av. LS11: Leeds 3D **40**
Cleveleys Ct. *LS11: Leeds 3D **40***
(off Cleveleys Av.)
Cleveleys Mt. LS11: Leeds 3D **40**
Cleveleys Rd. LS11: Leeds 3D **40**
Cleveleys St. *LS11: Leeds 3D **40***
(off Cleveleys Rd.)
Cleveleys Ter. LS11: Leeds 3D **40**
Cliff Ct. LS6: Leeds 1E **31**
Cliffdale Rd. LS7: Leeds 1F **31**
Cliffdale Rd. Light Ind. Est. LS7: Leeds 1F **31**
Cliffe Ct. *LS19: Yead 2E **9***
(off Harper La.)
Cliffe Dr. LS19: Yead 6C **8**
(not continuous)
Cliffe La. LS19: Yead 1E **17**
Cliffe Pk. Chase LS12: Leeds 1G **39**
Cliffe Pk. Cl. LS12: Leeds 1G **39**
Cliffe Pk. Cres. LS12: Leeds 1G **39**
Cliffe Pk. Dr. LS12: Leeds 1G **39**
Cliffe Pk. Mt. LS12: Leeds 1G **39**
Cliffe Pk. Ri. LS12: Leeds 1G **39**
Cliffe Pk. Way LS27: Morl 6D **48**
Cliffe Ter. WF3: Rothw 6C **52**
Cliffe Vw. LS27: Morl 6D **48**
Cliff La. LS6: Leeds 1D **30**
(not continuous)
Cliff Mt. LS6: Leeds 1E **31**
Cliff Mt. Ter. LS6: Leeds 1E **31**
Clifford Dr. LS29: Men 2D **6**
Clifford Pl. LS27: Morl 2H **49**
Cliff Rd. LS6: Leeds 1E **31**
Cliff Rd. Gdns. LS6: Leeds 1E **31**
Cliff Side Gdns. LS6: Leeds 1E **31**
Cliff Ter. LS6: Leeds 1E **31**
Clifton Av. LS9: Leeds 4C **32**
WF3: Wake 6G **59**
Clifton Ct. *LS28: Pud 5G **27***
(off Clifton Rd.)
Clifton Dr. LS28: Pud 5G **27**
Clifton Gro. LS9: Leeds 4C **32**
Clifton Hill LS28: Pud 5G **27**
Clifton M. LS28: Pud 5G **27**
Clifton Mt. LS9: Leeds 4C **32**
Clifton Pl. LS28: Pud 5H **27**
Clifton Rd. LS28: Pud 5G **27**
Clifton Ter. LS9: Leeds 4C **32**
Climax Works LS11: Leeds 5G **41**
Clipston Av. LS6: Leeds 5D **20**
Clipstone Mt. LS6: Leeds 5D **20**
Clipstone Ter. LS6: Leeds 5D **20**
Clipston St. LS6: Leeds 5D **20**
Clive Mt. Ho. *LS5: Leeds 2F **29***
(off Broad La.)
Cloberry St. LS2: Leeds 1A **4** (3E **31**)
Clock Bldgs. LS8: Leeds 1C **32**
Close, The LS9: Leeds 6A **32**
LS17: Leeds 4E **13**
LS20: Guis 5E **7**
WF3: E Ard 4H **57**
Cloth Hall St. LS2: Leeds 5F **5** (6G **31**)
Clough St. LS27: Morl 5H **49**
Clovelly Av. LS11: Leeds 4F **41**
Clovelly Gro. LS11: Leeds 4F **41**
Clovelly Pl. LS11: Leeds 4F **41**
Clovelly Row LS11: Leeds 4F **41**
Clovelly Ter. LS11: Leeds 4F **41**
Clover Ct. LS28: Pud 5C **16**
Clover Cres. LS28: Pud 4C **16**
Club La. LS13: Leeds 6G **17**
Club Row LS7: Leeds 4G **21**
LS19: Yead 2E **9**
Clumpcliffe LS26: Rothw 6D **54**
Clyde App. LS12: Leeds 1C **40**
Clyde Chase *LS12: Leeds 1C **40***
(off Clyde Vw.)
Clyde Ct. *LS12: Leeds 1C **40***
(off Clyde App.)
Clyde Gdns. LS12: Leeds 1C **40**
Clyde Grange *LS12: Leeds 1C **40***
(off Clyde App.)
Clyde Vw. LS12: Leeds 1C **40**
Clyde Wlk. LS12: Leeds 1C **40**
Coach Rd. LS12: Leeds 4E **39**
LS20: Guis 6F **7**
LS26: Swil 1F **55**
WF1: Wake 6E **59**
Coal Hill Dr. LS13: Leeds 1H **27**
Coal Hill Fold LS13: Leeds 1H **27**
Coal Hill Gdns. LS13: Leeds 1H **27**
Coal Hill Ga. *LS13: Leeds 1H **27***
(off Coal Hill Dr.)
Coal Hill Grn. LS13: Leeds 1H **27**
Coal Hill La. LS13: Leeds 1G **27**
LS28: Pud 1G **27**
Coal Rd. LS14: Leeds 1A **24**
LS17: Leeds, S'cft 1F **15**
Cobden Av. LS12: Leeds 3F **39**
Cobden Gro. LS12: Leeds 3F **39**
Cobden M. LS27: Morl 4G **49**
Cobden Pl. LS12: Leeds 3F **39**
Cobden Rd. LS12: Leeds 3F **39**
Cobden St. LS12: Leeds 3F **39**
LS27: Morl 4G **49**
Cobden Ter. LS12: Leeds 3F **39**
Cobham Wlk. LS15: Leeds 3F **35**
Cockburn Cl. LS11: Leeds 4G **41**
Cockburn Way LS11: Leeds 4G **41**
Cockcroft Ho. *LS6: Leeds 2B **30***
(off Chapel La.)
COCKERSDALE 1A **48**
Cockshott Cl. LS12: Leeds 4F **29**
Cockshott Dr. LS12: Leeds 4F **29**
Cockshott Hill LS28: Pud 2F **27**
Cockshott La. LS12: Leeds 4F **29**
(not continuous)
Colby Ri. LS15: Leeds 6G **33**
Coldcotes Av. LS9: Leeds 3D **32**
Coldcotes Cir. LS9: Leeds 3E **33**
Coldcotes Cl. LS9: Leeds 3E **33**
Coldcotes Cres. LS9: Leeds 3F **33**
Coldcotes Dr. LS9: Leeds 3E **33**
Coldcotes Gth. LS9: Leeds 3F **33**
Coldcotes Gro. LS9: Leeds 3F **33**
Coldcotes Vw. LS9: Leeds 3F **33**
Coldcotes Wlk. LS9: Leeds 3F **33**
Coldwell Rd. LS15: Leeds 4B **34**
Coldwell Sq. LS15: Leeds 4B **34**
Coleman St. LS12: Leeds 1D **40**
Colenso Gdns. LS11: Leeds 3D **40**
Colenso Gro. LS11: Leeds 3D **40**
Colenso Mt. LS11: Leeds 3D **40**
Colenso Pl. LS11: Leeds 3D **40**
Colenso Rd. LS11: Leeds 3D **40**
Colenso Ter. LS11: Leeds 3D **40**

72 A-Z Leeds

Coleridge Cl.—Cricketers, The

Coleridge Cl. LS26: Rothw 6C **54**
Coleridge La. LS28: Pud 2H **37**
Colindale Cl. BD10: B'frd 5A **16**
College Ct. LS27: Morl 3D **48**
College Lawns LS12: Leeds 5F **29**
College Rd. LS27: Morl 3D **48**
College Vw. LS12: Leeds 6F **29**
Colliers La. LS17: Leeds 5G **15**
Colliery App. WF3: Wake 5D **58**
Collin Rd. LS14: Leeds 4H **33**
Colmore Gro. LS12: Leeds 2B **40**
Colmore Rd. LS12: Leeds 2B **40**
Colmore St. LS12: Leeds 1B **40**
COLTON 1D **44**
Colton Ct. LS15: Leeds 6D **34**
Colton Cft. LS15: Leeds 6D **34**
Colton Gth. LS15: Leeds 6D **34**
Colton La. LS15: Leeds 6D **34**
Colton Lodges LS15: Leeds 6E **35**
Colton Mill LS15: Leeds 6F **35**
Colton Retail Pk. LS15: Leeds 6E **35**
Colton Rd. LS12: Leeds 6A **30**
LS15: Leeds 6C **34**
Colton Rd. E. LS15: Leeds 1E **45**
(not continuous)
Colton St. LS12: Leeds 6A **30**
Colville Ter. LS11: Leeds 3F **41**
WF3: E Ard 2A **58**
Colwyn Av. LS11: Leeds 5F **41**
Colwyn Mt. LS11: Leeds 5F **41**
Colwyn Pl. LS11: Leeds 5F **41**
Colwyn Rd. LS11: Leeds 5F **41**
Colwyn Ter. LS11: Leeds 5F **41**
Colwyn Vw. LS11: Leeds 5F **41**
Commercial Rd. LS5: Leeds 1G **29**
Commercial St. LS1: Leeds 4E **5** (5G **31**)
LS26: Rothw 4G **53**
LS27: Morl 5G **49**
Commercial Vs. LS28: Pud 1F **37**
Commercial Way LS28: Pud 5H **27**
Common La. WF3: E Ard 3F **57**
Common Rd. WF3: Wake 4H **59**
Compton Av. LS9: Leeds 3C **32**
Compton Cres. LS9: Leeds 3C **32**
Compton Gro. LS9: Leeds 3C **32**
Compton Mt. LS9: Leeds 3C **32**
Compton Pl. LS9: Leeds 3C **32**
Compton Rd. LS9: Leeds 3C **32**
Compton Row LS9: Leeds 3C **32**
Compton St. LS9: Leeds 3C **32**
Compton Ter. LS9: Leeds 3C **32**
Compton Vw. LS9: Leeds 3C **32**
Concept LS7: Leeds 4G **21**
Concordia St. LS1: Leeds 6E **5** (6G **31**)
Concord St. LS2: Leeds 2G **5** (4H **31**)
Coney Warren La. WF3: Wake 3G **59**
Conference Pl. LS12: Leeds 6G **29**
Conference Rd. LS12: Leeds 6G **29**
Conference Ter. LS12: Leeds 6G **29**
Congress Mt. LS12: Leeds 6G **29**
Congress St. LS12: Leeds 6G **29**
Coniston Av. LS6: Leeds 6C **20**
Coniston Ct. WF3: Wake 5D **58**
Coniston Gdns. LS15: Leeds 1G **43**
Coniston Rd. LS26: Rothw 2C **54**
Coniston Way LS26: Rothw 3C **54**
Consort St. LS3: Leeds 2A **4** (4D **30**)
Consort Ter. LS3: Leeds 4D **30**
Consort Vw. LS3: Leeds 4D **30**
Consort Wlk. LS3: Leeds 4D **30**
(not continuous)
Constable Gro. WF3: Wake 5G **59**
Constable Rd. WF3: E Ard 3C **56**
Constance Gdns. LS7: Leeds 3F **31**
Constance Way LS7: Leeds 3F **31**
Conway Av. LS8: Leeds 2B **32**
Conway Dr. LS8: Leeds 2B **32**
Conway Gro. LS8: Leeds 2B **32**
Conway Mt. LS8: Leeds 2B **32**
Conway Pl. LS8: Leeds 2B **32**
Conway Rd. LS8: Leeds 2B **32**
Conway St. LS8: Leeds 2B **32**
LS28: Pud 4F **27**
Conway Ter. LS8: Leeds 2B **32**
Conway Vw. LS8: Leeds 2B **32**
COOKRIDGE 4D **10**
Cookridge Av. LS16: Leeds 3E **11**
Cookridge Dr. LS16: Leeds 3D **10**
Cookridge Gro. LS16: Leeds 3E **11**
COOKRIDGE HOSPITAL 1E **19**
Cookridge La. LS16: Leeds 1D **10**
Cookridge St. LS1: Leeds 3D **4** (5F **31**)
LS2: Leeds 2D **4** (5F **31**)
Co-operation St. LS12: Leeds 3G **39**
Co-operative St. LS27: Morl 1A **50**
(Fountain St.)
LS27: Morl 4G **49**
(Queen's Prom.)
WF3: Rothw 2E **59**
Cooper Hill LS28: Pud 2H **37**
Copeland St. BD4: B'frd 2A **36**
Copgrove Cl. BD4: B'frd 4A **36**
Copgrove Ct. BD4: B'frd 4A **36**
Copgrove Rd. BD4: B'frd 4A **36**
LS8: Leeds 1C **32**
Copley Hill LS12: Leeds 1C **40**
Copley Hill Trad. Est. LS12: Leeds 2C **40**
Copley Hill Way LS12: Leeds 2C **40**
Copley La. WF3: Rothw 5D **52**
Copley St. LS12: Leeds 1C **40**
Copley Yd. LS12: Leeds 1C **40**
Copperfield Av. LS9: Leeds 1B **42**
Copperfield Cres. LS9: Leeds 1B **42**
Copperfield Dr. LS9: Leeds 1B **42**
Copperfield Gro. LS9: Leeds 1B **42**
Copperfield Mt. LS9: Leeds 1C **42**
Copperfield Pl. LS9: Leeds 1B **42**
Copperfield Row LS9: Leeds 1B **42**
Copperfield Ter. LS9: Leeds 1B **42**
Copperfield Vw. LS9: Leeds 1B **42**
Copperfield Wlk. LS9: Leeds 1B **42**
Coppice, The LS19: Yead 4B **8**
Coppice Grange LS19: Yead 1D **8**
Coppice Head LS26: Rothw 4H **53**
Coppice Way LS8: Leeds 5C **22**
Coppice Wood Av. LS19: Yead 1C **8**
LS20: Guis, Yead 1C **8**
Coppice Wood Cl. LS20: Guis 1C **8**
Coppice Wood Cres. LS19: Yead 1C **8**
Coppice Wood Gro. LS20: Guis 1C **8**
Coppice Wood Ri. LS19: Yead 1D **8**
Copplestone Wlk. BD4: B'frd 5A **36**
Coppy La. LS13: Leeds 1C **28**
Copse, The WF3: E Ard 4F **57**
Copt Royd Gro. LS19: Yead 2C **8**
Cordingley Cl. BD4: B'frd 6A **36**
Cordingley St. BD4: B'frd 6A **36**
Corner Ho. Shops LS17: Leeds 1H **21**
Corn Exchange LS2: Leeds 5F **5**
Corn Mill LS29: Men 1D **6**
Corn Mill Ct. LS13: Leeds 5D **28**
Corn Mill Vw. LS18: H'fth 3E **19**
Cornstone Fold LS12: Leeds 6C **28**
Cornus Gdns. LS10: Leeds 1H **51**
Cornwall Cl. LS26: Rothw 3F **53**
Cornwall Cres. LS26: Rothw 3F **53**
Coronation Av. BD17: B'frd 6A **8**
Coronation Pde. LS15: Leeds 1G **43**
Coronation St. WF3: Rothw 6F **53**
Corporation St. LS27: Morl 4F **49**
Cote, The LS28: Pud 3E **27**
Cotefields Av. LS28: Pud 2E **27**
Cote La. LS28: Pud 3E **27**
Coteroyd Av. LS27: Morl 1A **50**
Coteroyd Dr. LS27: Morl 2A **50**
Cotswold Dr. LS26: Rothw 3F **53**
Cotswold Rd. LS26: Rothw 3G **53**
Cottage Rd. BD10: B'frd 4A **16**
LS6: Leeds 5B **20**
Cottage Road Cinema 5B **20**
Cotterdale Vw. LS15: Leeds 1G **43**
COTTINGLEY 6B **40**
Cottingley App. LS11: Leeds 6B **40**
Cottingley Chase LS11: Leeds 6A **40**
Cottingley Ct. LS11: Leeds 6B **40**
Cottingley Cres. LS11: Leeds 6B **40**
Cottingley Dr. LS11: Leeds 5A **40**
Cottingley Fold LS11: Leeds 5A **40**
Cottingley Gdns. LS11: Leeds 6B **40**
Cottingley Grn. LS11: Leeds 6B **40**
Cottingley Gro. LS11: Leeds 6B **40**
Cottingley Hall Crematorium LS11: Leeds 5B **40**
Cottingley Hgts. LS11: Leeds 6B **40**
Cottingley Rd. LS11: Leeds 5A **40**
Cottingley Springs Cvn. Pk. LS27: Morl 6G **39**
Cottingley Station (Rail) 6A **40**
Cottingley Towers LS11: Leeds 6B **40**
Cottingley Va. LS11: Leeds 6B **40**
Cotton St. LS9: Leeds 5H **5** (6A **32**)
Coultas Cl. LS29: Men 1D **6**
County Arc. LS1: Leeds 4F **5** (5G **31**)
Coupland Pl. LS11: Leeds 3F **41**
Coupland Rd. LS11: Leeds 3F **41**
Coupland St. LS11: Leeds 4F **41**
Court, The LS17: Leeds 4D **12**
Courtenay Cl. BD3: B'frd 6A **26**
Courtenays LS14: Leeds 1B **34**
Courtyard, The LS10: Leeds 3H **41**
Courtyards, The LS14: Leeds 4B **24**
Coverdale Cl. LS12: Leeds 3F **29**
Coverley Gth. LS19: Yead 6H **7**
Coverley Ri. LS19: Yead 6H **7**
Cow Cl. Gro. LS12: Leeds 3G **39**
Cow Cl. Rd. LS12: Leeds 3F **39**
Cowley Rd. LS13: Leeds 6H **17**
Cowper Av. LS9: Leeds 3C **32**
Cowper Cres. LS9: Leeds 3C **32**
Cowper Gro. LS8: Leeds 2C **32**
Cowper Mt. LS9: Leeds 3C **32**
Cowper Rd. LS9: Leeds 3C **32**
Cowper St. LS7: Leeds 1H **31**
Cowper Ter. LS9: Leeds 3C **32**
Crab La. LS12: Leeds 5A **30**
Crabtree Way WF3: E Ard 4D **56**
Cragg Av. LS18: H'fth 3B **18**
Cragg Hill LS18: H'fth 3C **18**
Cragg Rd. LS18: H'fth 3C **18**
Cragg Ter. LS18: H'fth 3B **18**
(not continuous)
LS19: Yead 1D **16**
Craggwell Ter. *LS18: H'fth* *4C **18***
(off Wood La.)
Craggwood Cl. LS18: H'fth 4C **18**
Craggwood Rd. LS18: H'fth 4C **18**
Craggwood Ter. *LS18: H'fth* *4C **18***
(off Craggwood Rd.)
Crag Hill Av. LS16: Leeds 2E **11**
Crag Hill Vw. LS16: Leeds 3E **11**
Crag La. LS17: Leeds 4C **12**
Cragside Cl. LS5: Leeds 4E **19**
Cragside Cres. LS5: Leeds 4E **19**
Cragside Gdns. LS5: Leeds 4E **19**
Cragside Gro. LS5: Leeds 5D **18**
Cragside Mt. LS5: Leeds 4E **19**
Cragside Pl. LS5: Leeds 4E **19**
Cragside Wlk. LS5: Leeds 5D **18**
Craigmore Ct. BD4: B'frd 5B **36**
Cranbrook Av. LS11: Leeds 4E **41**
Cranbrook Vw. LS28: Pud 2A **38**
Cranewells Dr. LS15: Leeds 1D **44**
Cranewells Grn. LS15: Leeds 1C **44**
Cranewells Ri. LS15: Leeds 1C **44**
Cranewells Va. LS15: Leeds 1C **44**
Cranewells Vw. LS15: Leeds 6C **34**
Cranmer Bank LS17: Leeds 6E **13**
Cranmer Cl. LS17: Leeds 6E **13**
Cranmer Gdns. LS17: Leeds 6E **13**
Cranmer Ri. LS17: Leeds 5E **13**
Cranmer Rd. LS17: Leeds 6E **13**
(not continuous)
Cranmore Cres. LS10: Leeds 4B **52**
Cranmore Dr. LS10: Leeds 4B **52**
Cranmore Gdns. LS10: Leeds 4A **52**
Cranmore Gth. LS10: Leeds 4A **52**
Cranmore Grn. LS10: Leeds 4A **52**
Cranmore Gro. LS10: Leeds 4A **52**
Cranmore La. LS10: Leeds 4B **52**
Cranmore Ri. LS10: Leeds 4B **52**
Cranmore Rd. LS10: Leeds 4A **52**
Craven Pk. LS29: Men 1B **6**
Craven Rd. LS6: Leeds 2F **31**
Crawshaw Av. LS28: Pud 6H **27**
Crawshaw Cl. LS28: Pud 6G **27**
Crawshaw Gdns. LS28: Pud 6H **27**
Crawshaw Hill LS28: Pud 6G **27**
Crawshaw Pk. LS28: Pud 6G **27**
Crawshaw Ri. LS28: Pud 1G **37**
Crawshaw Rd. LS28: Pud 6G **27**
Crescent, The BD11: B'frd 2C **46**
LS6: Leeds *2E **31***
(off Woodhouse La.)
LS13: Leeds 2C **28**
LS15: Leeds 5B **34**
LS16: Leeds 5G **11**
LS17: Leeds 3D **12**
LS18: H'fth 2H **17**
LS20: Guis 5E **7**
LS28: Pud 5H **27**
LS29: Men 1D **6**
WF3: E Ard 3E **57**
Crescent Av. LS26: Rothw 2H **53**
Crescent Bungs. WF3: Leeds 1H **57**
Crescent Ct. LS17: Leeds 3D **12**
Crescent Gdns. LS17: Leeds 5H **13**
Crescent Grange LS11: Leeds 3G **41**
Crescent Towers LS11: Leeds 3G **41**
Crescent Vw. LS17: Leeds 3D **12**
Crest, The LS26: Swil 6G **45**
Cricketers, The LS5: Leeds 1H **29**

A-Z Leeds 73

Cricketers Fold—Dartmouth Way

Cricketers Fold LS17: Leeds 5G **15**
Cricketers Grn. LS19: Yead 3E **9**
Cricketers Ter. LS12: Leeds 6A **30**
Cricketers Vw. LS17: Leeds 5G **15**
Cricketers Wlk. LS15: Leeds 6E **35**
Cricklegate LS15: Leeds 5B **34**
CRIMBLES 6H 27
Crimbles Ct. LS28: Pud 6H **27**
Crimbles Pl. LS28: Pud 6H **27**
Crimbles Rd. LS28: Pud 6H **27**
Crimbles Ter. LS28: Pud 6H **27**
Croft, The BD11: B'frd 4G **47**
LS15: Leeds 4B **34**
LS26: Rothw 4C **54**
WF3: E Ard 6B **56**
Croft Av. LS28: Pud 2F **27**
WF3: E Ard 4H **57**
Croft Bank BD11: B'frd 4C **46**
Croft Bri. LS26: Rothw 4C **54**
Croft Cl. LS29: Men 1B **6**
Croft Cotts. LS12: Leeds 4E **39**
Croft Ct. LS18: H'fth 2C **18**
LS29: Men 1C **6**
Croftdale Gro. LS15: Leeds 3D **34**
Croft Dr. LS29: Men 1C **6**
Crofters Lea LS19: Yead 3B **8**
Croft Head LS20: Guis 4G **7**
Croft Ho. Av. LS27: Morl 4H **49**
Croft Ho. Cl. LS27: Morl 3H **49**
Croft Ho. Ct. LS28: Pud 5G **27**
Croft Ho. Dr. LS27: Morl 4H **49**
Croft Ho. Gdns. LS27: Morl 4H **49**
Croft Ho. Gro. LS27: Morl 4H **49**
Croft Ho. La. LS27: Morl 4H **49**
Croft Ho. M. LS27: Morl 4H **49**
Croft Ho. Mt. LS27: Morl 3H **49**
Croft Ho. Ri. LS27: Morl 3H **49**
Croft Ho. Rd. LS27: Morl 4H **49**
Croft Ho. Vw. LS27: Morl 4H **49**
Croft Ho. Wlk. LS27: Morl 3H **49**
Croft Ho. Way LS27: Morl 3H **49**
Crofton Ri. LS17: Leeds 5H **15**
Crofton Ter. LS17: Leeds 5H **15**
Croft Pk. LS29: Men 1B **6**
Croft Ri. LS29: Men 1C **6**
Croft's Ct. LS1: Leeds 4D **4** (5F **31**)
Croftside Cl. LS14: Leeds 2B **34**
Croft St. BD11: B'frd 4C **46**
(not continuous)
LS28: Pud 2F **27**
Croft Ter. LS12: Leeds 4E **39**
Croft Way LS29: Men 1C **6**
Cromack Vw. LS28: Pud 6E **27**
Cromer Pl. LS2: Leeds 3E **31**
(not continuous)
Cromer Rd. LS2: Leeds 1A **4** (3E **31**)
Cromer St. LS2: Leeds 1A **4** (3E **31**)
Cromer Ter. LS2: Leeds 1A **4** (4E **31**)
Crompton Dr. LS27: Morl 3F **49**
Cromwell Ct. BD11: B'frd 4F **47**
Cromwell Hgts. *LS9: Leeds 5A 32*
(off Cromwell St.)
Cromwell M. LS9: Leeds 4A **32**
Cromwell Mt. LS9: Leeds 4A **32**
LS10: Leeds 1H **51**
Cromwell St. LS9: Leeds 3H **5** (5A **32**)
Crooklands *LS20: Guis 4G 7*
(off Kelcliffe La.)
Cropper Ga. LS1: Leeds 4A **4** (5E **31**)
Crosby Av. LS11: Leeds 3D **40**
Crosby Pl. LS11: Leeds 2E **41**
Crosby Rd. LS11: Leeds 3D **40**
Crosby St. LS11: Leeds 2D **40**
Crosby Ter. LS11: Leeds 2E **41**
Crosby Vw. LS11: Leeds 2E **41**
Cross Albert Pl. LS12: Leeds 1B **40**
Cross Arc. LS1: Leeds 4F **5**
Cross Aston Gro. LS13: Leeds 3E **29**
Cross Av. LS26: Rothw 2H **53**
Cross Aysgarth Mt. LS9: Leeds 5B **32**
Cross Banstead St. LS8: Leeds 2B **32**
Cross Bath Rd. LS13: Leeds 3C **28**
Cross Belgrave St. LS2: Leeds 3F **5** (5G **31**)
Cross Bellbrooke Av. *LS9: Leeds 3D 32*
(off Bellbrooke Av.)
Cross Bell St. LS9: Leeds 3H **5**
Cross Bentley La. LS6: Leeds 5D **20**
Cross Burley Lodge Rd. *LS6: Leeds 3C 30*
(off Burley Rd.)
Cross Cardigan Ter. LS4: Leeds 4A **30**
Cross Catherine St. LS9: Leeds 6A **32**
Cross Chancellor St. LS6: Leeds 2F **31**
Cross Chapel St. LS6: Leeds 6B **20**
Cross Chestnut Gro. *LS6: Leeds 2C 30*
(off Chestnut Av.)
Cross Cliff Rd. LS6: Leeds 1D **30**
Cross Conway Mt. LS8: Leeds 2B **32**
Cross Cowper St. LS7: Leeds 2H **31**
Cross Dawlish Gro. LS9: Leeds 5D **32**
Cross Easy Rd. LS9: Leeds 1B **42**
Cross Elford St. LS8: Leeds 2B **32**
Crossfield St. LS2: Leeds 2E **31**
Cross Flatts Av. LS11: Leeds 5E **41**
Cross Flatts Cres. LS11: Leeds 5D **40**
Cross Flatts Dr. LS11: Leeds 4D **40**
Cross Flatts Gro. LS11: Leeds 5D **40**
Cross Flatts Mt. LS11: Leeds 5E **41**
Cross Flatts Pde. LS11: Leeds 5D **40**
Cross Flatts Pl. LS11: Leeds 5D **40**
Cross Flatts Rd. LS11: Leeds 5D **40**
Cross Flatts Row LS11: Leeds 5D **40**
Cross Flatts St. LS11: Leeds 5D **40**
Cross Flatts Ter. LS11: Leeds 5D **40**
Cross Francis St. LS7: Leeds 2H **31**
CROSS GATES 3C 34
Cross Gates Av. LS15: Leeds 2C **34**
Cross Gates La. LS15: Leeds 2B **34**
Cross Gates Rd. LS15: Leeds 3A **34**
(not continuous)
Crossgates Shop. Cen. LS15: Leeds 3C **34**
Cross Gates Station (Rail) 4C 34
Cross Glen Rd. LS16: Leeds 4A **20**
Cross Granby Ter. LS6: Leeds 6B **20**
Cross Grange Av. LS7: Leeds 2A **32**
Cross Grasmere St. LS12: Leeds 6B **30**
CROSS GREEN 2C 42
Cross Grn. BD4: B'frd 3A **36**
Cross Grn. App. LS9: Leeds 2C **42**
Cross Grn. Av. LS9: Leeds 1B **42**
Cross Grn. Cl. LS9: Leeds 2C **42**
Cross Grn. Ct. LS9: Leeds 2D **42**
Cross Grn. Cres. LS9: Leeds 1B **42**
Cross Grn. Dr. LS9: Leeds 2C **42**
Cross Grn. Gth. LS9: Leeds 2C **42**
Cross Grn. Gro. LS9: Leeds 1B **42**
Cross Grn. Ind. Est. LS9: Leeds 2D **42**
Cross Grn. Ind. Pk. LS9: Leeds 1E **43**
Cross Grn. La. LS9: Leeds 1A **42**
LS15: Leeds 5A **34**
Cross Grn. Ri. LS9: Leeds 2C **42**
Cross Grn. Rd. LS9: Leeds 1B **42**
Cross Grn. Row LS6: Leeds 4C **20**
Cross Grn. Va. LS9: Leeds 3C **42**
Cross Grn. Way LS9: Leeds 2C **42**
Cross Greenwood Mt. LS6: Leeds 4C **20**
Cross Hartley Av. *LS6: Leeds 1E 31*
(off Delph La.)
Cross Heath Gro. LS11: Leeds 4C **40**
Cross Henley Rd. LS13: Leeds 3C **28**
Cross Hill LS11: Leeds 6C **40**
Cross Hilton Gro. LS8: Leeds 6B **22**
Cross Ingledew Cres. LS8: Leeds 1D **22**
Cross Ingram Rd. LS11: Leeds 2D **40**
Cross Kelso Rd. LS2: Leeds 1A **4** (4D **30**)
Crossland Ct. LS11: Leeds 1E **41**
Crossland Rd. LS27: Morl 2H **49**
Crossland Ter. LS11: Leeds 4G **41**
Cross La. BD4: B'frd 2D **46**
LS12: Leeds 2E **39**
(Stonebridge La.)
LS12: Leeds 6H **29**
(Up. Wortley Rd.)
LS20: Guis 1H **7**
Cross Lea Farm Rd. LS5: Leeds 4F **19**
Cross Lidgett Pl. LS8: Leeds 3B **22**
Cross Louis St. LS7: Leeds 2H **31**
Cross Maude St. LS2: Leeds 5G **5**
Cross Mitford Rd. LS12: Leeds 6B **30**
Cross Osmondthorpe La. LS9: Leeds 5E **33**
Cross Pk. St. LS15: Leeds 5A **34**
Cross Peel St. LS27: Morl 5H **49**
Cross Quarry St. LS6: Leeds 1E **31**
Cross Reginald Mt. LS7: Leeds 1H **31**
Cross Rd. LS18: H'fth 3A **18**
Cross Roseville Rd. *LS8: Leeds 2A 32*
(off Bayswater Rd.)
Cross Roundhay Av. LS8: Leeds 6B **22**
Cross Row LS15: Swil 1G **45**
Cross St Michaels La. LS6: Leeds 1B **30**
Cross Speedwell St. LS6: Leeds 2F **31**
Cross Stamford St. LS7: Leeds 1H **5** (4H **31**)
Cross St. LS15: Leeds 5A **34**
LS26: Rothw 4G **53**
WF3: E Ard 3A **58**
Cross Ter. LS26: Rothw 4G **53**
Cross Valley Dr. LS15: Leeds 4B **34**
Cross Westfield Rd. *LS3: Leeds 4D 30*
(off Westfield Rd.)
Cross Wingham St. LS7: Leeds 3H **31**
Cross Woodstock St. *LS2: Leeds 3F 31*
(off Blenheim Wlk.)
Cross Woodview St. *LS11: Leeds 5F 41*
(off Woodview St.)
Cross York St. LS2: Leeds 5G **5** (6H **31**)
Crown Ct. LS2: Leeds 5F **5** (6G **31**)
Crow Nest Dr. LS11: Leeds 5C **40**
Crow Nest La. LS11: Leeds 5B **40**
Crow Nest M. LS11: Leeds 5C **40**
CROWN POINT 6G 5 (6H 31)
Crown Point Retail Pk. LS10: Leeds 1G **41**
Crown Point Rd. LS2: Leeds 6G **5** (1G **41**)
LS9: Leeds 6H **5** (1G **41**)
LS10: Leeds 6G **5** (1G **41**)
Crown St. LS2: Leeds 5F **5** (6G **31**)
Crown St. Bldg. LS2: Leeds 5F **5**
Crowther Av. LS28: Pud 5B **16**
Crowther Pl. LS6: Leeds 2F **31**
Crowther St. BD10: B'frd 4A **16**
Crowthers Yd. LS28: Pud 1G **37**
Crowtrees Ct. LS19: Yead 5E **9**
Crow Trees Pk. LS19: Yead 5D **8**
Croxall Dr. WF3: Wake 6G **59**
Croydon St. LS11: Leeds 1D **40**
Crozier Ho. LS10: Leeds 1H **41**
Cudbear St. LS10: Leeds 1H **41**
Cumberland Ct. LS6: Leeds 2B **30**
Cumberland Rd. LS6: Leeds 1D **30**
Curlew Ri. LS27: Morl 6B **50**
Czar St. LS11: Leeds 1E **41**

D

Daffil Av. LS27: Morl 2H **49**
Daffil Grange M. LS27: Morl 2H **49**
Daffil Grange Way LS27: Morl 2H **49**
Daffil Gro. LS27: Morl 2H **49**
Daffil Rd. LS27: Morl 2H **49**
Daisyfield Grange *LS13: Leeds 4D 28*
(off Rossefield App.)
Daisyfield Rd. LS13: Leeds 3D **28**
DAISY HILL 4A 50
Daisy Hill LS27: Morl 4A **50**
Daisy Hill Av. LS27: Morl 3A **50**
Daisy Hill Cl. LS27: Morl 3H **49**
Daisy Row LS13: Leeds 4D **28**
Daisy Va. M. WF3: E Ard 2A **58**
Daisy Va. Ter. WF3: E Ard 2A **58**
Dale Cl. LS20: Guis 5D **6**
Dale Pk. Av. LS16: Leeds 5D **10**
Dale Pk. Cl. LS16: Leeds 5D **10**
Dale Pk. Gdns. LS16: Leeds 5D **10**
Dale Pk. Ri. LS16: Leeds 5D **10**
Dale Pk. Vw. LS16: Leeds 5D **10**
Dale Pk. Wlk. LS16: Leeds 5D **10**
Dale Rd. BD11: B'frd 6A **38**
Dales Dr. LS20: Guis 5D **6**
Daleside Av. LS28: Pud 5C **26**
Daleside Cl. LS28: Pud 4B **26**
Daleside Gro. LS28: Pud 5C **26**
Daleside Rd. LS28: Pud 4B **26**
Dales Way LS20: Guis 5D **6**
Dale Vs. LS18: H'fth 4D **18**
Dalton Av. LS11: Leeds 5E **41**
Dalton Gro. LS11: Leeds 5E **41**
Dalton Rd. LS11: Leeds 5E **41**
Dam La. LS19: Yead 2E **9**
Damon Av. BD10: B'frd 1A **26**
Danby Wlk. LS9: Leeds 6B **32**
Dane Ct. Rd. BD4: B'frd 4A **36**
Dane Hill Dr. BD4: B'frd 3A **36**
Daniel Ct. BD4: B'frd 5B **36**
Darcy Ct. LS15: Leeds 5C **34**
Darfield Av. LS8: Leeds 2C **32**
Darfield Cres. LS8: Leeds 2C **32**
Darfield Gro. LS8: Leeds 2B **32**
Darfield Pl. LS8: Leeds 2C **32**
Darfield Rd. LS8: Leeds 2C **32**
Darfield St. LS8: Leeds 2C **32**
Dark La. WF17: Bat 6H **47**
Darkwood Cl. LS17: Leeds 5C **14**
Darkwood Way LS17: Leeds 5C **14**
Darley Av. LS10: Leeds 2H **51**
Darnley La. LS15: Leeds 1C **44**
Darnley Rd. LS16: Leeds 4H **19**
Darren St. BD4: B'frd 1A **36**
Darthmouth M. LS27: Morl 6F **49**
Dartmouth Av. LS27: Morl 6G **49**
Dartmouth Way LS11: Leeds 5G **41**

74 A-Z Leeds

David Lloyd Leisure
Moortown 1F 21
David St. LS11: Leeds 1F 41
Davies Av. LS8: Leeds 3B 22
Dawlish Av. LS9: Leeds 5D 32
Dawlish Cres. LS9: Leeds 5D 32
Dawlish Gro. LS9: Leeds 6D 32
Dawlish Mt. LS9: Leeds 5D 32
Dawlish Pl. LS9: Leeds 5D 32
Dawlish Rd. LS9: Leeds 5D 32
Dawlish Row LS9: Leeds 5D 32
Dawlish St. LS9: Leeds 5D 32
Dawlish Ter. LS9: Leeds 5D 32
Dawlish Wlk. LS9: Leeds 5D 32
Dawson Hill LS27: Morl 4G 49
Dawson La. BD4: B'frd 5G 37
LS26: Rothw 3G 53
Dawson Rd. LS11: Leeds 4E 41
Dawsons Cnr. LS28: Pud 3E 27
Dawsons Ct. LS14: Leeds 1B 34
Dawsons Mdw. LS28: Pud 3E 27
Dawsons Ter. LS28: Pud 3E 27
Dawson St. LS28: Pud 4F 27
WF3: E Ard 2B 56
Dean Av. LS8: Leeds 5C 22
Dean Ct. LS8: Leeds 5C 22
Deanfield Av. LS27: Morl 4F 49
Dean Hall Cl. LS27: Morl 5F 49
Dean Head LS18: H'fth 1A 10
Deanhurst Gdns. LS27: Morl 3D 48
Deanhurst Ind. Cen.
LS27: Morl 3D 48
Dean La. LS18: H'fth, Yead 1A 10
LS20: Guis 5B 6
Dean M. LS18: H'fth 1B 10
Dean Pk. Av. BD11: B'frd 2G 47
Dean Pk. Dr. BD11: B'frd 2G 47
Dean Pastures BD11: B'frd 3G 47
Deansway LS27: Morl 3F 49
Deanswood Cl. LS17: Leeds 6E 13
Deanswood Dr. LS17: Leeds 6D 12
Deanswood Gdns. LS17: Leeds 6D 12
Deanswood Gth. LS17: Leeds 6E 13
Deanswood Grn. LS17: Leeds 6D 12
Deanswood Hill LS17: Leeds 6D 12
Deanswood Pl. LS17: Leeds 6E 13
Deanswood Ri. LS17: Leeds 6E 13
Deanswood Vw. LS17: Leeds 6E 13
Dean Vw. WF17: Bat 6H 47
Deighton Vw. LS6: Leeds 2C 20
De Lacies Ct. LS26: Rothw 2A 54
De Lacies Rd. LS26: Rothw 2A 54
De Lacy Mt. LS5: Leeds 1G 29
Delius Av. BD10: B'frd 6A 16
Delph Ct. LS6: Leeds 1E 31
DELPH END 6E 27
Delph End LS28: Pud 6D 26
Delph La. LS6: Leeds 1E 31
Delph Mt. LS6: Leeds 1E 31
Delph Vw. LS6: Leeds 1E 31
Demontfort Ho. BD4: B'frd 3A 36
(off Ned La.)
Denbigh App. LS9: Leeds 3F 33
Denbigh Cft. LS9: Leeds 3F 33
Denbigh Hgts. LS9: Leeds 3F 33
Denbrook Av. BD4: B'frd 6B 36
Denbrook Cl. BD4: B'frd 6B 36
Denbrook Cres. BD4: B'frd 1B 46
Denbrook Wlk. BD4: B'frd 6B 36
Denbrook Way BD4: B'frd 6B 36
Denbury Mt. BD4: B'frd 5A 36
Denby Ho. BD4: B'frd 6B 36
Dence Grn. BD4: B'frd 2A 36
Dence Pl. LS15: Leeds 5G 33
Dene Ho. Ct. LS2: Leeds 3F 31
Deneway LS28: Pud 3E 27
Denham Av. LS27: Morl 6G 49
Denison Hall LS3: Leeds 2A 4 (4E 31)
Denison Rd. LS3: Leeds 3A 4 (5E 31)
Denison St. LS19: Yead 2D 8
Dennil Cres. LS15: Leeds 1D 34
Dennil Rd. LS15: Leeds 2D 34
Dennison Fold BD4: B'frd 2A 36
Dennistead Cres. LS6: Leeds 6B 20
Denshaw Dr. LS27: Morl 5A 50
Denshaw Gro. LS27: Morl 5A 50
Denshaw La. WF3: Leeds 6D 50
Denton Av. LS8: Leeds 3B 22
Denton Gro. LS8: Leeds 3B 22
Denton Row LS12: Leeds 1G 39
Denton Ter. LS27: Morl 6G 49
Dent St. LS9: Leeds 6B 32
Derby Pl. BD3: B'frd 6A 26

Derby Pl. LS19: Yead 5D 8
(off North St.)
Derby Rd. BD3: B'frd 6A 26
LS19: Yead 5D 8
Derbyshire St. LS10: Leeds 4B 42
Derby Ter. BD10: B'frd 3A 16
Derry Hill LS29: Men 2B 6
Derry Hill Gdns. LS29: Men 1B 6
Derry La. LS29: Men 1B 6
Derwent Av. LS26: Rothw 3C 54
Derwent Dr. LS16: Leeds 5B 12
Derwent Pl. LS11: Leeds 1E 41
Derwentwater Gro. LS6: Leeds 6B 20
Derwentwater Ter. LS6: Leeds 6B 20
Detroit Av. LS15: Leeds 5D 34
Detroit Dr. LS15: Leeds 5E 35
Devon Cl. LS2: Leeds 3F 31
Devon Rd. LS2: Leeds 3F 31
Devonshire Av. LS8: Leeds 2C 22
Devonshire Cl. LS8: Leeds 2C 22
(not continuous)
Devonshire Cres. LS8: Leeds 2C 22
Devonshire Gdns. LS2: Leeds 2F 31
Devonshire La. LS8: Leeds 1C 22
Devonshire Pl. LS19: Yead 2D 8
Devro Ct. LS9: Leeds 3D 42
Dewsbury Rd. BD19: Cleck 6D 46
LS11: Leeds 1G 41
(Meadow La.)
LS11: Leeds 2D 50
(Pk. Wood Cl.)
WF3: Dew, Leeds, Morl, E Ard ..1C 56
WF12: Dew, E Ard 5A 56
Diadem Dr. LS14: Leeds 4G 33
Dial St. LS9: Leeds 1A 42
Dibb La. LS19: Yead 6H 7
Dib Cl. LS8: Leeds 6F 23
Dib La. LS8: Leeds 6F 23
Dickinson St. LS18: H'fth 1C 18
Dick La. BD3: B'frd 6A 26
BD4: B'frd 3A 36
Dick's Gth. Rd. LS29: Men 1B 6
Digby Rd. LS29: Men 1C 6
Digpal Rd. LS27: Leeds 6A 40
Dinsdale Bldgs. LS19: Yead 3C 8
(off Back La.)
Disraeli Gdns. LS11: Leeds 3F 41
Disraeli Ter. LS11: Leeds 3F 41
Dixon Ct. LS12: Leeds 4H 39
Dixon La. LS12: Leeds 2A 40
Dixon La. Rd. LS12: Leeds 2A 40
Dobson Av. LS11: Leeds 4G 41
Dobson Gro. LS11: Leeds 4G 41
Dobson Pl. LS11: Leeds 4G 41
Dobsons Row WF3: Rothw 1F 59
Dobson Ter. LS11: Leeds 4G 41
Dobson Vw. LS11: Leeds 4G 41
Dock St. LS10: Leeds 6F 5 (6G 31)
Dodgson Av. LS7: Leeds 2A 32
Dolly La. LS9: Leeds 4A 32
Dolphin Ct. LS9: Leeds 6A 32
LS13: Leeds 4B 28
Dolphin La. WF3: E Ard, Leeds 1A 58
(not continuous)
Dolphin Rd. LS10: Leeds 4A 52
Dolphin St. LS9: Leeds 6A 32
Domestic Rd. LS12: Leeds 2D 40
Domestic St. LS11: Leeds 1D 40
Dominion Av. LS7: Leeds 5H 21
Dominion Cl. LS7: Leeds 5H 21
Donald St. LS28: Pud 3F 27
Donisthorpe St. LS10: Leeds 2A 42
Dorchester Ct. BD4: B'frd 4A 36
Dorchester Cres. BD4: B'frd 4A 36
Dorchester Dr. LS19: Yead 3F 9
Dorset Av. LS8: Leeds 1C 32
Dorset Gro. LS28: Pud 5G 27
Dorset Mt. LS8: Leeds 2C 32
Dorset Rd. LS8: Leeds 1C 32
Dorset St. LS8: Leeds 1C 32
Dorset Ter. LS8: Leeds 2C 32
Dortmund Sq. LS2: Leeds 3E 5
Dotterel Glen LS27: Morl 6B 50
Dovedale Gdns. LS15: Leeds 3F 35
Dovedale Gth. LS15: Leeds 2F 35
Dragon Ct. LS12: Leeds 1D 40
Dragon Cres. LS12: Leeds 2B 40
Dragon Dr. LS12: Leeds 2A 40
Dragon Rd. LS12: Leeds 2B 40
Dragons Health Club
Yeadon 2D 8
Drake La. BD11: B'frd 4G 47
Draycott Wlk. BD4: B'frd 5A 36

Drayton Mnr. Yd. LS11: Leeds 3G 41
(off Moor La.)
Driftholme Rd. BD11: B'frd 2H 47
DRIGHLINGTON 3G 47
Drighlington By-Pass BD4: B'frd ...2E 47
BD11: B'frd 4F 47
WF17: B'frd 4F 47
Drive, The LS8: Leeds 3B 22
LS9: Leeds 6A 32
LS15: Leeds 3D 34
LS16: Leeds 6G 11
LS17: Leeds 3D 12
LS26: Swil 6G 45
Driver Pl. LS12: Leeds 1C 40
Driver St. LS12: Leeds 1D 40
Driver Ter. LS12: Leeds 1C 40
DRUB 6A 46
Drub La. BD19: Cleck 6A 46
Drummond Av. LS16: Leeds 5A 20
Drummond Ct. LS16: Leeds 5A 20
Drummond Rd. LS16: Leeds 4A 20
Drury Av. LS18: H'fth 3B 18
Drury Cl. LS18: H'fth 3B 18
Drury La. LS18: H'fth 3B 18
(not continuous)
Duckett Gro. LS28: Pud 5B 26
Dudley Gro. BD4: B'frd 2A 36
Dudley St. BD4: B'frd 2A 36
Dufton App. LS14: Leeds 2A 34
Duke St. LS9: Leeds 5H 5 (6H 31)
Dulverton Cl. LS11: Leeds 6B 40
Dulverton Ct. LS11: Leeds 6B 40
Dulverton Gdns. LS11: Leeds 5A 40
Dulverton Gth. LS11: Leeds 6A 40
Dulverton Grn. LS11: Leeds 6A 40
(Dulverton Cl.)
LS11: Leeds 6A 40
(Dulverton Gro.)
Dulverton Gro. BD4: B'frd 4A 36
LS11: Leeds 6A 40
Dulverton Pl. LS11: Leeds 6A 40
Dulverton Sq. LS11: Leeds 6B 40
Duncan St. LS1: Leeds 5F 5 (6G 31)
Duncombe St. LS1: Leeds 3A 4 (5E 31)
Dungeon La. LS26: Rothw 2H 59
Dunhill Cres. LS9: Leeds 5G 33
Dunhill Ri. LS9: Leeds 5G 33
Dunkirk Hill LS12: Leeds 4B 30
Dunlin Cl. LS27: Morl 6B 50
Dunlin Ct. LS10: Leeds 4H 51
Dunlin Cft. LS10: Leeds 4H 51
Dunlin Dr. LS10: Leeds 4H 51
Dunlin Fold LS10: Leeds 4H 51
Dunlop Av. LS12: Leeds 3G 39
Dunningley La. WF3: Leeds 6D 50
Dunnock Cft. LS27: Morl 6A 50
Dunstarn Ct. LS16: Leeds 6B 12
Dunstarn Dr. LS16: Leeds 6B 12
Dunstarn Gdns. LS16: Leeds 6C 12
Dunstarn La. LS16: Leeds 1B 20
Durban Av. LS11: Leeds 5D 40
Durban Cres. LS11: Leeds 5D 40
Durham Ct. LS28: Pud 2F 27
Dutton Grn. LS14: Leeds 3A 24
Dutton Way LS14: Leeds 4A 24
Duxbury Ri. LS7: Leeds 3F 31
Dyehouse La. LS28: Pud 3G 37
(not continuous)
Dyers Ct. LS6: Leeds 1D 30
Dyer St. LS2: Leeds 4G 5 (5H 31)
Dyson Ho. LS4: Leeds 2H 29

E

Earlsmere Dr. LS27: Morl 4F 49
Earlswood Av. LS8: Leeds 1B 22
Earlswood Chase LS28: Pud 1G 37
Earlswood Mead LS28: Pud 1F 37
Easdale Cl. LS14: Leeds 6H 23
Easdale Cres. LS14: Leeds 6A 24
Easdale Mt. LS14: Leeds 1H 33
Easdale Rd. LS14: Leeds 1H 33
EAST ARDSLEY 4G 57
EAST BIERLEY 2B 46
East C'way. LS16: Leeds 4B 12
East C'way. Cl. LS16: Leeds 4B 12
East C'way. Cres. LS16: Leeds 5B 12
East C'way. Va. LS16: Leeds 5C 12
East Ct. LS28: Pud 2F 27
(off Ebenezer St.)
Eastdean Bank LS14: Leeds 5A 24
Eastdean Dr. LS14: Leeds 5A 24

Eastdean Gdns.—Eskdale Cl.

Eastdean Gdns. LS14: Leeds . . . 5B **24**
Eastdean Ga. LS14: Leeds . . . 6B **24**
Eastdean Grange LS14: Leeds . . . 6B **24**
Eastdean Gro. LS14: Leeds . . . 5B **24**
Eastdean Ri. LS14: Leeds . . . 5B **24**
Eastdean Rd. LS14: Leeds . . . 5A **24**
Easterly Av. LS8: Leeds . . . 1C **32**
Easterly Cl. LS8: Leeds . . . 2D **32**
Easterly Cres. LS8: Leeds . . . 1C **32**
Easterly Cross LS8: Leeds . . . 1D **32**
Easterly Gth. LS8: Leeds . . . 1D **32**
Easterly Gro. LS8: Leeds . . . 1C **32**
Easterly Mt. LS8: Leeds . . . 1D **32**
Easterly Rd. LS8: Leeds . . . 1C **32**
Easterly Sq. LS8: Leeds . . . 1D **32**
Easterly Vw. LS8: Leeds . . . 1D **32**
Eastfield Cres. LS26: Rothw . . . 3B **54**
Eastfield Dr. LS26: Rothw . . . 3B **54**
Eastfield Gdns. BD4: B'frd . . . 4A **36**
East Fld. St. LS9: Leeds . . . 6A **32**
Eastgate LS2: Leeds . . . 4F **5** (5G **31**)
E. Grange Cl. LS10: Leeds . . . 6A **42**
E. Grange Dr. LS10: Leeds . . . 6A **42**
E. Grange Gth. LS10: Leeds . . . 6A **42**
E. Grange Ri. LS10: Leeds . . . 6A **42**
E. Grange Rd. LS10: Leeds . . . 6A **42**
E. Grange Sq. LS10: Leeds . . . 6A **42**
E. Grange Vw. LS10: Leeds . . . 6A **42**
E. King St. LS9: Leeds . . . 6H **5** (6A **32**)
Eastland Wlk. LS13: Leeds . . . 4E **29**
East Leeds Leisure Cen. . . . **6G 33**
Eastleigh WF3: E Ard . . . 3E **57**
Eastleigh Ct. WF3: E Ard . . . 3E **57**
Eastleigh Dr. WF3: E Ard . . . 3D **56**
EAST MOOR . . . **5B 12**
E. Moor Av. LS8: Leeds . . . 2B **22**
E. Moor Cl. LS8: Leeds . . . 2B **22**
E. Moor Cres. LS8: Leeds . . . 1B **22**
E. Moor Dr. LS8: Leeds . . . 2C **22**
Eastmoor Ho. BD4: B'frd . . . 5B **36**
E. Moor La. LS16: Leeds . . . 5B **12**
E. Moor Rd. LS8: Leeds . . . 1B **22**
East Pde. LS1: Leeds . . . 4D **4** (5F **31**)
LS29: Men . . . 1C **6**
East Pk. Dr. LS9: Leeds . . . 6B **32**
East Pk. Gro. LS9: Leeds . . . 6C **32**
East Pk. Mt. LS9: Leeds . . . 6C **32**
East Pk. Pde. LS9: Leeds . . . 6C **32**
East Pk. Pl. LS9: Leeds . . . 6C **32**
East Pk. Rd. LS9: Leeds . . . 6B **32**
East Pk. St. LS9: Leeds . . . 6C **32**
LS27: Morl . . . 6F **49**
East Pk. Ter. LS9: Leeds . . . 6C **32**
East Pk. Vw. LS9: Leeds . . . 6C **32**
E. Side Ct. LS28: Pud . . . 2B **38**
East St. LS9: Leeds . . . 6H **5** (6H **31**)
East Vw. LS15: Leeds . . . 3C **34**
LS19: Yead . . . 3E **9**
LS26: Rothw . . . 4C **54**
LS27: Morl . . . 4C **48**
LS28: Pud . . . 2G **37**
East Vw. Cotts. *LS28: Pud . . . 5H 27*
(off Lane End)
East Vw. Rd. LS19: Yead . . . 3E **9**
Eastwood Cres. LS14: Leeds . . . 1D **34**
Eastwood Dr. LS14: Leeds . . . 6D **24**
Eastwood Gdns. LS14: Leeds . . . 1C **34**
Eastwood Gth. LS14: Leeds . . . 1D **34**
Eastwood La. LS14: Leeds . . . 1D **34**
Eastwood Nook LS14: Leeds . . . 1D **34**
Easy Rd. LS9: Leeds . . . 1B **42**
Eaton Hill LS16: Leeds . . . 6E **11**
Eaton M. LS10: Leeds . . . 4G **51**
Eaton Sq. LS10: Leeds . . . 5G **51**
Ebberston Gro. LS6: Leeds . . . 2D **30**
Ebberston Pl. LS6: Leeds . . . 2D **30**
Ebberston Ter. LS6: Leeds . . . 2D **30**
Ebenezer St. LS28: Pud . . . 2F **27**
WF3: Rothw . . . 6D **52**
Ebenzer Ho. *LS27: Morl . . . 5G 49*
(off Fountain St.)
Ebor Mt. LS6: Leeds . . . 3D **30**
Ebor Pl. LS6: Leeds . . . 3D **30**
Ebor St. LS6: Leeds . . . 3D **30**
Ebor Ter. *LS10: Leeds . . . 5A 42*
(off Woodhouse Hill Rd.)
Ecclesburn Av. LS9: Leeds . . . 6C **32**
Ecclesburn Rd. LS9: Leeds . . . 6C **32**
Ecclesburn St. LS9: Leeds . . . 6C **32**
Ecclesburn Ter. LS9: Leeds . . . 6C **32**
Eccleshill Swimming Pool . . . **5A 16**
Eccup La. LS16: Leeds . . . 3B **12**
Eccup Moor Rd. LS16: Leeds . . . 1C **12**
Edale Way LS16: Leeds . . . 6F **11**
Eddison Cl. LS16: Leeds . . . 4B **12**
Eddison St. LS28: Pud . . . 3F **27**
Eddison Wlk. LS16: Leeds . . . 4B **12**
Eden Cres. LS4: Leeds . . . 1H **29**
Eden Dr. LS4: Leeds . . . 2H **29**
Eden Gdns. LS4: Leeds . . . 2H **29**
Eden Gro. LS4: Leeds . . . 2H **29**
Eden Mt. LS4: Leeds . . . 2H **29**
Eden Rd. LS4: Leeds . . . 1H **29**
Eden Wlk. LS4: Leeds . . . 2H **29**
Eden Way LS4: Leeds . . . 2H **29**
Ederoyd Av. LS28: Pud . . . 4D **26**
Ederoyd Cres. LS28: Pud . . . 4C **26**
Ederoyd Dr. LS28: Pud . . . 4D **26**
Ederoyd Gro. LS28: Pud . . . 4D **26**
Ederoyd Mt. LS28: Pud . . . 4D **26**
Ederoyd Ri. LS28: Pud . . . 4C **26**
Edgbaston Cl. LS17: Leeds . . . 3E **13**
Edgbaston Wlk. LS17: Leeds . . . 3E **13**
Edgemoor Cl. BD4: B'frd . . . 1A **46**
Edgerton Rd. LS16: Leeds . . . 3H **19**
Edgware Av. LS8: Leeds . . . 3B **32**
Edgware Gro. LS8: Leeds . . . 3B **32**
Edgware Mt. LS8: Leeds . . . 3B **32**
Edgware Pl. LS8: Leeds . . . 3B **32**
Edgware Row LS8: Leeds . . . 3B **32**
Edgware St. LS8: Leeds . . . 3B **32**
Edgware Ter. LS8: Leeds . . . 3B **32**
Edgware Vw. LS8: Leeds . . . 3B **32**
Edinburgh Av. LS12: Leeds . . . 5G **29**
Edinburgh Gro. LS12: Leeds . . . 5G **29**
Edinburgh Pl. LS12: Leeds . . . 5G **29**
Edinburgh Rd. LS12: Leeds . . . 5G **29**
Edinburgh Ter. LS12: Leeds . . . 5G **29**
Edlington Cl. BD4: B'frd . . . 4A **36**
Edmonton Pl. LS7: Leeds . . . 5H **21**
Edroyd Pl. LS28: Pud . . . 2F **27**
Edroyd St. LS28: Pud . . . 2F **27**
Education Rd. LS7: Leeds . . . 2G **31**
Edward Ct. WF2: Wake . . . 6A **58**
Edward Dr. WF1: Wake . . . 6D **58**
Edward St. BD4: B'frd . . . 6A **36**
LS2: Leeds . . . 3F **5** (5G **31**)
Edwin Av. LS20: Guis . . . 4F **7**
Edwin Rd. LS6: Leeds . . . 3C **30**
Eeast Vw. *LS28: Pud . . . 5H 27*
(off Lane End)
Egerton Ter. *LS19: Yead . . . 6F 9*
(off Town St.)
Eggleston Dr. BD4: B'frd . . . 5B **36**
Eggleston St. LS13: Leeds . . . 6H **17**
Eighth Av. LS12: Leeds . . . 1B **40**
LS26: Rothw . . . 2A **54**
Eightlands Av. LS13: Leeds . . . 3D **28**
Eightlands La. LS13: Leeds . . . 3D **28**
Ekota Pl. LS8: Leeds . . . 1B **32**
Elba LS12: Leeds . . . 5A **4** (6E **31**)
Elder Cft. LS13: Leeds . . . 4C **28**
Elder Mt. LS13: Leeds . . . 4C **28**
Elder Pl. LS13: Leeds . . . 4C **28**
Elder Ri. LS26: Rothw . . . 3E **55**
Elder Rd. LS13: Leeds . . . 4C **28**
Elder St. BD10: B'frd . . . 4A **16**
LS13: Leeds . . . 4C **28**
Elderwood Gdns. BD10: B'frd . . . 6A **16**
Eldon Ct. LS2: Leeds . . . 3F **31**
Eldon Mt. LS20: Guis . . . 4G **7**
Eldon Ter. *LS2: Leeds . . . 3F 31*
(off Woodhouse La.)
Eleanor Dr. LS28: Pud . . . 4B **16**
Elford Gro. LS8: Leeds . . . 2B **32**
Elford Pl. E. LS8: Leeds . . . 2B **32**
Elford Pl. W. LS8: Leeds . . . 2B **32**
Elford Rd. LS8: Leeds . . . 2B **32**
Elgar Wlk. WF3: Wake . . . 6G **59**
Eliot Gro. LS20: Guis . . . 5H **7**
Elizabeth Gro. LS27: Morl . . . 4A **50**
Elizabeth Pl. LS14: Leeds . . . 6A **24**
Elizabeth St. LS6: Leeds . . . 2C **30**
Elland Road . . . **4C 40**
Elland Rd. LS11: Leeds . . . 5B **40**
(Crow Nest La.)
LS11: Leeds . . . 2H **49**
(Millshaw Pk. Way)
LS11: Leeds . . . 3D **40**
(Tilbury Rd.)
LS27: Morl . . . 2H **49**
Elland Rd. Ind. Pk. LS11: Leeds . . . 4B **40**
Elland Ter. LS11: Leeds . . . 2F **41**
Elland Way LS11: Leeds . . . 5B **40**
Ellerby La. LS9: Leeds . . . 1A **42**
Ellerby Rd. LS9: Leeds . . . 6A **32**
Eller Ct. LS8: Leeds . . . 5E **23**
Ellers Gro. LS8: Leeds . . . 1B **32**
Ellers Rd. LS8: Leeds . . . 1B **32**
Ellicott Ct. LS29: Men . . . 1C **6**
Ellis Fold LS12: Leeds . . . 6H **29**
Ellis Ter. *LS16: Leeds . . . 5B 20*
(off Glebe Ter.)
Ellwood Cl. LS7: Leeds . . . 4D **20**
Elm Av. WF3: Wake . . . 6H **59**
Elm Ct. BD11: B'frd . . . 5D **46**
Elm Cft. LS14: Leeds . . . 3C **24**
Elmete Av. LS8: Leeds . . . 4E **23**
LS15: Scho . . . 5F **25**
Elmete Cl. LS8: Leeds . . . 5F **23**
Elmete Ct. LS8: Leeds . . . 5E **23**
Elmete Cft. LS15: Scho . . . 5F **25**
Elmete Dr. LS8: Leeds . . . 4F **23**
Elmete Grange LS29: Men . . . 1C **6**
Elmete Gro. LS8: Leeds . . . 4E **23**
Elmete Hill LS8: Leeds . . . 5F **23**
Elmete La. LS8: Leeds . . . 4F **23**
LS17: Leeds . . . 6G **15**
Elmete Mt. LS8: Leeds . . . 5F **23**
Elmete Wlk. LS8: Leeds . . . 5E **23**
Elmete Way LS8: Leeds . . . 5F **23**
Elmet Towers LS14: Leeds . . . 1C **34**
Elmfield LS26: Rothw . . . 4D **54**
Elmfield Ct. BD11: B'frd . . . 5C **46**
LS27: Morl . . . 6H **49**
Elmfield Gro. LS12: Leeds . . . 1B **40**
Elmfield Pde. LS27: Morl . . . 6H **49**
Elmfield Pl. LS12: Leeds . . . 1B **40**
Elmfield Rd. LS12: Leeds . . . 1B **40**
LS27: Morl . . . 6H **49**
Elmfield Way LS13: Leeds . . . 4D **28**
Elm Ho. *LS7: Leeds . . . 4A 22*
(off Allerton Pk.)
LS15: Leeds . . . 1G **43**
Elmhurst Cl. LS17: Leeds . . . 5C **14**
Elmhurst Gdns. LS17: Leeds . . . 5C **14**
Elmroyd LS26: Rothw . . . 5H **53**
Elms, The LS7: Leeds . . . 5H **21**
LS13: Leeds . . . 4E **29**
LS20: Guis . . . 4G **7**
Elm St. LS6: Leeds . . . 1F **31**
Elmton Cl. LS10: Leeds . . . 2H **51**
Elm Tree Cl. LS15: Leeds . . . 1E **45**
LS28: Pud . . . 1G **37**
Elmtree La. LS10: Leeds . . . 3H **41**
Elm Wlk., The LS15: Leeds . . . 2B **44**
Elmwood La. LS7: Leeds . . . 1F **5** (4G **31**)
Elmwood Rd. LS2: Leeds . . . 1E **5** (4G **31**)
Elsham Ter. LS4: Leeds . . . 3A **30**
Elsworth Ho. LS5: Leeds . . . 2F **29**
Elsworth St. LS12: Leeds . . . 6B **30**
Eltham Av. LS6: Leeds . . . 2F **31**
Eltham Cl. LS6: Leeds . . . 2F **31**
Eltham Ct. LS6: Leeds . . . 2F **31**
Eltham Dr. LS6: Leeds . . . 2F **31**
Eltham Gdns. LS6: Leeds . . . 2F **31**
Eltham Ri. LS6: Leeds . . . 2F **31**
Elvaston Rd. LS27: Morl . . . 6G **49**
Elwell St. WF3: E Ard . . . 2A **58**
Ely St. LS12: Leeds . . . 5A **30**
Embankment, The LS1: Leeds . . . 6E **5** (6G **31**)
Emmanuel Trad. Est. LS12: Leeds . . . 1E **41**
Emmet Cl. BD11: B'frd . . . 4D **46**
Emmott Dr. LS19: Yead . . . 6F **9**
Emmott Vw. LS19: Yead . . . 6F **9**
Emsley Pl. LS10: Leeds . . . 2A **42**
Emsley's Vis. Cen. . . . **4C 8**
Emville Av. LS17: Leeds . . . 4E **15**
Endecliffe M. LS6: Leeds . . . 1E **31**
Enfield LS19: Yead . . . 3D **8**
Enfield Av. LS7: Leeds . . . 3A **32**
Enfield St. LS7: Leeds . . . 3H **31**
Enfield Ter. LS7: Leeds . . . 3A **32**
Engine Fields Nature Reserve . . . **3C 8**
Englefield Cl. BD4: B'frd . . . 5A **36**
Englefield Cres. BD4: B'frd . . . 5A **36**
Ennerdale Rd. LS12: Leeds . . . 5D **38**
Ennerdale Way LS12: Leeds . . . 4D **38**
Enterprise Pk. Ind. Est. LS11: Leeds . . . 6D **40**
Enterprise Way LS10: Leeds . . . 6B **42**
Envoy St. LS11: Leeds . . . 3G **41**
Epworth Pl. LS10: Leeds . . . 3A **42**
Eric St. LS13: Leeds . . . 6C **18**
Eshald La. LS26: Rothw . . . 4D **54**
Eshald Mans. LS26: Rothw . . . 3D **54**
Eshald Pl. LS26: Rothw . . . 3D **54**
Esholt Av. LS20: Guis . . . 6F **7**
Esholt Hall Est. BD17: B'frd . . . 5A **8**
Eskdale Cl. LS20: Guis . . . 5G **7**

76 A-Z Leeds

First Av.—Garnet Vw.

First Av. LS12: Leeds 6B **30**
LS19: Yead 4E **9**
LS26: Rothw 2H **53**
LS28: Pud 4G **27**
First Av. Ind. Est. LS28: Pud 4G **27**
Firth Av. LS11: Leeds 5E **41**
Firth Cl. WF3: Wake 6G **59**
Firth Gro. LS11: Leeds 5E **41**
Firth Mt. LS11: Leeds 5E **41**
Firth Rd. LS11: Leeds 5E **41**
Firth St. LS7: Leeds 1H **5** (4H **31**)
Firth Ter. LS9: Leeds 1H **5** (4A **32**)
Firth Vw. LS11: Leeds 5E **41**
Fir Tree App. LS17: Leeds 5F **13**
Fir Tree Cl. LS17: Leeds 5G **13**
Fir Tree Gdns. LS17: Leeds 5F **13**
Fir Tree Grn. LS17: Leeds 5G **13**
Fir Tree Gro. LS17: Leeds 6G **13**
Fir Tree La. LS17: Leeds 6H **13**
Fir Tree Ri. LS17: Leeds 6G **13**
Fir Tree Va. LS17: Leeds 6G **13**
Fish St. LS1: Leeds 4F **5** (5G **31**)
Fitness First Health Club
Leeds **3A 30**
Fitzroy Dr. LS8: Leeds 5C **22**
Flats, The LS19: Yead 3E **9**
Flawith Dr. BD2: B'frd 3A **26**
Flax Mill Rd. LS10: Leeds 4A **42**
Flax Pl. LS9: Leeds 6H **5** (6A **32**)
Flaxton Cl. LS11: Leeds 4F **41**
Flaxton Gdns. LS11: Leeds 4F **41**
Flaxton St. LS11: Leeds 4F **41**
Flaxton Vw. LS11: Leeds 4F **41**
Fleet La. LS26: Mick 5G **55**
LS26: Mick, Rothw 4D **54**
(not continuous)
Fleet Thro' Rd. LS18: H'fth 5B **18**
Flexbury Av. LS27: Morl 6G **49**
Flinton Gro. BD2: B'frd 2A **26**
Floral Av. LS7: Leeds 5G **21**
Florence Av. LS9: Leeds 3C **32**
Florence Gro. LS9: Leeds 3C **32**
Florence Mt. LS9: Leeds 3C **32**
Florence Pl. LS9: Leeds 3C **32**
Florence St. LS9: Leeds 3C **32**
Florence Ter. *LS27: Morl 6H **49***
(off South Pde.)
Flossmore Way LS27: Morl 2C **48**
Flower Chase LS20: Guis 4H **7**
Flower Cl. LS19: Yead 2C **8**
Flower Ct. LS18: H'fth 4B **18**
Flower Gth. *LS18: H'fth 4B **18***
(off Regent Rd.)
Flower Mt. *LS19: Yead 2E **9***
(off Alexandra Ter.)
Fold, The LS15: Leeds 1E **35**
Folkton Holme BD2: B'frd 3A **26**
Folly Hall Mt. WF3: E Ard 3C **56**
Folly Hall Rd. WF3: E Ard 3C **56**
Folly La. LS11: Leeds 3F **41**
Fontmell Cl. BD4: B'frd 5A **36**
Football LS19: Yead 2E **9**
Football Cen. **4A 30**
Football World **2D 42**
Forber Gro. BD4: B'frd 2A **36**
Forber Pl. LS15: Leeds 6G **33**
Forbes Ho. *BD4: B'frd 4A **36***
(off Stirling Cres.)
Forest Bank LS27: Morl 2C **48**
Forest Ridge WF3: E Ard 2G **57**
Forge La. LS12: Leeds 5B **30**
LS17: Leeds 1F **15**
Forge Row LS12: Leeds 4D **38**
Forman's Dr. WF3: Rothw 6C **52**
Forrester Ct. WF3: Rothw 6D **52**
Forster Pl. LS12: Leeds 3G **39**
Forster St. LS10: Leeds 2A **42**
Forsythia Av. WF3: E Ard 3G **57**
Forth Ct. LS11: Leeds 1E **41**
Foster Cl. LS27: Morl 4G **49**
Foster Cres. LS27: Morl 4G **49**
Foster Sq. LS10: Leeds 1H **51**
Foster St. LS27: Morl 4G **49**
Foster Ter. LS13: Leeds 2D **28**
Foston Cl. BD2: B'frd 3A **26**
Foundry App. LS9: Leeds 3D **32**
Foundry Av. LS8: Leeds 2D **32**
LS9: Leeds 2D **32**
Foundry Dr. LS9: Leeds 2D **32**
Foundry Ind. Est. LS28: Pud 4G **27**
Foundry La. LS9: Leeds 2F **33**
LS14: Leeds 2F **33**
LS28: Pud 3G **27**
Foundry Mill Cres. LS14: Leeds 2H **33**
Foundry Mill Dr. LS14: Leeds 2G **33**
(not continuous)
Foundry Mill Gdns. LS14: Leeds 6G **23**
Foundry Mill Mt. LS14: Leeds 2H **33**
Foundry Mill St. LS14: Leeds 2H **33**
Foundry Mill Ter. LS14: Leeds 2H **33**
Foundry Mill Vw. LS14: Leeds 2H **33**
Foundry Mill Wlk. LS14: Leeds 2H **33**
Foundry Pl. LS9: Leeds 2D **32**
Foundry Rd. LS28: Pud 4G **27**
Foundry St. LS9: Leeds 5H **5** (6A **32**)
LS11: Leeds 1F **41**
Foundry Wlk. LS8: Leeds 2C **32**
Fountain Ct. LS27: Morl 5E **49**
Fountain Hall *LS27: Morl 6F **49***
(off Fountain St.)
Fountain St. LS1: Leeds 3B **4** (5E **31**)
LS27: Morl 6F **49**
(Britannia Rd.)
LS27: Morl 1A **50**
(William St.)
Fourteenth Av. LS12: Leeds 1B **40**
Fourth Av. LS26: Rothw 2A **54**
Fowler's Pl. LS28: Pud 3G **27**
Foxcroft Cl. LS6: Leeds 6H **19**
Foxcroft Grn. LS6: Leeds 6H **19**
Foxcroft Mt. LS6: Leeds 6H **19**
Foxcroft Rd. LS6: Leeds 6H **19**
Foxcroft Wlk. LS6: Leeds 6H **19**
Foxcroft Way LS6: Leeds 6H **19**
Foxglove Av. LS8: Leeds 5E **23**
Foxglove Rd. WF17: Bat 6G **47**
Foxhill Av. LS16: Leeds 2A **20**
Foxhill Ct. LS16: Leeds 2A **20**
Foxhill Cres. LS16: Leeds 2B **20**
Foxhill Dr. LS16: Leeds 2A **20**
Foxhill Grn. LS16: Leeds 2B **20**
Foxhill Gro. LS16: Leeds 2B **20**
Foxhills, The LS16: Leeds 5D **10**
Foxholes Cres. LS28: Pud 5D **16**
Foxholes La. LS28: Pud 5D **16**
Foxton Gdns. LS27: Morl 6F **49**
Fox Way LS10: Leeds 2A **42**
Foxwood LS8: Leeds 3E **23**
Foxwood Av. LS8: Leeds 6G **23**
Foxwood Cl. LS8: Leeds 6G **23**
Foxwood Farm Way LS8: Leeds 6G **23**
Foxwood Gro. LS8: Leeds 6G **23**
Foxwood Ri. LS8: Leeds 6G **23**
Foxwood Wlk. LS8: Leeds 6G **23**
Fraisthorpe Mead BD2: B'frd 3A **26**
Frances St. LS28: Pud 3F **27**
Francis Ct. *LS7: Leeds 2H **31***
(off Francis St.)
Francis Gro. LS11: Leeds 4F **41**
Francis St. LS7: Leeds 2H **31**
Frankland Gro. LS7: Leeds 2A **32**
Frankland Pl. LS7: Leeds 2A **32**
(not continuous)
Frank Parkinson Ct. *LS20: Guis 4G **7***
(off Kelcliffe Av.)
Frank Parkinson Homes *LS20: Guis 4G **7***
(off Oxford St.)
Fraser Av. LS18: H'fth 3H **17**
Fraser Rd. LS28: Pud 5B **16**
Fraser St. LS9: Leeds 4B **32**
Frederick Av. LS9: Leeds 1C **42**
Frederick St. LS28: Pud 2E **27**
Freemantle Pl. LS15: Leeds 6G **33**
Freemont St. LS13: Leeds 3A **28**
Freestone M. LS12: Leeds 6C **28**
Fremantle Gro. BD4: B'frd 2A **36**
Frensham Av. LS27: Morl 6F **49**
Frodingham Vs. BD2: B'frd 3A **26**
Frontline Cl. LS8: Leeds 5C **22**
Front Row LS11: Leeds 1F **41**
(not continuous)
Front St. LS11: Leeds 1F **41**
Fuchsia Cft. LS26: Rothw 3E **55**
Fulford Wlk. BD2: B'frd 3A **26**
Fulham Pl. LS11: Leeds 4F **41**
Fulham Sq. *LS11: Leeds 4F **41***
(off Fulham St.)
Fulham St. LS11: Leeds 4F **41**
Fulmar Ct. LS10: Leeds 4H **51**
FULNECK **2G 37**
Fulneck LS28: Pud 3F **37**
Fulneck Cl. LS11: Leeds 2E **51**
Fulneck Ct. LS28: Pud 2H **37**
Fulneck M. LS28: Pud 2H **37**
Fulneck Moravian Settlement & Moravian Mus.
2G 37
Fulton Pl. LS16: Leeds 4A **20**
Furnace La. BD11: B'frd 3C **46**
Future Bodies Gym & Fitness Cen. ***5H 49***
(in Peel Mills Business Cen.)

G

Gable End Ter. LS28: Pud 6H **27**
Gables, The LS17: Leeds 5C **14**
LS18: H'fth 1C **18**
Gabriel Ct. *LS10: Leeds 3H **41***
(off Hunslet Grn. Way)
Gainsborough Pl. *LS12: Leeds 4E **39***
(off Well Holme Mead)
Gainsborough Way WF3: Wake 6G **59**
Gainsbro' Av. LS16: Leeds 4H **11**
Gainsbro' Dr. LS16: Leeds 4H **11**
Gaitskell Ct. LS11: Leeds 2E **41**
Gaitskell Grange LS11: Leeds 2E **41**
Gaitskell Wlk. LS11: Leeds 2E **41**
Gala Bingo
Silver Royd Hill **1F 39**
Tong Street **6A 36**
Gala Casino **4A 4 (5D 30)**
Gallagher Leisure Pk. BD3: Pud 5B **26**
Gallery & Studio Theatre **1D 4 (4F 31)**
Galloway Ct. LS28: Pud 5C **26**
Galloway La. LS28: Pud 4C **26**
Galloway Rd. BD10: B'frd 4A **16**
GAMBLE HILL **5D 28**
Gamble Hill LS13: Leeds 5D **28**
Gamble Hill Chase LS13: Leeds 5D **28**
Gamble Hill Cl. LS13: Leeds 5D **28**
Gamble Hill Cft. *LS13: Leeds 5D **28***
(off Gamble Hill Vw.)
Gamble Hill Cross *LS13: Leeds 5D **28***
(off Gamble Hill Lawn)
Gamble Hill Dr. LS13: Leeds 5D **28**
Gamble Hill Fold *LS13: Leeds 5D **28***
(off Gamble Hill Dr.)
Gamble Hill Grange *LS13: Leeds 5D **28***
(off Gamble Hill Lawn)
Gamble Hill Grn. LS13: Leeds 5D **28**
Gamble Hill Lawn LS13: Leeds 5D **28**
Gamble Hill Path *LS13: Leeds 5D **28***
(off Gamble Hill Grn.)
Gamble Hill Pl. LS13: Leeds 5D **28**
Gamble Hill Ri. LS13: Leeds 5D **28**
Gamble Hill Va. LS13: Leeds 5D **28**
Gamble Hill Vw. LS13: Leeds 5D **28**
Gamble Hill Wlk. *LS13: Leeds 5D **28***
(off Gamble Hill Ri.)
Gamble La. LS12: Leeds 1C **38**
Gambles Hill LS28: Pud 2F **27**
Gang, The *LS12: Leeds 6A **30***
(off Town St.)
Gangster's Gym & Smokey's Place **3B 30**
Ganners Cl. LS13: Leeds 1C **28**
Ganners Gth. LS13: Leeds 1D **28**
Ganners Grn. LS13: Leeds 1C **28**
Ganners Gro. LS13: Leeds 1D **28**
Ganners Hill LS13: Leeds 1D **28**
Ganners La. LS13: Leeds 1C **28**
Ganners Mt. LS13: Leeds 1C **28**
Ganners Ri. LS13: Leeds 1D **28**
Ganners Rd. LS13: Leeds 1C **28**
Ganners Wlk. LS13: Leeds 1C **28**
Ganners Way LS13: Leeds 1C **28**
Ganton Cl. LS6: Leeds 1F **31**
Gardeners Ct. LS10: Leeds 3H **41**
Garden Ho. La. WF3: E Ard 3E **57**
Gardenhurst LS6: Leeds 1C **30**
Gardens, The LS10: Leeds 5G **51**
LS28: Pud 2E **27**
Garden Vw. Ct. LS8: Leeds 2D **22**
GARFORTH BRIDGE **2H 45**
Gargrave App. LS9: Leeds 5B **32**
Gargrave Ct. LS9: Leeds 4B **32**
Gargrave Pl. LS9: Leeds 4B **32**
Garibaldi St. BD3: B'frd 6A **26**
(not continuous)
Garland Dr. LS15: Leeds 6D **34**
Garmont M. LS7: Leeds 5H **21**
Garmont Rd. LS7: Leeds 5H **21**
Garnet Av. LS11: Leeds 4G **41**
Garnet Cres. LS11: Leeds 4G **41**
Garnet Gro. LS11: Leeds 4G **41**
Garnet Pde. LS11: Leeds 4G **41**
Garnet Pl. LS11: Leeds 4G **41**
Garnet Rd. LS11: Leeds 5G **41**
Garnet Ter. LS11: Leeds 4G **41**
Garnet Vw. LS11: Leeds 4G **41**

78 A-Z Leeds

Garth, The—Grange Pk. Way

Garth, The LS9: Leeds 6A 32
Garth Av. LS17: Leeds 2F 21
Garth Dr. LS17: Leeds 2F 21
Garth Gro. LS29: Men 1C 6
Garth Rd. LS17: Leeds 2F 21
Garth Wlk. LS17: Leeds 2F 21
Garton Av. LS9: Leeds 6C 32
Garton Gro. LS9: Leeds 6C 32
Garton Rd. LS9: Leeds 6C 32
Garton Ter. LS9: Leeds 6C 32
Garton Vw. LS9: Leeds 6C 32
Gascoigne Rd. WF3: E Ard 2A 58
Gas Works Yd. LS26: Rothw 4H 53
(off Commercial St.)
Gate Ho. Ct. LS26: Rothw 2E 55
Gateland Dr. LS17: Leeds 5G 15
Gateland La. LS17: Leeds 6G 15
Gate Way Dr. LS19: Yead 2C 8
Gateways WF1: Wake 6E 59
Gathorne Cl. LS8: Leeds 2A 32
Gathorne St. LS8: Leeds 2A 32
(not continuous)
Gathorne Ter. LS8: Leeds 2A 32
Gaunts Pl. LS28: Pud 2G 27
Gavin Cl. BD3: B'frd 6A 26
Gelderd Bus. Pk. LS12: Leeds 3B 40
Gelderd Cl. LS12: Leeds 3B 40
Gelderd La. LS12: Leeds 3B 40
Gelderd Pl. LS12: Leeds 1C 40
Gelderd Rd. LS12: Leeds 4B 40
LS12: Morl 6G 39
LS27: Leeds, Morl 4C 48
WF17: Bat 6H 47
Gelderd Trad. Est. LS12: Leeds 2C 40
Gelder Rd. LS12: Leeds 6H 29
Gemini Bus. Pk. LS7: Leeds 2H 31
Genista Dr. LS10: Leeds 1H 51
George Mann Rd. LS10: Leeds 4C 42
George Mann Way LS10: Leeds 4B 42
George St. LS2: Leeds 4F 5 (5G 31)
LS19: Yead 5D 8
WF1: Wake 6D 58
Gerard Av. LS27: Morl 5F 49
Ghyll Beck Dr. LS19: Yead 6G 9
Ghyll Mt. LS19: Yead 3B 8
Ghyll Rd. LS6: Leeds 5G 19
Ghyll Royd LS20: Guis 6G 7
(not continuous)
Ghyllroyd LS19: Yead 4C 8
Ghyllroyd Av. BD11: B'frd 4D 46
Ghyllroyd Dr. BD11: B'frd 4D 46
Gibraltar Island Rd. LS10: Leeds 3B 42
Gibraltar Rd. LS28: Pud 6D 26
Gibson Ct. WF3: E Ard 6B 56
Gibson Dr. LS15: Leeds 6C 34
Gilbert Chase LS5: Leeds 2G 29
Gilbert Cl. LS5: Leeds 2H 29
Gilbert Mt. LS5: Leeds 2H 29
Gilbert St. LS28: Pud 3F 27
GILDERSOME 2C 48
Gildersome La. LS12: Morl 6B 38
LS27: Morl 1B 48
Gildersome Spur LS27: Morl 4D 48
GILDERSOME STREET 4B 48
Gillett Dr. LS26: Rothw 4H 53
Gillett La. LS26: Rothw 4H 53
Gillingham Grn. BD4: B'frd 4A 36
Gill La. LS19: Yead 5A 8
Gillroyd Mt. LS27: Morl 5A 50
Gillroyd Pde. LS27: Morl 6H 49
Gillroyd Pl. LS27: Morl 6H 49
Gillroyd Ter. LS27: Morl 5A 50
Gills, The LS27: Morl 5A 50
Gilpin Pl. LS12: Leeds 1B 40
Gilpin St. LS12: Leeds 1B 40
Gilpin Ter. LS12: Leeds 1B 40
Gilpin Vw. LS12: Leeds 1B 40
GILROYD 5A 50
Gipsy Hill LS26: Rothw 3B 54
Gipsy La. LS11: Leeds 1E 51
LS26: Rothw 3B 54
Gipsy Mead LS26: Rothw 3B 54
Gipsy St. BD3: B'frd 5A 26
GIPTON 2D 32
Gipton App. LS9: Leeds 4E 33
Gipton Av. LS7: Leeds 2A 32
Gipton Ga. E. LS9: Leeds 2E 33
Gipton Ga. W. LS9: Leeds 2D 32
Gipton Sq. LS9: Leeds 4F 33
Gipton St. LS8: Leeds 2A 32
GIPTON WOOD 6D 22
Gipton Wood Av. LS8: Leeds 6D 22
Gipton Wood Cres. LS8: Leeds 6D 22
Gipton Wood Gro. LS8: Leeds 6D 22
Gipton Wood Pl. LS8: Leeds 6D 22
Gipton Wood Rd. LS8: Leeds 6D 22
Glade, The LS28: Pud 3C 26
Gladstone Ct. LS28: Pud 3H 27
(off Gladstone Ter.)
Gladstone Cres. LS19: Yead 4D 8
Gladstone Rd. LS19: Yead 5D 8
Gladstone Sq. LS27: Morl 5H 49
(off Middleton Rd.)
Gladstone St. LS28: Pud 2F 27
Gladstone Ter. LS27: Morl 5G 49
LS28: Pud 3H 27
Gladstone Vs. LS17: Leeds 6G 15
Glanville Ter. LS26: Rothw 4G 53
Glasshouse St. LS10: Leeds 2H 41
Glasshouse Vw. LS10: Leeds 5F 51
Glebe Av. LS5: Leeds 1H 29
Glebe Ct. LS26: Rothw 4D 52
Glebelands Dr. LS6: Leeds 5B 20
Glebe Mt. LS28: Pud 1G 37
Glebe Pl. LS5: Leeds 1H 29
Glebe St. LS28: Pud 1G 37
Glebe Ter. LS16: Leeds 4B 20
GLEDHOW 4B 22
Gledhow Av. LS8: Leeds 3B 22
Gledhow Ct. LS7: Leeds 4A 22
Gledhow Grange Vw. LS8: Leeds 4B 22
Gledhow Grange Wlk. LS8: Leeds 4B 22
Gledhow La. LS7: Leeds 4H 21
LS8: Leeds 4A 22
Gledhow La. End LS7: Leeds 4H 21
Gledhow Mt. LS8: Leeds 3A 32
Gledhow Pk. Av. LS7: Leeds 5A 22
Gledhow Pk. Cres. LS7: Leeds 5A 22
Gledhow Pk. Dr. LS7: Leeds 5H 21
Gledhow Pk. Gro. LS7: Leeds 5A 22
Gledhow Pk. Rd. LS7: Leeds 5A 22
Gledhow Pk. Vw. LS7: Leeds 5A 22
Gledhow Pl. LS8: Leeds 3A 32
Gledhow Ri. LS8: Leeds 5D 22
Gledhow Rd. LS8: Leeds 3A 32
Gledhow Ter. LS8: Leeds 3A 32
Gledhow Towers LS8: Leeds 4A 22
Gledhow Valley Rd. LS7: Leeds 3H 21
LS8: Leeds 4A 22
Gledhow Wood Av. LS8: Leeds 4B 22
Gledhow Wood Cl. LS8: Leeds 4B 22
Gledhow Wood Ct. LS8: Leeds 6C 22
Gledhow Wood Gro. LS8: Leeds 4B 22
Gledhow Wood Rd. LS8: Leeds 4B 22
Glencoe Vw. LS9: Leeds 1B 42
Glendale Ho. LS27: Morl 6H 49
Glen Dene LS29: Men 1D 6
Glendower Pk. LS16: Leeds 1B 20
Gleneagles Rd. LS17: Leeds 5F 13
Glenfield Cvn. Pk. LS17: Bard 1H 15
Glen Gro. LS27: Morl 6H 49
Glenholme Rd. LS28: Pud 3E 27
Glenhurst BD4: B'frd 6A 36
Glenlea Cl. LS28: Leeds 2A 28
Glenlea Gdns. LS28: Leeds 2A 28
Glenmere Mt. LS19: Yead 2F 9
Glen Mt. LS27: Morl 6H 49
LS29: Men 2D 6
Glenmount Ter. LS27: Morl 1A 56
Glen Rd. LS16: Leeds 4A 20
LS27: Morl 6A 50
Glenroyd Cl. LS28: Pud 6E 27
Glensdale Gro. LS9: Leeds 6B 32
Glensdale Mt. LS9: Leeds 6B 32
Glensdale Rd. LS9: Leeds 6B 32
Glensdale St. LS9: Leeds 6B 32
Glensdale Ter. LS9: Leeds 6B 32
Glenthorpe Av. LS9: Leeds 5C 32
Glenthorpe Cres. LS9: Leeds 5C 32
Glenthorpe Ter. LS9: Leeds 5C 32
Global Av. LS11: Leeds 6C 40
Global Ct. LS11: Leeds 1C 50
Globe Rd. LS11: Leeds 6A 4 (6E 31)
Glossop Gro. LS6: Leeds 1F 31
(off Glossop Vw.)
Glossop Mt. LS6: Leeds 1F 31
Glossop St. LS6: Leeds 1F 31
Glossop Vw. LS6: Leeds 1F 31
Gloucester Ct. LS12: Leeds 6C 30
Gloucester Ter. LS12: Leeds 5C 30
Glover Way LS11: Leeds 5G 41
Goffee Way LS27: Morl 1A 50
Golden Bank LS18: H'fth 2C 18
Golden Ter. LS12: Leeds 3G 39
Goldsmith Dr. WF3: Rothw 6D 52
Gomersall Ho. BD11: B'frd 3F 47
Goodman St. LS10: Leeds 2A 42
Goodrick La. LS17: Leeds 3F 13
Goodwin Rd. LS12: Leeds 1A 40
Goodwood LS10: Leeds 6H 51
Goody Cross La. LS26: Swil 5H 45
Goody Cross Va. LS26: Swil 5H 45
Goosedale Ct. BD4: B'frd 6C 36
Gordon Dr. LS6: Leeds 5C 20
Gordon Pl. LS6: Leeds 5D 20
Gordon St. WF3: E Ard 3A 58
Gordon Ter. LS6: Leeds 5D 20
Gordon Vw. LS6: Leeds 5D 20
Gorse Lea LS10: Leeds 1H 51
Gotts Pk. Av. LS12: Leeds 4F 29
Gotts Pk. Cres. LS12: Leeds 4F 29
Gotts Pk. Vw. LS12: Leeds 3F 29
Gotts Rd. LS12: Leeds 5A 4 (6D 30)
Gower St. LS2: Leeds 3G 5 (5H 31)
Grace St. LS1: Leeds 4B 4 (5E 31)
Grafton St. LS7: Leeds 2F 5 (4G 31)
Grafton Vs. LS15: Leeds 1D 34
Graham Av. LS4: Leeds 2B 30
Graham Gro. LS4: Leeds 2B 30
Graham Ho. LS5: Leeds 2F 29
(off Broad La.)
Graham Mt. LS4: Leeds 2B 30
Graham St. LS4: Leeds 2B 30
Graham Ter. LS4: Leeds 2B 30
Graham Vw. LS4: Leeds 2B 30
Graham Wlk. LS27: Morl 2D 48
Graingers Way LS12: Leeds 6A 4 (6D 30)
Granary Wharf LS1: Leeds 6D 4 (6F 31)
Granby Av. LS6: Leeds 6B 20
Granby Cl. LS6: Leeds 1B 30
Granby Gro. LS6: Leeds 1B 30
Granby Mt. LS6: Leeds 6B 20
Granby Pl. LS6: Leeds 6B 20
Granby Rd. LS6: Leeds 1B 30
Granby St. LS6: Leeds 6B 20
Granby Ter. LS6: Leeds 6B 20
Granby Vw. LS6: Leeds 6B 20
Grand Arc. LS1: Leeds 3F 5
Grandstand Rd. WF2: Wake 6A 58
WF3: Wake 6A 58
Grand Theatre & Opera House 3F 5 (5G 31)
Grange, The LS6: Leeds 6C 20
LS11: Leeds 5E 41
LS12: Leeds 4F 29
LS13: Leeds 4C 28
WF3: Rothw 6F 53
Grange Av. BD3: Pud 5B 26
BD4: B'frd 1C 46
LS7: Leeds 1A 32
LS19: Yead 3E 9
LS29: Men 1B 6
Grange Bldgs. LS27: Morl 2A 56
(off Hodgson St.)
Grange Cl. LS10: Leeds 3H 41
LS18: H'fth 3H 17
Grange Ct. LS6: Leeds 6D 20
LS15: Scho 5F 25
LS17: Leeds 4G 13
LS26: Rothw 2C 54
Grange Cres. LS7: Leeds 1A 32
LS19: Yead 3E 9
Grange Cft. LS17: Leeds 4G 13
Grange Dr. LS18: H'fth 3H 17
Grange Farm Cl. LS29: Men 1B 6
Grangefield Ind. Est. LS28: Pud 4G 27
Grangefield Rd. LS28: Pud 3G 27
(not continuous)
Grange Flds. Mt. LS10: Leeds 2B 52
Grange Flds. Rd. LS10: Leeds 3B 52
Grange Flds. Way LS10: Leeds 3B 52
Grange Gro. BD3: Pud 5B 26
Grange Holt LS17: Leeds 4G 13
Grange Mt. LS19: Yead 3E 9
Grange Pk. Av. LS8: Leeds 6F 23
Grange Pk. Cl. LS8: Leeds 6G 23
LS27: Morl 2H 49
Grange Pk. Ct. LS27: Morl 2H 49
(off Grange Pk. Dr.)
Grange Pk. Cres. LS8: Leeds 6F 23
Grange Pk. Dr. LS27: Morl 2H 49
Grange Pk. Gro. LS8: Leeds 6F 23
Grange Pk. M. LS8: Leeds 6F 23
LS27: Morl 2H 49
Grange Pk. Pl. LS8: Leeds 6F 23
Grange Pk. Ri. LS8: Leeds 6F 23
Grange Pk. Rd. LS8: Leeds 6F 23
Grange Pk. Ter. LS8: Leeds 6G 23
Grange Pk. Wlk. LS8: Leeds 6F 23
Grange Pk. Way LS27: Morl 2H 49

A-Z Leeds 79

Grange Rd.—Haigh Gdns.

Grange Rd. LS10: Leeds 3H **41**
LS19: Yead 3E **9**
Grange Rd., The LS16: Leeds 2H **19**
Grange St. LS27: Morl 1A **50**
Grange Ter. LS7: Leeds 1H **31**
LS19: Yead 3E 9
(off Grange Rd.)
LS27: Morl 2H **49**
LS28: Pud 5G **27**
Grange Vw. BD3: Pud 5B **26**
LS7: Leeds 1A **32**
LS15: Leeds 1D **44**
LS28: Pud 5G **27**
Grange Vw. Gdns. LS17: Leeds 2H **23**
Grangewood Ct. LS16: Leeds 2H **19**
WF1: Wake 6F **59**
Grangewood Gdns. LS16: Leeds 2H **19**
Granhamthorpe LS13: Leeds 3C **28**
Granny Av. LS27: Morl 1A **50**
Granny La. LS12: Leeds 2G **39**
Granny Pl. LS27: Morl 1A **50**
Grant Av. LS7: Leeds 3A **32**
Grantham Towers *LS9: Leeds 4A 32*
(off Lindsey Gdns.)
Granton Rd. LS7: Leeds 6H **21**
Granville Rd. LS9: Leeds 4A **32**
Granville St. LS28: Pud 5E **27**
(Cemetery Rd.)
LS28: Pud 3H **27**
(Gladstone Ter.)
Granville Ter. LS19: Yead 2E **9**
LS20: Guis 3H **7**
Grape St. LS10: Leeds 2H **41**
Grasmere Cl. LS12: Leeds 1B **40**
Grasmere Ct. LS12: Leeds 6B **30**
Grasmere Rd. LS12: Leeds 1B **40**
GRAVELEYTHORPE 5A **34**
Graveleythorpe Ri. LS15: Leeds 4B **34**
Graveleythorpe Rd. LS15: Leeds 4B **34**
Gray Ct. LS15: Leeds 5D **34**
Grayrigg Cl. LS15: Leeds 6G **33**
Grayshon St. BD11: B'frd 4H **47**
Grayson Crest LS4: Leeds 2H **29**
Grayson Hgts. LS4: Leeds 2H **29**
Grayswood Dr. BD4: B'frd 3A **36**
Gt. George St. LS1: Leeds 3C **4** (5F **31**)
LS2: Leeds 3C **4** (5F **31**)
Gt. Northern St. LS27: Morl 6G **49**
Gt. Wilson St. LS11: Leeds 1F **41**
Greaves Yd. LS28: Pud 2G **37**
Greek St. LS1: Leeds 4D **4** (5F **31**)
GREEN, THE
Leeds 1A **34**
Pudsey 1F **27**
Green, The BD4: B'frd 2B **46**
LS14: Leeds 6A **24**
(not continuous)
LS17: Leeds 1A **22**
LS18: H'fth 3B **18**
LS20: Guis 5G **7**
LS27: Morl 2D **48**
LS28: Pud 1F **27**
Greenacre Pk. LS19: Yead 4D **8**
Greenacre Pk. Av. LS19: Yead 4D **8**
Greenacre Pk. M. LS19: Yead 4E **9**
Greenacre Pk. Ri. LS19: Yead 4D **8**
Greenacres Dr. WF17: Bat 6A **48**
Green Bank WF3: Rothw 2F **59**
Greenbanks Av. LS18: H'fth 1C **18**
Greenbanks Cl. LS18: H'fth 1C **18**
Greenbanks Dr. LS18: H'fth 1B **18**
GREENBOTTOM 5G **7**
Green Chase LS6: Leeds 4C **20**
Green Cl. LS6: Leeds 4D **20**
Green Ct. LS15: Scho 4F **25**
LS17: Leeds 1H **21**
Green Cres. LS6: Leeds 4C **20**
Greencroft M. *LS20: Guis 4G 7*
(off The Green)
Grn. Dragon Yd. LS1: Leeds 4D **4**
Greenfield Av. LS20: Guis 6D **6**
LS27: Morl 2B **48**
Greenfield Ct. LS16: Leeds 5H **11**
Greenfield Dr. LS27: Morl 2B **48**
Greenfield La. LS20: Guis 6C **6**
Greenfield Rd. LS9: Leeds 6A **32**
Greengate LS26: Rothw 3C **54**
GREENGATES 4A **16**
Greenhead Rd. LS16: Leeds 3H **19**
Grn. Hill Chase LS12: Leeds 1H **39**
Grn. Hill Cl. LS12: Leeds 4F **29**
Grn. Hill Cres. LS12: Leeds 1H **39**
Grn. Hill Cft. LS12: Leeds 1H **39**
Grn. Hill Dr. LS13: Leeds 4E **29**
Grn. Hill Gdns. LS12: Leeds 1H **39**
Grn. Hill Holt LS12: Leeds 1H **39**
Grn. Hill La. LS12: Leeds 2G **39**
Grn. Hill Mt. LS13: Leeds 4E **29**
Grn. Hill Pl. LS13: Leeds 4E **29**
Grn. Hill Rd. LS12: Leeds 4F **29**
Grn. Hill Rd. LS13: Leeds 4E **29**
Greenhills LS19: Yead 6E **9**
Grn. Hill Way LS13: Leeds 4E **29**
Greenholme Ct. BD4: B'frd 5B **36**
Greenhow Cl. LS4: Leeds 3B **30**
Greenhow Gdns. LS4: Leeds 3B **30**
Greenhow Rd. LS4: Leeds 3B **30**
Greenhow Wlk. LS4: Leeds 3B **30**
Greenland Ct. LS26: Rothw 4C **54**
Green La. LS11: Leeds 6D **40**
LS12: Leeds 1C **40**
(Sutherland St.)
LS12: Leeds 2C **38**
(Tong Rd.)
LS14: Leeds 3A **24**
LS15: Leeds 4B **34**
LS16: Leeds 5D **10**
LS18: H'fth 4B **18**
LS19: Yead 4D **8**
LS28: Pud 1F **37**
WF3: Rothw 2E **59**
Green Lea LS26: Rothw 3B **54**
Greenlea Av. LS19: Yead 3B **8**
Greenlea Cl. LS19: Yead 4B **8**
Greenlea Fold LS19: Yead 4B **8**
Greenlea Mt. LS19: Yead 3B **8**
Greenlea Rd. LS19: Yead 3B **8**
Greenmoor Av. LS12: Leeds 6D **28**
WF3: Rothw 2E **59**
Greenmoor Cl. WF3: Rothw 2E **59**
Greenmoor Cres.
WF3: Rothw 2F **59**
Greenmount Ct. *LS11: Leeds 4F 41*
(off Fulham St.)
Greenmount La. LS11: Leeds 4F **41**
Greenmount Pl. LS11: Leeds 4F **41**
Greenmount St. LS11: Leeds 4F **41**
Greenmount Ter. LS11: Leeds 4F **41**
Greenock Pl. LS12: Leeds 5G **29**
Greenock Rd. LS12: Leeds 5G **29**
Greenock St. LS12: Leeds 5G **29**
Greenock Ter. LS12: Leeds 5G **29**
Green Pk. LS17: Leeds 1A **22**
Grn. Pasture Cl. LS9: Leeds 5E **33**
Green Rd. LS6: Leeds 3C **20**
Green Row LS6: Leeds 4C **20**
Greenroyd Av. BD19: Cleck 6A **46**
Greenshank M. LS27: Morl 5B **50**
Greenshaw Ter. LS20: Guis 4F **7**
Greenside *LS19: Yead 4C 8*
(off Warm La.)
LS28: Pud 1F **37**
Grn. Side Av. LS12: Leeds 2H **39**
Greenside Cl. LS12: Leeds 2A **40**
Greenside Ct. LS27: Morl 2D **48**
Greenside Dr. LS12: Leeds 2A **40**
Greenside Gro. LS28: Pud 1F **37**
Greenside Rd. LS12: Leeds 2A **40**
Grn. Side Ter. LS12: Leeds 2H **39**
Greenside Wlk. LS12: Leeds 2H **39**
Green Ter. LS11: Leeds 4G **41**
LS20: Guis 5G **7**
Greenthorpe Ct. LS13: Leeds 6E **29**
Greenthorpe Hill LS13: Leeds 6E **29**
Greenthorpe Mt. LS13: Leeds 5E **29**
Greenthorpe Rd. LS13: Leeds 5E **29**
Greenthorpe St. LS13: Leeds 6E **29**
Greenthorpe Wlk. LS13: Leeds 5E **29**
Green Top LS12: Leeds 2H **39**
Greentop LS28: Pud 1F **37**
Grn. Top Gdns. LS12: Leeds 2H **39**
Green Vw. LS6: Leeds 4C **20**
Greenview Cl. LS9: Leeds 3E **33**
Greenview Ct. LS8: Leeds 3C **22**
Greenview Mt. LS9: Leeds 3E **33**
Greenville Av. LS12: Leeds 2H **39**
Greenville Gdns.
LS12: Leeds 2H **39**
Greenway LS15: Leeds 4C **34**
LS20: Guis 6E **7**
Greenway Cl. LS15: Leeds 4C **34**
Greenwell Ct. LS9: Leeds 5E **33**
Greenwood Ct. LS6: Leeds 3C **20**
Greenwood Mt. LS6: Leeds 4C **20**
Greenwood Pk. LS6: Leeds 4C **20**
Greenwood Rd. WF3: E Ard 3D **56**
Greenwood Row *LS27: Morl 5H 49*
(off Commercial St.)
LS28: Pud 6H **27**
Gresley Ho. *LS18: H'fth 6C 10*
(off Sussex Av.)
Greyshiels Av. LS6: Leeds 1A **30**
Greyshiels Cl. LS6: Leeds 1A **30**
Greystone Mt. LS15: Leeds 6G **33**
Greystones Ct. LS8: Leeds 4E **23**
LS17: Leeds 5G **13**
Griff Ho. La. WF3: E Ard 3F **57**
Grimthorpe Av. LS6: Leeds 6A **20**
Grimthorpe Pl. LS6: Leeds 6B **20**
Grimthorpe St. LS6: Leeds 6A **20**
Grimthorpe Ter. LS6: Leeds 6B **20**
Grosmont Pl. LS13: Leeds 2C **28**
Grosmont Rd. LS13: Leeds 3C **28**
Grosmont Ter. LS13: Leeds 2C **28**
Grosvenor Ct. *LS16: Leeds 5D 10*
(off Tinshill Rd.)
Grosvenor Hill LS7: Leeds 3G **31**
Grosvenor M. LS19: Yead 5C **8**
Grosvenor Mt. LS6: Leeds 1D **30**
Grosvenor Pk. LS7: Leeds 4G **21**
Grosvenor Pk. Gdns. LS6: Leeds 1D **30**
Grosvenor Rd. LS6: Leeds 1D **30**
Grosvenor Ter. LS6: Leeds 1D **30**
Grove, The BD10: B'frd 4A **16**
LS17: Leeds 4D **12**
LS18: H'fth 3B **18**
LS19: Yead 3D **8**
LS26: Swil 5H **45**
LS27: Morl 2D **48**
LS28: Pud 6F **27**
WF3: E Ard 3F **57**
Grove Av. LS6: Leeds 5C **20**
LS28: Pud 6F **27**
Grove Ct. LS6: Leeds 5C **20**
LS28: Pud 6F **27**
Grove Farm Cl. LS16: Leeds 5F **11**
Grove Farm Cres. LS16: Leeds 6E **11**
Grove Farm Cft. LS16: Leeds 5E **11**
Grove Farm Dr. LS16: Leeds 5E **11**
Grove Gdns. LS6: Leeds 5C **20**
Grovehall Av. LS11: Leeds 6D **40**
Grovehall Dr. LS11: Leeds 6D **40**
Grovehall Pde. LS11: Leeds 6D **40**
Grovehall Rd. LS11: Leeds 6D **40**
Grove Ho. *LS7: Leeds 1A 32*
(off Woodland Gro.)
Grove Ho. Ct. *LS8: Leeds 5F 23*
(off Nth. Grove Cl.)
Grove La. LS6: Leeds 5B **20**
Grove Ri. LS17: Leeds 4D **12**
Grove Rd. LS6: Leeds 6C **20**
LS10: Leeds 4A **42**
LS15: Leeds 6A **34**
LS18: H'fth 3B **18**
LS28: Pud 6F **27**
LS29: Men 1C **6**
Grove St. LS1: Leeds 4A **4**
LS28: Pud 3G **27**
Grove Ter. BD11: B'frd 5C **46**
LS28: Pud 6F **27**
Grovewood LS6: Leeds 5B **20**
Grunberg Pl. LS6: Leeds 6B **20**
Grunberg St. LS6: Leeds 6B **20**
Guardian M. *LS12: Leeds 2A 40*
(off Lynwood Vw.)
Guillemot App. LS27: Morl 6B **50**
GUISELEY 4G **7**
Guiseley Dr. LS29: Men 3D **6**
Guiseley Retail Pk. LS20: Guis 5G **7**
Guiseley Station (Rail) 4F **7**
Guiseley Theatre 5G **7**
Gurbax Ct. BD3: B'frd 6A **26**
Gwynne Av. BD3: B'frd 4A **26**
Gym and Tonic 1B **22**
Gym Health & Fitness Club, The 3C **32**
Gypsy Wood Cl. LS15: Leeds 6D **34**
Gypsy Wood Crest LS15: Leeds 6D **34**

H

Haddon Av. LS4: Leeds 3A **30**
Haddon Pl. LS4: Leeds 3A **30**
Haddon Rd. LS4: Leeds 3B **30**
Hadleigh Ct. LS17: Leeds 1H **21**
Hadley's Ct. *LS27: Morl 3D 48*
(off Gelderd Rd.)
Haigh Av. LS26: Rothw 2E **53**
Haigh Gdns. LS26: Rothw 2E **53**

80 A-Z Leeds

Haigh Hall—Hawkhills

Haigh Hall BD10: B'frd 4A **16**
Haigh Hall Rd. BD10: B'frd 4A **16**
HAIGH MOOR **5C 56**
Haigh Moor Av. WF3: E Ard 5C **56**
Haigh Moor Cres. WF3: E Ard 5C **56**
Haigh Moor Rd. WF3: E Ard 6C **56**
Haigh Moor Vw. WF3: E Ard 5C **56**
Haigh Pk. Rd. LS10: Leeds 5D **42**
Haigh Rd. LS26: Rothw 3G **53**
Haighside LS26: Rothw 3E **53**
Haighside Cl. LS26: Rothw 3E **53**
Haighside Dr. LS26: Rothw 3E **53**
Haighside Way LS26: Rothw 3E **53**
Haigh Ter. LS26: Rothw 2E **53**
Haigh Vw. LS26: Rothw 2E **53**
Haigh Wood Cres. LS16: Leeds 6D **10**
Haigh Wood Grn. LS16: Leeds 1D **18**
Haigh Wood Rd. LS16: Leeds 6C **10**
Haines Pk. LS7: Leeds 3A **32**
Hainsworth Ct. *LS28: Pud 2F **27***
(off Ebenezer St.)
Hainsworth Sq. LS28: Pud 2F **27**
Hainsworth St. LS12: Leeds 1C **40**
LS26: Rothw 5G **53**
Halcyon Hill LS7: Leeds 3G **21**
Hales Rd. LS12: Leeds 2H **39**
Halesworth Cres. BD4: B'frd 4A **36**
Haley's Yd. LS13: Leeds 2C **28**
HALF MILE **2H 27**
Half Mile LS13: Pud 3H **27**
LS28: Pud 3H **27**
Half Mile Cl. LS28: Pud 3H **27**
Half Mile Ct. LS28: Pud 3H **27**
Half Mile Gdns. LS13: Pud 3H **27**
Half Mile Grn. LS28: Pud 3H **27**
Half Mile La. LS13: Pud 2H **27**
LS28: Pud 2H **27**
Hall, The LS7: Leeds 4G **21**
Hallamfield LS20: Guis 5G **7**
Hallam St. LS20: Guis 5F **7**
Hall Ct. LS7: Leeds 1H **31**
Hall Gro. LS6: Leeds 3D **30**
Halliday Av. LS12: Leeds 5G **29**
Halliday Dr. LS12: Leeds 5G **29**
Halliday Gro. LS12: Leeds 5G **29**
Halliday Mt. LS12: Leeds 5G **29**
Halliday Pl. LS12: Leeds 5G **29**
Halliday Rd. LS12: Leeds 5G **29**
Halliday St. LS28: Pud 5G **27**
Hall La. LS7: Leeds 6H **21**
LS12: Leeds 1C **38**
(Green La.)
LS12: Leeds 6A **30**
(Strawberry Rd.)
LS16: Leeds 3E **11**
LS18: H'fth 3H **17**
Hall Pk. Av. LS18: H'fth 2A **18**
Hall Pk. Cl. LS18: H'fth 2A **18**
Hall Pk. Gth. LS18: H'fth 2A **18**
Hall Pk. Mt. LS18: H'fth 2A **18**
Hall Pk. Ri. LS18: H'fth 2A **18**
Hall Pl. LS9: Leeds 6B **32**
Hall Rd. LS12: Leeds 6A **30**
LS26: Swil 6H **45**
Hall Sq. LS28: Pud 4D **16**
Hallwood Grn. BD10: B'frd 6A **16**
HALTON **5H 33**
Halton Dr. LS15: Leeds 5A **34**
Halton Hill LS15: Leeds 5H **33**
HALTON MOOR **6G 33**
Halton Moor Av. LS9: Leeds 1F **43**
Halton Moor Rd. LS9: Leeds 1C **42**
(not continuous)
LS15: Leeds 1G **43**
Hamilton Av. LS7: Leeds 1A **32**
Hamilton Gdns. LS7: Leeds 2H **31**
Hamilton Pl. LS7: Leeds 2A **32**
Hamilton Ter. LS7: Leeds 1A **32**
Hamilton Vw. LS7: Leeds 1A **32**
Hammerton Gro. LS28: Pud 6H **27**
Hammerton St. LS28: Pud 6G **27**
Hammond Cres. BD11: B'frd 2F **47**
Hampton Pl. LS9: Leeds 6B **32**
Hampton St. LS9: Leeds 6A **32**
Hampton Ter. LS9: Leeds 6B **32**
Hanley Rd. LS27: Morl 6G **49**
Hanover Av. LS3: Leeds 2A **4** (5E **31**)
Hanover Ct. LS27: Morl 4H **49**
Hanover Ho. *LS19: Yead 2E **9***
(off Harper La.)
Hanover La. LS3: Leeds 3B **4** (5E **31**)
Hanover Mt. LS3: Leeds 2A **4** (4E **31**)
Hanover Sq. LS3: Leeds 2A **4** (4E **31**)
Hanover Wlk. LS3: Leeds 3B **4** (5E **31**)
(not continuous)
Hanover Way LS3: Leeds 3A **4** (5E **31**)
Hansby Av. LS14: Leeds 6B **24**
Hansby Bank LS14: Leeds 6B **24**
Hansby Cl. LS14: Leeds 1B **34**
Hansby Dr. LS14: Leeds 6B **24**
Hansby Gdns. LS14: Leeds 1B **34**
Hansby Ga. LS14: Leeds 6B **24**
Hansby Grange LS14: Leeds 6B **24**
Hansby Pl. LS14: Leeds 6B **24**
Harborough Grn. *BD10: B'frd 3A **16***
(off The Leavens)
Harcourt Dr. LS27: Morl 4F **49**
Harcourt Pl. LS1: Leeds 4A **4** (5D **30**)
Harden Gro. BD10: B'frd 2A **26**
Hardrow Grn. LS12: Leeds 2B **40**
Hardrow Gro. LS12: Leeds 2B **40**
Hardrow Rd. LS12: Leeds 2A **40**
Hardrow Ter. LS12: Leeds 2B **40**
Hardwick Cft. LS7: Leeds 5H **21**
Hardy Av. LS27: Morl 1A **50**
Hardy Ct. LS27: Morl 5H **49**
Hardy Gro. LS11: Leeds 4E **41**
Hardy St. LS11: Leeds 4E **41**
LS27: Morl 5H **49**
Hardy Ter. LS11: Leeds 4F **41**
Hardy Vw. LS11: Leeds 4E **41**
Hare Farm Av. LS12: Leeds 6D **28**
Hare Farm Cl. LS12: Leeds 5D **28**
Harefield E. LS15: Leeds 6G **33**
Harefield W. LS15: Leeds 6G **33**
HAREHILLS **3D 32**
Harehills Av. LS7: Leeds 1A **32**
LS8: Leeds 1A **32**
HAREHILLS CORNER **1B 32**
Harehills La. LS7: Leeds 6A **22**
LS8: Leeds 1B **32**
LS9: Leeds 1C **32**
Harehills Pk. Av. LS9: Leeds 3D **32**
Harehills Pk. Cotts. LS9: Leeds 3E **33**
Harehills Pk. Rd. LS9: Leeds 3D **32**
Harehills Pk. Ter. LS9: Leeds 3D **32**
Harehills Pk. Vw. LS9: Leeds 3D **32**
Harehills Pl. LS8: Leeds 2B **32**
Harehills Rd. LS8: Leeds 1B **32**
Hare La. LS28: Pud 2G **37**
Hare Pk. Mt. LS12: Leeds 6C **28**
Hares Av. LS8: Leeds 1B **32**
Hares Mt. LS8: Leeds 1A **32**
Hares Rd. LS8: Leeds 1A **32**
Hares Ter. LS8: Leeds 1B **32**
Hares Vw. LS8: Leeds 1B **32**
Harewood Ct. LS14: Leeds 1A **34**
LS17: Leeds 2H **21**
Harewood St. LS2: Leeds 4F **5** (5G **31**)
Harewood Way LS13: Leeds 5B **28**
Hargrave Cres. LS29: Men 1B **6**
Hargreaves Av. WF3: Wake 6G **59**
Hargreaves Cl. LS27: Morl 2F **49**
Hargreaves St. LS26: Rothw 4H **53**
Harker Ter. LS28: Pud 4F **27**
Harland Sq. *LS2: Leeds 2E **31***
(off Moorfield St.)
Harlech Av. LS11: Leeds 5F **41**
Harlech Cres. LS11: Leeds 5F **41**
Harlech Gro. LS11: Leeds 5F **41**
Harlech Mt. LS11: Leeds 5F **41**
Harlech Pk. Ct. LS11: Leeds 5F **41**
Harlech Rd. LS11: Leeds 5F **41**
Harlech St. LS11: Leeds 5F **41**
Harlech Ter. LS11: Leeds 5F **41**
Harley Cl. LS13: Leeds 5A **28**
Harley Ct. LS13: Leeds 5A **28**
Harley Dr. LS13: Leeds 5A **28**
Harley Gdns. LS13: Leeds 5A **28**
Harley Grn. LS13: Leeds 5A **28**
Harley Ri. LS13: Leeds 5A **28**
Harley Rd. LS13: Leeds 5A **28**
Harley Ter. LS13: Leeds 5A **28**
Harley Vw. LS13: Leeds 5A **28**
Harley Wlk. LS13: Leeds 5A **28**
Harlington Ct. LS27: Morl 6G **49**
Harlington Rd. LS27: Morl 6G **49**
Harlow Ct. LS8: Leeds 4E **23**
Harold Av. LS6: Leeds 3C **30**
Harold Gdns. LS27: Morl 5A **50**
Harold Gro. LS6: Leeds 3C **30**
Harold Mt. LS6: Leeds 3C **30**
Harold Pl. LS6: Leeds 3C **30**
Harold Rd. LS6: Leeds 3C **30**
Harold Sq. LS6: Leeds 3C **30**
Harold St. LS6: Leeds 3C **30**
Harold Ter. LS6: Leeds 3C **30**
Harold Vw. LS6: Leeds 3C **30**
Harold Wlk. LS6: Leeds 3C **30**
Harper Ga. BD4: B'frd 3B **36**
Harper La. LS19: Yead 3D **8**
Harper Rock *LS19: Yead 3D **8***
(off Harper La.)
Harper St. LS2: Leeds 5G **5** (6H **31**)
Harper Ter. *LS19: Yead 3D **8***
(off Harper La.)
Harrier Way LS27: Morl 5B **50**
Harriet St. LS7: Leeds 2H **31**
Harrison and Potter Trust Homes, The
LS2: Leeds 2F **5**
Harrison Cres. LS9: Leeds 4F **33**
Harrison Potter Trust Almshouse
*LS2: Leeds 2E **31***
(off Raglan Rd.)
Harrison's Av. LS28: Pud 3H **27**
Harrison St. LS1: Leeds 3F **5** (5G **31**)
Harrogate Pde. LS17: Leeds 1H **21**
Harrogate Rd. LS7: Leeds 3G **21**
LS17 . . . . 6H **13**
LS17: Leeds 2G **21**
LS19: B'hpe, Yead 1G **9**
LS19: Yead 5D **8**
(not continuous)
Harrogate Vw. LS17: Leeds 4E **15**
Harrowby Cres. LS16: Leeds 4H **19**
Harrowby Rd. LS16: Leeds 4H **19**
Harthill LS27: Morl 2D **48**
Harthill Av. LS27: Morl 2D **48**
Harthill Cl. LS27: Morl 2D **48**
Harthill La. LS27: Morl 2D **48**
Harthill Paddock LS27: Morl 2D **48**
Harthill Pde. *LS27: Morl 2D **48***
(off Town St.)
Harthill Ri. LS27: Morl 2D **48**
Hartland Rd. BD4: B'frd 3A **36**
Hartley Av. LS6: Leeds 1E **31**
Hartley Cres. LS6: Leeds 1E **31**
Hartley Gdns. LS6: Leeds 1F **31**
Hartley Gro. LS6: Leeds 1E **31**
Hartley Hill LS2: Leeds 2F **5** (4G **31**)
Hartley Pl. LS27: Morl 6H **49**
Hartley's Bldgs. LS27: Morl 6H **49**
Hartley St. LS27: Morl 5H **49**
(California St.)
LS27: Morl 2H **49**
(Grange Pk. Dr.)
Hartley's Yd. LS12: Leeds 6H **29**
Hartwell Rd. LS6: Leeds 3C **30**
Harwill App. LS27: Morl 2A **50**
Harwill Av. LS27: Morl 2A **50**
Harwill Cft. LS27: Morl 2A **50**
Harwill Gro. LS27: Morl 2A **50**
Harwill Ri. LS27: Morl 2A **50**
Harwill Rd. LS27: Morl 2A **50**
Haslewood Cl. LS9: Leeds 5A **32**
Haslewood Ct. LS9: Leeds 5B **32**
Haslewood Dene LS9: Leeds 5B **32**
Haslewood Dr. LS9: Leeds 5A **32**
Haslewood Gdns. LS9: Leeds 5B **32**
Haslewood Grn. LS9: Leeds 5B **32**
Haslewood M. LS9: Leeds 5B **32**
Haslewood Pl. LS9: Leeds 5B **32**
Haslewood Sq. LS9: Leeds 5B **32**
Haslewood Vw. LS9: Leeds 5B **32**
Hastings Ct. LS17: Leeds 5G **15**
Hathaway Dr. LS14: Leeds 2B **24**
Hathaway La. LS14: Leeds 3B **24**
Hathaway M. LS14: Leeds 2B **24**
Hathaway Wlk. LS14: Leeds 3B **24**
Hauxwell Dr. LS19: Yead 3D **8**
Haven, The LS15: Leeds 5D **34**
Haven Chase LS16: Leeds 6E **11**
Haven Cl. LS16: Leeds 5F **11**
Haven Ct. LS16: Leeds 6F **11**
Haven Cft. LS16: Leeds 6F **11**
Haven Gdns. LS16: Leeds 6E **11**
Haven Gth. LS16: Leeds 6E **11**
Haven Grn. LS16: Leeds 6E **11**
Haven Mt. LS16: Leeds 6E **11**
Haven Ri. LS16: Leeds 6E **11**
Haven Vw. LS16: Leeds 6E **11**
Havercroft LS12: Leeds 2E **39**
Havercroft Gdns. LS12: Leeds 2E **39**
Haw Av. LS19: Yead 1E **9**
Hawkhill Av. LS15: Leeds 3B **34**
LS20: Guis 5F **7**
Hawkhill Dr. LS15: Leeds 2B **34**
Hawkhill Gdns. LS15: Leeds 2B **34**
Hawkhills LS7: Leeds 4A **22**

A-Z Leeds 81

Hawkhurst Rd.—Highcliffe Rd.

Hawkhurst Rd. LS12: Leeds 1A **40**
Hawkins Dr. LS7: Leeds 3G **31**
Hawkshead Cres. LS14: Leeds 2H **33**
Hawksley Ct. LS27: Morl 2F **49**
Hawk's Nest Gdns. E. LS17: Leeds 5H **13**
Hawk's Nest Gdns. Sth. LS17: Leeds 5H **13**
Hawk's Nest Gdns. W. LS17: Leeds 5H **13**
Hawk's Nest Ri. LS17: Leeds 5H **13**
Hawkstone Av. LS20: Guis 6E **7**
Hawkstone Vw. LS20: Guis 6E **7**
Hawkswood Av. LS5: Leeds 4E **19**
Hawkswood Cres. LS5: Leeds 4E **19**
Hawkswood Gro. LS5: Leeds 4E **19**
Hawkswood Mt. LS5: Leeds 4E **19**
Hawkswood Pl. LS5: Leeds 5E **19**
Hawkswood St. LS5: Leeds 5F **19**
Hawkswood Ter. LS5: Leeds 5F **19**
Hawkswood Vw. LS5: Leeds 4E **19**
HAWKSWORTH
LS5 **5E 19**
LS20 **5B 6**
Hawksworth Av. LS20: Guis 6F **7**
Hawksworth Cl. LS29: Men 2C **6**
Hawksworth Commercial Pk.
LS13: Leeds 4C **28**
Hawksworth Dr. LS20: Guis 6F **7**
LS29: Men 1B **6**
Hawksworth Gro. LS5: Leeds 5D **18**
Hawksworth La. LS20: Guis 5B **6**
Hawksworth Rd. LS18: H'fth 4D **18**
Haw La. LS19: Yead 2D **8**
Hawley Cl. LS27: Morl 6F **49**
Hawley Ter. BD10: B'frd 1A **26**
Hawley Way LS27: Morl 6F **49**
Haworth Ct. *LS19: Yead 2D 8*
(off Chapel La.)
Haworth La. LS19: Yead 2D **8**
Haworth Rd. WF17: Bat 6H **47**
Hawthorn Av. LS19: Yead 2D **8**
Hawthorn Cres. LS7: Leeds 4H **21**
LS19: Yead 2D **8**
Hawthorn Cft. WF3: Rothw 2E **59**
Hawthorn Dr. LS13: Leeds 5F **17**
LS19: Yead 1E **9**
Hawthorne Av. BD3: B'frd 5A **26**
Hawthorne Cl. LS27: Morl 2D **48**
Hawthorne Dr. LS27: Morl 2E **49**
Hawthorne Gdns. LS16: Leeds 4H **11**
Hawthorne Mills *LS12: Leeds 3G 39*
(off Cow Cl. Gro.)
Hawthorne Sq. WF3: E Ard 3A **58**
Hawthorne Vw. LS27: Morl 2E **49**
Hawthorn Gro. LS13: Leeds 6F **17**
LS26: Rothw 5H **53**
Hawthorn La. LS7: Leeds 4H **21**
Hawthorn Mt. LS7: Leeds 4H **21**
Hawthorn Pk. LS14: Leeds 3B **24**
Hawthorn Ri. LS14: Leeds 3C **24**
Hawthorn Rd. LS7: Leeds 4H **21**
LS19: Yead 2D **8**
Hawthorns, The WF1: Wake 6F **59**
Hawthorn St. BD3: B'frd 5A **26**
Hawthorn Ter. LS25: Swil 2H **45**
Hawthorn Va. LS7: Leeds 4H **21**
Hawthorn Vw. LS7: Leeds 4H **21**
Haw Vw. LS19: Yead 1E **9**
Haydn Av. WF3: Wake 5G **59**
Haydn Cl. LS27: Morl 5G **49**
Haydn Ct. LS27: Morl 5G **49**
Haydn's Ter. LS28: Pud 3G **27**
Hayfield Ter. LS12: Leeds 1A **40**
Hayleigh Av. LS13: Leeds 2C **28**
Hayleigh Mt. LS13: Leeds 2C **28**
Hayleigh St. LS13: Leeds 2C **28**
Hayleigh Ter. LS13: Leeds 3C **28**
Hazel Av. LS14: Leeds 3C **24**
Hazel Cl. BD11: B'frd 3C **46**
Hazel Ct. LS26: Rothw 5H **53**
Hazelhurst Ct. LS28: Pud 6H **27**
Hazel La. WF3: E Ard 3B **58**
Hazelwood Ct. WF1: Wake 6F **59**
Hazelwood Rd. WF1: Wake 6F **59**
HEADINGLEY **6B 20**
Headingley **1B 30**
Headingley Av. LS6: Leeds 6A **20**
Headingley Ct. LS6: Leeds 1D **30**
Headingley Cres. LS6: Leeds 1B **30**
HEADINGLEY HILL **1C 30**
Headingley La. LS6: Leeds 1C **30**
Headingley Mt. LS6: Leeds 6A **20**
Headingley Office Pk. LS6: Leeds 1D **30**
Headingley Ri. *LS6: Leeds 2D 30*
(off Welton Rd.)
Headingley Stadium **1B 30**
Headingley Station (Rail) **1H 29**
Headingley Ter. LS6: Leeds 1D **30**
Headingley Vw. LS6: Leeds 1B **30**
Headrow, The LS1: Leeds 3D **4** (5F **31**)
Headrow Cen., The LS1: Leeds 4E **5** (5G **31**)
Healey Cft. WF3: E Ard 4F **57**
Healey Cft. La. WF3: E Ard 4F **57**
Heathcliffe Cl. WF17: Bat 6H **47**
Heath Cres. LS11: Leeds 4C **40**
Heathcroft Bank LS11: Leeds 5C **40**
Heathcroft Cres. LS11: Leeds 5C **40**
Heathcroft Dr. LS11: Leeds 5C **40**
Heathcroft Lawn LS11: Leeds 5C **40**
Heathcroft Ri. LS11: Leeds 5C **40**
Heathcroft Va. LS11: Leeds 5C **40**
Heather Cl. WF1: Wake 6F **59**
Heather Ct. WF1: Wake 6G **59**
Heathercroft LS7: Leeds 5A **22**
Heatherdale Ct. WF3: E Ard 3C **56**
Heatherdale Dr. WF3: E Ard 3C **56**
Heatherdale Fold WF3: E Ard 3C **56**
Heatherdale Rd. WF3: E Ard 3B **56**
Heather Gdns. LS13: Leeds 5E **29**
Heather Gro. LS13: Leeds 4E **29**
Heathfield LS16: Leeds 5G **11**
Heathfield Cl. WF3: E Ard 4D **56**
Heathfield Ter. LS6: Leeds 5B **20**
Heathfield Wlk. LS16: Leeds 4G **11**
Heath Gro. LS11: Leeds 4C **40**
LS28: Pud 1E **37**
Heath Mt. LS11: Leeds 4C **40**
Heath Pl. LS11: Leeds 4C **40**
Heath Ri. LS11: Leeds 5C **40**
Heath Rd. LS11: Leeds 4C **40**
Heaton Av. LS12: Leeds 2A **40**
Heaton's Ct. LS1: Leeds 6E **5** (6G **31**)
Hebden App. LS14: Leeds 5B **24**
Hebden Chase LS14: Leeds 5B **24**
Hebden Cl. LS14: Leeds 5B **24**
Hebden Grn. LS14: Leeds 5B **24**
Hebden Path LS14: Leeds 5B **24**
Hebden Pl. LS14: Leeds 5B **24**
Hebden Wlk. LS14: Leeds 5B **24**
Heddon Pl. LS6: Leeds 5C **20**
Heddon St. LS6: Leeds 5C **20**
Hedley Chase LS12: Leeds 6C **30**
Hedley Gdns. LS12: Leeds 6C **30**
Hedley Grn. LS12: Leeds 6C **30**
Heights Bank LS12: Leeds 6F **29**
Heights Cl. LS12: Leeds 6E **29**
Heights Dr. LS12: Leeds 5E **29**
Heights E., The LS12: Leeds 6F **29**
Heights Gth. LS12: Leeds 6E **29**
Heights Grn. LS12: Leeds 6F **29**
Heights La. LS12: Leeds 6F **29**
Heights Pde. LS12: Leeds 6E **29**
Heights Wlk. LS12: Leeds 6F **29**
Heights Way LS12: Leeds 6E **29**
Heights W., The LS12: Leeds 6E **29**
Helmsley Ct. LS10: Leeds 5G **51**
Helmsley Dr. LS16: Leeds 4H **19**
Helmsley Rd. LS16: Leeds 4H **19**
Helston Cft. LS10: Leeds 4E **51**
Helston Gth. LS10: Leeds 4E **51**
Helston Grn. LS10: Leeds 4E **51**
Helston Pl. LS10: Leeds 4E **51**
Helston Rd. LS10: Leeds 3E **51**
Helston Sq. LS10: Leeds 3D **50**
Helston St. LS10: Leeds 3D **50**
Helston Wlk. LS10: Leeds 4E **51**
(not continuous)
Helston Way LS10: Leeds 3E **51**
Hembrigg Gdns. LS27: Morl 6H **49**
Hembrigg Ter. LS27: Morl 6G **49**
Hemingway Cl. LS10: Leeds 3A **42**
Hemingway Gth. LS10: Leeds 4A **42**
Hemingway Grn. LS10: Leeds 4A **42**
Henbury St. LS7: Leeds 1H **5** (4H **31**)
Henconner Av. LS7: Leeds 5G **21**
Henconner Cres. LS7: Leeds 5G **21**
Henconner Dr. LS7: Leeds 5G **21**
Henconner Gdns. LS7: Leeds 5G **21**
Henconner Gth. LS7: Leeds 5G **21**
Henconner Gro. LS7: Leeds 5G **21**
Henconner La. LS7: Leeds 5G **21**
LS13: Leeds 4E **29**
Henconner Rd. LS7: Leeds 5G **21**
Henley Av. LS13: Leeds 3C **28**
LS19: Yead 6F **9**
Henley Cl. LS19: Yead 6F **9**
Henley Cres. LS13: Leeds 3C **28**
LS19: Yead 6F **9**
Henley Dr. LS19: Yead 6E **9**
Henley Gro. LS13: Leeds 3C **28**
Henley Hill LS19: Yead 6E **9**
Henley Mt. LS19: Yead 6F **9**
Henley Pl. LS13: Leeds 3C **28**
Henley Rd. LS13: Leeds 3C **28**
Henley St. LS13: Leeds 3C **28**
Henley Ter. LS13: Leeds 3C **28**
Henley Vw. LS13: Leeds 3C **28**
LS19: Yead 6E **9**
Henley Vs. *LS19: Yead 6E 9*
(off Well La.)
Henry Av. LS12: Leeds 2A **40**
Henry Moore Institute **3D 4**
Henry Pl. LS27: Morl 5G **49**
Henry Price Bldgs.
LS2: Leeds 3E **31**
Henry Ter. LS19: Yead 6H **7**
HENSHAW **3C 8**
Henshaw Av. LS19: Yead 3D **8**
Henshaw Cres. LS19: Yead 3D **8**
Henshaw La. LS19: Yead 4C **8**
Henshaw M. LS19: Yead 4D **8**
Henshaw Oval LS19: Yead 3D **8**
Hepton Ct. LS9: Leeds 5D **32**
Hepworth Av. LS27: Morl 1H **49**
Hepworth Cres. LS27: Morl 1H **49**
Herbalist St. LS12: Leeds 1C **40**
Herbert Pl. BD3: B'frd 5A **26**
Hereford St. LS12: Leeds 5A **30**
Hermon Rd. LS15: Leeds 4B **34**
Hermon St. LS15: Leeds 4B **34**
Heron Cl. LS17: Leeds 5B **14**
Heron Ct. LS27: Morl 5B **50**
Heron Gro. LS17: Leeds 5B **14**
Herries Ct. *LS29: Men 1D 6*
(off Leathley Rd.)
Hertford Chase LS15: Leeds 1C **44**
Hertford Cl. LS15: Leeds 1D **44**
Hertford Cft. LS15: Leeds 1D **44**
Hertford Fold LS15: Leeds 1C **44**
Hertford Lawn LS15: Leeds 1C **44**
Hesketh Av. LS5: Leeds 6G **19**
WF3: E Ard 3B **56**
Hesketh La. WF3: E Ard 3B **56**
Hesketh Mt. LS5: Leeds 6G **19**
Hesketh Pl. LS5: Leeds 6G **19**
Hesketh Rd. LS5: Leeds 6G **19**
Hesketh Ter. LS5: Leeds 1G **29**
Hessle Av. LS6: Leeds 2C **30**
Hessle Mt. LS6: Leeds 2C **30**
Hessle Pl. LS6: Leeds 2C **30**
Hessle Rd. LS6: Leeds 2C **30**
Hessle St. LS6: Leeds 2C **30**
Hessle Ter. LS6: Leeds 2C **30**
Hessle Vw. LS6: Leeds 2C **30**
Hessle Wlk. LS6: Leeds 2C **30**
Hetton Ct. LS10: Leeds 4H **41**
Hetton Dr. BD3: B'frd 1A **36**
Hetton Rd. LS8: Leeds 6D **22**
Heyback La. WF3: E Ard 6A **56**
WF12: E Ard 6A **56**
HEY BECK **6A 56**
Hey Beck La. WF3: E Ard 6B **56**
Heybeck Wlk. BD4: B'frd 5B **36**
Heydon Cl. LS6: Leeds 2D **20**
Heysham Dr. BD4: B'frd 4A **36**
High Ash Av. LS17: Leeds 4A **14**
High Ash Cres. LS17: Leeds 4A **14**
High Ash Dr. LS17: Leeds 4A **14**
High Ash Mt. LS17: Leeds 4A **14**
High Bank App. LS15: Leeds 6D **34**
High Bank Cl. LS15: Leeds 6D **34**
High Bank Gdns. LS15: Leeds 6E **35**
High Bank Ga. LS15: Leeds 6D **34**
High Bank Pl. LS15: Leeds 6D **34**
High Bank St. *LS28: Pud 2F 27*
(off Low Bank St.)
High Bank Vw. LS15: Leeds 6D **34**
High Bank Way LS15: Leeds 6D **34**
High Brook Fall WF3: Wake 5E **59**
Highbury Cl. LS6: Leeds 5C **20**
Highbury La. LS6: Leeds 5C **20**
Highbury Mt. LS6: Leeds 5C **20**
Highbury Pl. LS6: Leeds 5C **20**
LS13: Leeds 5A **28**
Highbury Rd. LS6: Leeds 5C **20**
Highbury St. LS6: Leeds 5C **20**
Highbury Ter. LS6: Leeds 5C **20**
High Cliffe *LS4: Leeds 2A 30*
(off St Michael's La.)
Highcliffe Ind. Est. LS27: Morl 4F **49**
Highcliffe Rd. LS27: Morl 5F **49**

82 A-Z Leeds

Holtdale Grn.—Irwin St.

Holtdale Grn. LS16: Leeds 4F 11
Holtdale Gro. LS16: Leeds 4E 11
Holtdale Lawn LS16: Leeds 4F 11
Holtdale Pl. LS16: Leeds 4F 11
Holtdale Rd. LS16: Leeds 4F 11
Holtdale Vw. LS16: Leeds 4F 11
Holtdale Way LS16: Leeds 4F 11
Holt Dr. LS16: Leeds 4G 11
Holt Farm Cl. LS16: Leeds 4F 11
Holt Farm Ri. LS16: Leeds 4F 11
Holt Gdns. LS16: Leeds 4A 12
Holt Gth. LS16: Leeds 4G 11
Holt Ga. LS16: Leeds 4G 11
Holt Grn. LS16: Leeds 4G 11
Holt La. LS16: Leeds 4E 11
Holt La. Ct. LS16: Leeds 5H 11
HOLT PARK 4F 11
Holt Pk. App. LS16: Leeds 4G 11
Holt Pk. Av. LS16: Leeds 4G 11
Holt Pk. Cl. LS16: Leeds 4G 11
Holt Pk. Cres. LS16: Leeds 4F 11
Holt Pk. Dr. LS16: Leeds 4G 11
Holt Pk. Gdns. LS16: Leeds 4G 11
Holt Pk. Ga. LS16: Leeds 4G 11
Holt Pk. Grange LS16: Leeds 4G 11
Holt Pk. Grn. LS16: Leeds 4G 11
Holt Pk. Gro. LS16: Leeds 4F 11
Holt Pk. La. LS16: Leeds 4G 11
Holt Pk. Leisure Cen. 4F 11
Holt Pk. Ri. LS16: Leeds 4G 11
Holt Pk. Rd. LS16: Leeds 4G 11
Holt Pk. Va. LS16: Leeds 4G 11
Holt Pk. Vw. LS16: Leeds 4F 11
Holt Pk. Way LS16: Leeds 4G 11
Holt Ri. LS16: Leeds 4G 11
Holt Rd. LS16: Leeds 4G 11
Holt Va. LS16: Leeds 4G 11
Holt Wlk. LS16: Leeds 4G 11
Holt Way LS16: Leeds 4G 11
Holybrook Av. BD10: B'frd 5A 16
Holywell La. LS17: Leeds 4F 15
Holywell Vw. LS17: Leeds 4F 15
Home Farm Dr. LS29: Men 2B 6
Home Farm M. LS29: Men 2C 6
Home Lea LS26: Rothw 2F 53
Home Lea Dr. LS26: Rothw 3F 53
Hopefield Chase
LS26: Rothw 5D 52
Hopefield Cl. LS26: Rothw 5D 52
Hopefield Ct. LS26: Rothw 5D 52
WF3: E Ard 4G 57
Hopefield Cres. LS26: Rothw 5D 52
Hopefield Dr. LS26: Rothw 5D 52
Hopefield Gdns. LS26: Rothw 5D 52
Hopefield Grn. LS26: Rothw 5D 52
Hopefield Gro. LS26: Rothw 5D 52
Hopefield M. LS26: Rothw 5D 52
Hopefield Pl. LS26: Rothw 5D 52
Hopefield Vw. LS26: Rothw 5D 52
Hopefield Wlk. LS26: Rothw 5D 52
Hopefield Way LS26: Rothw 5D 52
Hope Pastures 1A 20
Hope Rd. LS9: Leeds 3H 5 (5H 31)
Hopes Farm Mt. LS10: Leeds 2B 52
Hopes Farm Rd. LS10: Leeds 2B 52
Hopes Farm Vw. LS10: Leeds 2B 52
Hope St. LS27: Morl 5G 49
Hopewell Pl. LS6: Leeds 3C 30
Hopewell Ter. LS18: H'fth 4B 18
Hopewell Vw. LS10: Leeds 4H 51
Hopkin St. BD4: B'frd 6A 36
Hopton Ct. *LS12: Leeds* *6H 29*
(off Hopton M.)
Hopton M. LS12: Leeds 6H 29
Hopwood Bank LS18: H'fth 1C 18
Hopwood Cl. LS18: H'fth 1C 18
Hopwood Rd. LS18: H'fth 1C 18
Hornbeam Way LS14: Leeds 3C 24
Horsfall St. LS27: Morl 3F 49
HORSFORTH 3B 18
Horsforth New Rd.
LS13: Leeds 5G 17
Horsforth Station (Rail) 6C 10
Horsforth Village Mus. *3B 18*
(off The Green)
Horsham Rd. BD4: B'frd 5A 36
Horsman St. BD4: B'frd 6A 36
Horton Cl. LS13: Leeds 1H 27
Horton Gth. LS13: Leeds 1H 27
Horton Ri. LS13: Leeds 1H 27
Hospital La. LS16: Leeds 6F 11
Hough Cl. LS13: Leeds 5B 28
HOUGH END 5C 28
Hough End Av. LS13: Leeds 4D 28
Hough End Cl. LS13: Leeds 4D 28
Hough End Ct. LS13: Leeds 4D 28
Hough End Cres. LS13: Leeds 4C 28
Hough End Gdns. LS13: Leeds 4D 28
Hough End Gth. LS13: Leeds 4C 28
Hough End La. LS13: Leeds 4C 28
Hough Gro. LS13: Leeds 3C 28
Hough La. LS13: Leeds 3C 28
Houghley Av. LS12: Leeds 3F 29
Houghley Cl. LS13: Leeds 3E 29
Houghley Cres. LS12: Leeds 3F 29
Houghley La. LS13: Leeds 3E 29
Houghley Rd. LS12: Leeds 3F 29
Houghley Sq. LS12: Leeds 3F 29
HOUGH SIDE 6B 28
Hough Side Cl. LS28: Pud 6B 28
Hough Side La. LS28: Pud 6A 28
Hough Side Rd. LS28: Pud 6H 27
Hough Ter. LS13: Leeds 3C 28
Hough Top LS13: Leeds 6A 28
Hough Tree Rd. LS13: Leeds 5C 28
Hough Tree Ter. LS13: Leeds 5C 28
Hovingham Av. LS8: Leeds 1C 32
Hovingham Gro. LS8: Leeds 1C 32
Hovingham Mt. LS8: Leeds 1C 32
Hovingham Ter. LS8: Leeds 1C 32
Howard Av. LS15: Leeds 6H 33
Howard Ct. LS15: Leeds 6H 33
Howden Cl. BD4: B'frd 6B 36
HOWDEN CLOUGH 6B 48
Howden Clough Ind. Est.
WF17: Bat 6B 48
Howden Clough Rd. LS27: Morl 6C 48
Howden Gdns. LS6: Leeds 3C 30
Howden Pl. LS6: Leeds 3C 30
Howden Way LS27: Morl 6D 48
Howley Pk. Vw. LS27: Morl 2A 56
Howson Cl. LS20: Guis 4H 7
Hoxton Mt. LS11: Leeds 4D 40
Hudson Gro. LS9: Leeds 4C 32
Hudson Pl. LS9: Leeds 4C 32
Hudson Rd. LS9: Leeds 3C 32
Hudson's Ter. LS19: Yead 2E 9
Hudson St. LS9: Leeds 4C 32
LS28: Pud 4F 27
Hudswell Rd. LS10: Leeds 3H 41
Huggan Row *LS28: Pud* *6H 27*
(off Hammerton Gro.)
Hughenden Vw. LS27: Morl 3G 49
Hull St. LS27: Morl 5H 49
Hunger Hill LS27: Morl 6G 49
Hunger Hills Av. LS18: H'fth 2A 18
Hunger Hills Dr. LS18: H'fth 2A 18
HUNSLET 3H 41
Hunslet Bus. Pk. LS10: Leeds 2A 42
HUNSLET CARR 6H 41
Hunslet Distributor LS10: Leeds 3H 41
Hunslet Grn. Retail Cen.
LS10: Leeds 4H 41
Hunslet Grn. Way LS10: Leeds 3H 41
Hunslet Hall Rd. LS11: Leeds 3F 41
Hunslet Hawks RLFC 1G 51
Hunslet La. LS10: Leeds 1G 41
(Crown Point Rd.)
LS10: Leeds 6F 5 (1G 41)
(Hunslet Rd., not continuous)
Hunslet Rd. LS10: Leeds 1H 41
(Crown Point Rd., not continuous)
LS10: Leeds 6F 5 (6G 31)
(Waterloo St.)
Hunslet Trad. Est.
LS10: Leeds 3B 42
Hunsworth La. BD4: B'frd 5A 46
Hunters Ct. LS15: Leeds 6A 34
Hunters Way LS15: Leeds 6A 34
Huntington Cres. LS16: Leeds 4A 20
Huntsman Ho. LS10: Leeds 1G 41
Hurstville Av. BD4: B'frd 3B 46
Husler Gro. LS7: Leeds 2H 31
Husler Pl. LS7: Leeds 2H 31
Hustler's Row LS6: Leeds 3B 20
Hutchinson Pl. LS5: Leeds 2G 29
Hutton Ter. LS28: Pud 6G 27
HYDE PARK 2C 30
Hyde Pk. Cl. LS6: Leeds 3D 30
Hyde Pk. Cnr. LS6: Leeds 2D 30
Hyde Pk. Pl. LS6: Leeds 2D 30
Hyde Pk. Rd. LS6: Leeds 3D 30
Hyde Pk. Ter. LS6: Leeds 2D 30
Hyde Pl. LS2: Leeds 2A 4 (4E 31)
Hyde St. LS2: Leeds 2A 4 (4E 31)
Hyde Ter. LS2: Leeds 1A 4 (4E 31)

I

Ibbetson Cl. LS27: Morl 2G 49
Ibbetson Ct. LS27: Morl 2G 49
Ibbetson Cft. LS27: Morl 2G 49
Ibbetson Dr. LS27: Morl 2G 49
Ibbetson M. LS27: Morl 2G 49
Ibbetson Oval LS27: Morl 2G 49
Ibbetson Ri. LS27: Morl 2G 49
Ibbetson Rd. LS27: Morl 2G 49
Ida's, The LS10: Leeds 5C 42
Ida St. LS10: Leeds 5C 42
Ilford St. LS27: Morl 5H 49
Illingworth Cl. LS19: Yead 4E 9
Imperial Ter. LS12: Leeds 5H 29
Industrial St. LS9: Leeds 4B 32
Infirmary St. LS1: Leeds 4D 4 (5F 31)
Inghams Av. LS28: Pud 6D 26
Inghams Ter. LS28: Pud 5D 26
Inghams Vw. LS28: Pud 5D 26
Ingle Av. LS27: Morl 3F 49
Ingleborough Cl. BD4: B'frd 4A 36
Ingleborough Dr. LS27: Morl 6A 50
(not continuous)
Ingleby Way LS10: Leeds 2A 52
Ingle Ct. LS27: Morl 4F 49
(Earlsmere Dr.)
LS27: Morl 3F 49
(Ingle Av.)
Ingle Cres. LS27: Morl 3G 49
Ingledew Ct. LS17: Leeds 5H 13
Ingledew Cres. LS8: Leeds 1D 22
Ingledew Dr. LS8: Leeds 2D 22
Ingle Gro. LS27: Morl 4F 49
Ingle Row LS7: Leeds 5H 21
Ingleton Cl. LS11: Leeds 4F 41
Ingleton Dr. LS15: Leeds 6G 33
Ingleton Gro. LS11: Leeds 4F 41
Ingleton Ho. *BD4: B'frd* *5A 36*
(off Arlesford Rd.)
Ingleton Pl. LS11: Leeds 4F 41
Ingleton St. LS11: Leeds 4F 41
Inglewood App. LS14: Leeds 2B 34
Inglewood Dr. LS14: Leeds 2B 34
Inglewood Pl. LS14: Leeds 2B 34
Inglewood Ter. *LS6: Leeds* *1E 31*
(off Delph La.)
Ingram Cl. LS11: Leeds 2D 40
Ingram Ct. LS11: Leeds 2D 40
Ingram Cres. LS11: Leeds 3D 40
Ingram Gdns. LS11: Leeds 2D 40
Ingram Pde. LS26: Rothw 4G 53
Ingram Rd. LS11: Leeds 3D 40
Ingram Row LS11: Leeds 1F 41
Ingram St. LS11: Leeds 1F 41
Ingram Vw. LS11: Leeds 2D 40
Ings Av. LS20: Guis 3F 7
Ings Ct. LS20: Guis 3E 7
Ings Cres. LS9: Leeds 6D 32
LS20: Guis 4E 7
Ings La. LS20: Guis 4E 7
Ings Rd. LS9: Leeds 6D 32
Inmoor Rd. BD4: B'frd 2D 46
Inner Ring Rd. LS1: Leeds 2B 4 (4E 31)
INTAKE 1A 28
Intake Cl. WF3: Wake 6H 59
Intake La. LS10: Leeds 6G 51
LS13: Leeds 2H 27
LS14: T'ner 1D 24
LS19: Yead 6F 9
LS28: Leeds 2H 27
WF3: Wake 6H 59
(not continuous)
Intake Mt. LS10: Leeds 5G 51
Intake Rd. LS28: Pud 5H 27
Intake Sq. LS10: Leeds 5G 51
Intake Vw. LS10: Leeds 5G 51
LS13: Leeds 2A 28
Intercity Way LS13: Leeds 4H 27
Intermezzo Dr. LS10: Leeds 6D 42
Invertrees Av. LS19: Yead 5E 9
Iqbal Ct. BD3: B'frd 1A 36
Ireland Cres. LS16: Leeds 6F 11
IRELAND WOOD 2F 19
Iron Stone Dr. LS12: Leeds 3G 39
Iron Stone Gdns. LS12: Leeds 4G 39
Ironwood App. LS14: Leeds 2A 34
Ironwood Cres. LS14: Leeds 2A 34
Ironwood Vw. LS14: Leeds 1A 34
Irwin App. LS15: Leeds 6H 33
Irwin St. LS28: Pud 3F 27
(not continuous)

84 A-Z Leeds

Langbar Grn. LS14: Leeds 5D 24
Langbar Gro. LS14: Leeds 6D 24
Langbar Pl. LS14: Leeds 5D 24
Langbar Rd. LS14: Leeds 6D 24
Langbar Sq. LS14: Leeds 6D 24
Langbar Towers *LS14: Leeds* 6D *24*
                    (off Swarcliffe Av.)
Langbar Vw. LS14: Leeds 5D 24
Langdale Av. LS6: Leeds 6A 20
  WF1: Wake 6F 59
Langdale Gdns. LS6: Leeds 1A 30
Langdale Rd. BD10: B'frd 1A 26
  LS26: Rothw 3B 54
Langdale Ter. LS6: Leeds 1A 30
LANGLEY 3D 58
Langley Av. LS13: Leeds 1A 28
Langley Cl. LS13: Leeds 1A 28
Langley Cres. LS13: Leeds 1B 28
Langley Gth. LS13: Leeds 1A 28
Langley Mt. LS13: Leeds 1B 28
Langley Pl. LS13: Leeds 1A 28
Langley Rd. LS13: Leeds 1A 28
Langley Ter. LS13: Leeds 1A 28
Langthorne Ct. LS27: Morl 1A 56
Langton Grn. LS12: Leeds 2A 40
Langtons Wharf LS2: Leeds 6G 5
Lanrick Ho. *BD4: B'frd* 3A *36*
                (off Broadstone Way)
Lansdale Ct. BD4: B'frd 5B 36
Lansdowne St. LS12: Leeds 1A 40
Lanshaw Cl. LS10: Leeds 3A 52
Lanshaw Cres. LS10: Leeds 4A 52
Lanshaw Pl. LS10: Leeds 3A 52
Lanshaw Rd. LS10: Leeds 3A 52
Lanshaw Ter. LS10: Leeds 4A 52
Lanshaw Vw. LS10: Leeds 3A 52
Lanshaw Wlk. LS10: Leeds 4A 52
Larchfield Home LS10: Leeds 3A 42
Larchfield Rd. LS10: Leeds 2A 42
Larchwood LS19: Yead 1E 17
LARKFIELD 5E 9
Larkfield Av. LS19: Yead 5E 9
Larkfield Cres. LS19: Yead 5E 9
Larkfield Dr. LS19: Yead 5E 9
Larkfield Mt. LS19: Yead 5E 9
Larkfield Rd. LS19: Yead 5E 9
  LS28: Pud 5G 27
Larkhill Cl. LS8: Leeds 3A 22
Larkhill Grn. LS8: Leeds 2A 22
Larkhill Rd. LS8: Leeds 2A 22
Larkhill Vw. LS8: Leeds 3A 22
Larkhill Wlk. LS8: Leeds 2A 22
Larkhill Way LS8: Leeds 2A 22
Larwood Av. BD10: B'frd 1A 26
La Salle LS10: Leeds 1H 41
Lascelles Mt. *LS8: Leeds* 2B *32*
                (off Lascelles Rd. E.)
Lascelles Pl. LS8: Leeds 2B 32
Lascelles Rd. E. LS8: Leeds 2B 32
Lascelles Rd. W. LS8: Leeds 2B 32
Lascelles St. LS8: Leeds 2B 32
Lascelles Ter. LS8: Leeds 2B 32
Lascelles Vw. LS8: Leeds 2B 32
Lastingham Rd. LS13: Leeds 6H 17
Latchmere Av. LS16: Leeds 3F 19
Latchmere Cl. LS16: Leeds 3G 19
Latchmere Crest LS16: Leeds 3F 19
Latchmere Cross LS16: Leeds 3F 19
Latchmere Dr. LS16: Leeds 3F 19
Latchmere Gdns. LS16: Leeds 2G 19
Latchmere Grn. LS16: Leeds 3F 19
Latchmere Rd. LS16: Leeds 3F 19
Latchmere Vw. LS16: Leeds 3F 19
                (not continuous)
Latchmere Wlk. LS16: Leeds 2G 19
Latchmore Rd. LS12: Leeds 3C 40
Latchmore Rd. Ind. Pk.
  LS12: Leeds 3B 40
Latham La. BD19: Cleck 6C 46
Launceston Dr. BD4: B'frd 5A 36
Laura St. LS12: Leeds 1D 40
Laurel Bank LS15: Leeds 1D 34
Laurel Bank Ct. LS6: Leeds 1A 30
Laurel Fold LS12: Leeds 6A 30
Laurel Gro. LS12: Leeds 6A 30
Laurel Hill Av. LS15: Leeds 6D 34
Laurel Hill Cft. LS15: Leeds 6D 34
Laurel Hill Gdns. LS15: Leeds 6D 34
Laurel Hill Gro. LS15: Leeds 6D 34
Laurel Hill Vw. LS15: Leeds 6D 34
Laurel Hill Way LS15: Leeds 1D 44
Laurel Mt. LS7: Leeds 6H 21
  LS28: Pud 5G 27

Laurel Pl. LS10: Leeds 6F 51
  LS12: Leeds 6A 30
Laurels, The LS8: Leeds 5B 22
Laurel St. LS12: Leeds 6A 30
Laurel Ter. LS12: Leeds 6A 30
  LS15: Leeds 1D *34*
                (off Laurel Bank)
  LS28: Pud 5G 27
Laurence Ct. LS26: Rothw 2D 54
Lavender Wlk. LS9: Leeds 6B 32
Lawfield Av. LS26: Rothw 3E 53
LAWNS 5A 58
Lawns WF2: Wake 5A 58
Lawns Av. LS12: Leeds 4D 38
Lawns Cl. LS12: Leeds 4D 38
Lawns Ct. WF2: Wake 6A 58
Lawns Cres. LS12: Leeds 4D 38
Lawns Cft. LS12: Leeds 4D 38
Lawns Dene LS12: Leeds 4D 38
Lawns Dr. LS12: Leeds 4D 38
Lawns Grn. LS12: Leeds 4D 38
Lawns Hall Cl. LS16: Leeds 6H 11
Lawns La. LS10: Leeds 4A 42
  LS12: Leeds 3D 38
  WF2: Wake 6A 58
Lawns Sq. LS12: Leeds 4D 38
Lawns Ter. LS12: Leeds 4D 38
  WF3: E Ard 4H 57
LAWNSWOOD 1G 19
Lawnswood Bus. Pk. LS16: Leeds 2G 19
Lawns Wood Crematorium LS16: Leeds 6H 11
Lawnswood Gdns. LS16: Leeds 1H 19
Lawrence Av. LS8: Leeds 1E 33
Lawrence Ct. LS28: Pud 1F 37
Lawrence Cres. LS8: Leeds 1E 33
Lawrence Gdns. LS8: Leeds 6E 23
Lawrence Rd. LS8: Leeds 1E 33
Lawrence Wlk. LS8: Leeds 1E 33
Lawson Ct. LS28: Pud 2G 27
Lawson St. LS12: Leeds 6H 29
Lawson Wood Ct. LS6: Leeds 2D 20
Lawson Wood Dr. LS6: Leeds 2D 20
Laycock Pl. LS7: Leeds 2H 31
Lay Gth. LS26: Rothw 4G 53
Lay Gth. Cl. LS26: Rothw 4G 53
Lay Gth. Ct. LS26: Rothw 5G 53
Lay Gth. Fold LS26: Rothw 5G 53
Lay Gth. Gdns. LS26: Rothw 5G 53
Lay Gth. Grn. LS26: Rothw 5G 53
Lay Gth. Mead LS26: Rothw 5G 53
Lay Gth. Pl. LS26: Rothw 5G 53
Lay Gth. Sq. LS26: Rothw 5G 53
Layton Av. LS19: Yead 6F 9
Layton Cl. LS19: Yead 1G 17
Layton Cres. LS19: Yead 6F 9
Layton Dr. LS19: Yead 6G 9
Layton La. LS19: Yead 1G 17
Layton Mt. LS19: Yead 6F 9
Layton Pk. Av. LS19: Yead 1G 17
Layton Pk. Cl. LS19: Yead 6F 9
Layton Pk. Cft. LS19: Yead 6F 9
Layton Pk. Dr. LS19: Yead 6F 9
Layton Ri. LS18: H'fth 6H 9
Layton Rd. LS18: H'fth 6H 9
  LS19: H'fth, Yead 6G 9
Leadwell La. LS26: Rothw 6D 52
  WF3: Rothw 6D 52
Lea Farm Cres. LS5: Leeds 5F 19
Lea Farm Dr. LS5: Leeds 4F 19
Lea Farm Gro. LS5: Leeds 5F 19
Lea Farm Mt. LS5: Leeds 4F 19
Lea Farm Pl. LS5: Leeds 5F 19
Lea Farm Rd. LS5: Leeds 5F 19
Lea Farm Row LS5: Leeds 5F 19
Lea Farm Wlk. LS5: Leeds 4F 19
Leafield Cl. LS17: Leeds 1F 21
Leafield Dr. LS17: Leeds 1F 21
  LS28: Pud 2H 37
Leafield Grange LS17: Leeds 1F 21
Leafield Towers LS17: Leeds 1F 21
Leafield Vs. *LS19: Yead* 6H *7*
                (off Leafield Pl.)
Leah Pl. LS12: Leeds 1D 40
Leah Row LS12: Leeds 1D 40
Lea Mill Pk. Cl. LS19: Yead 2C 8
Lea Mill Pk. Dr. LS19: Yead 2C 8
Leamside Wlk. BD4: B'frd 5A 36
Lea Pk. Cl. LS10: Leeds 2B 52
Lea Pk. Cft. LS10: Leeds 2C 52
Lea Pk. Dr. LS10: Leeds 2B 52
Lea Pk. Gdns. LS10: Leeds 2B 52

Lea Pk. Gth. LS10: Leeds 2B 52
Lea Pk. Gro. LS10: Leeds 2B 52
Lea Pk. Va. LS10: Leeds 2C 52
Leasowe Av. LS10: Leeds 5A 42
Leasowe Cl. LS10: Leeds 5A 42
Leasowe Ct. *LS10: Leeds* 5A *42*
             (off Woodhouse Hill Rd.)
Leasowe Gdns. LS10: Leeds 5B 42
Leasowe Gth. LS10: Leeds 5A 42
Leasowe Rd. LS10: Leeds 5A 42
Lea Ter. LS12: Leeds 2G 21
Leathley Av. LS29: Men 2D 6
Leathley Cres. LS29: Men 2D 6
Leathley La. LS29: Men 1D 6
Leathley Rd. LS10: Leeds 2G 41
  LS29: Men 1D 6
Leavens, The BD10: B'frd 3A 16
Lea Vw. LS18: H'fth 2B 18
Ledbury Av. LS10: Leeds 5B 52
Ledbury Cl. LS10: Leeds 5B 52
Ledbury Cft. LS10: Leeds 5B 52
Ledbury Dr. LS10: Leeds 5B 52
Ledbury Grn. LS10: Leeds 5B 52
Ledbury Gro. LS10: Leeds 5A 52
Ledgard Way LS12: Leeds 5A 30
Ledger La. WF1: Wake 6D 58
  WF3: Rothw 2E 59
Lee Beck Gro. WF3: Wake 1E 59
LEEDS 5D 4 (6F 31)
Leeds 27 Ind. Est. LS27: Morl 5E 49
Leeds and Bradford Rd. LS5: Leeds 6C 18
  LS13: Leeds 2A 28
  LS28: Leeds, Pud 3H 27
LEEDS BRADFORD INTERNATIONAL AIRPORT 2G 9
LEEDS BUPA HOSPITAL 3C 22
Leeds Bus. Cen., The LS27: Morl 4E 49
LEEDS CHEST CLINIC 3F 5 (5G 31)
Leeds City Art Gallery 3D 4
Leeds City Office Pk. LS11: Leeds 1G 41
Leeds Civic Theatre 2D 4 (4F 31)
LEEDS DENTAL INSTITUTE 2B 4 (4F 31)
LEEDS GENERAL INFIRMARY 2C 4 (4F 31)
Leeds International Swimming Pool 4B 4 (3E 31)
Leeds La. LS26: Swil 2G 45
Leeds Metropolitan University
  Beckett Pk. Campus 5H 19
  Calverley St. 1D 4 (4F 31)
LEEDS NUFFIELD HOSPITAL 3B 4 (5E 31)
Leeds Rd. BD3: B'frd 6A 26
  LS15: Bar E, Scho 6H 25
  LS15: Leeds, Scho 1E 35
  LS16: B'hpe 1G 11
  LS19: Yead 5D 8
  LS20: Guis 5G 7
  LS26: Mick 6G 55
  LS26: Rothw 2H 53
                (Mount, The)
  WF1: Wake 6E 59
  LS26: Rothw 5D 52
                (Wakefield Rd.)
  WF1: Wake 6E 59
  WF3: Rothw 2E 59
  WF17: Bat 6B 48
Leeds Shop. Plaza LS1: Leeds 5E 5 (6G 31)
Leeds Station (Rail) 5D 4 (6F 31)
Leeds United FC 4C 40
Leeds University Business School 3D 30
Leeds Wall, The 2C 40
Lee Fair Ct. WF3: E Ard 5B 56
Lee La. E. LS18: H'fth 1B 18
Lee La. W. LS18: H'fth 1H 17
LEE MOOR 4G 59
Lee Moor La. WF3: Wake 3G 59
Lee Moor Rd. WF3: Wake 5G 59
LEE MOUNT 5H 59
Lees La. LS28: Pud 1F 27
Leicester Cl. LS7: Leeds 3F 31
Leicester Gro. LS7: Leeds 3F 31
Leicester Pl. LS2: Leeds 3F 31
  LS7: Leeds 3F 31
Leigh Av. WF3: E Ard 3E 57
Leigh Rd. WF3: E Ard 3E 57
Leighton Cl. LS1: Leeds 3B 4
Leighton Pl. LS1: Leeds 3C 4
Leighton St. LS1: Leeds 3B 4 (5F 31)
Leigh Vw. WF3: E Ard 3D 56
Leith Ho. *BD4: B'frd* 4A *36*
                (off Stirling Cres.)
Lenham Cl. LS27: Morl 6G 49
Lenhurst Av. LS12: Leeds 2F 29
Lennox Gdns. LS15: Leeds 6C 34

Lovell Ho. LS7: Leeds	.1G 5
Lovell Pk. Cl. LS7: Leeds	.1G 5 (4H 31)
Lovell Pk. Ct. LS7: Leeds	.1F 5 (4G 31)
Lovell Pk. Ga. LS7: Leeds	.1F 5 (4G 31)
Lovell Pk. Grange LS7: Leeds	.1G 5
Lovell Pk. Hgts. LS7: Leeds	.1G 5
Lovell Pk. Hill LS7: Leeds	.1F 5 (4G 31)
Lovell Pk. M. LS7: Leeds	.1G 5 (4H 31)
Lovell Pk. Rd. LS2: Leeds	.2F 5 (4G 31)
LS7: Leeds	.2F 5 (4G 31)
Lovell Pk. Towers LS7: Leeds	.1F 5
Lovell Pk. Vw. LS7: Leeds	.1G 5 (4H 31)
Low Bank St. LS28: Pud	.2F 27
Low Cl. St. LS2: Leeds	.2E 31
Lowell Gro. LS13: Leeds	.5A 28
Lowell Pl. LS13: Leeds	.5A 28
Lwr. Bankhouse LS28: Pud	.3F 37
Lwr. Basinghall St. LS1: Leeds	.4D 4 (5F 31)
Lwr. Brunswick St. LS2: Leeds	.2G 5 (4H 31)
LOWER FAGLEY	.2A 26
Lower La. BD4: B'frd	.4A 46
Lwr. Rushton Rd. BD3: B'frd	.3A 46
Lwr. Tofts Rd. LS28: Pud	.6G 27
Lwr. Town St. LS13: Leeds	.2D 28
LOWER WORTLEY	.2A 40
Lwr. Wortley Rd. LS12: Leeds	.3G 39
LOW FARM	.5F 11
Low Flds. Av. LS12: Leeds	.3C 40
Low Flds. Rd. LS12: Leeds	.3C 40
(not continuous)	
Low Flds. Way LS12: Leeds	.3C 40
LOW FOLD	
LS12	.1E 39
LS18	.3A 18
Low Fold LS9: Leeds	.1A 42
LS18: H'fth	.4A 18
LS19: Yead	.5D 8
Low Gipton Cres. LS8: Leeds	.2F 33
Low Grange Cres. LS10: Leeds	.6A 42
Low Grange Vw. LS10: Leeds	.1A 52
LOW GREEN	.6E 9
Low Grn. LS19: Yead	.6E 9
Low Hall Cl. LS29: Men	.1C 6
Low Hall Pl. LS11: Leeds	.1E 41
Low Hall Rd. LS18: H'fth	.3G 17
LS19: H'fth	.3G 17
LS29: Men	.1D 6
Low La. LS18: H'fth	.1C 18
Low Mills Rd. LS12: Leeds	.3H 39
LOW MOOR SIDE	.5C 38
Low Moor Side LS12: Leeds	.4D 38
Low Moorside Cl. LS12: Leeds	.4E 39
Low Moorside Ct. LS12: Leeds	.4E 39
Low Moor Side La. LS12: Leeds	.5C 38
Low Moor Ter. LS11: Leeds	.5F 41
Lowood La. WF17: Bat	.6G 47
Low Rd. LS10: Leeds	.3A 42
Lowry Rd. WF3: E Ard	.3B 56
Low Shops La. LS26: Rothw	.3E 53
Low St. WF3: E Ard	.2D 56
Lowther Cres. LS26: Swil	.5G 45
Lowther Dr. LS26: Swil	.5F 45
Lowther St. LS8: Leeds	.1B 32
Lowther Ter. LS15: Swil	.1G 45
Lowtown LS28: Pud	.5H 27
LOW TOWN END	.6H 49
Low Whitehouse Row LS10: Leeds	.2H 41
Lucas Ct. LS6: Leeds	.2G 31
Lucas Pl. LS6: Leeds	.1E 31
Lucas St. LS6: Leeds	.1E 31
Lucy Av. LS15: Leeds	.5G 33
Ludgate Hill LS2: Leeds	.4F 5 (5G 31)
Ludolf Dr. LS17: Leeds	.5G 15
Lulworth Av. LS15: Leeds	.4D 34
Lulworth Cl. LS15: Leeds	.4D 34
Lulworth Cres. LS15: Leeds	.4D 34
Lulworth Dr. LS15: Leeds	.5D 34
Lulworth Gth. LS15: Leeds	.5D 34
Lulworth Vw. LS15: Leeds	.4D 34
Lulworth Wlk. LS15: Leeds	.4D 34
Lumb Bottom BD11: B'frd	.2H 47
Lumb Hall Way BD11: B'frd	.2H 47
Lumby Cl. LS28: Pud	.2H 37
Lumby La. LS28: Pud	.2H 37
Lumley Av. LS4: Leeds	.2B 30
Lumley Gro. LS4: Leeds	.2B 30
Lumley Mt. LS4: Leeds	.2B 30
Lumley Pl. LS4: Leeds	.2B 30
Lumley Rd. LS4: Leeds	.2B 30
Lumley St. LS4: Leeds	.2B 30
Lumley Ter. LS4: Leeds	.2B 30
Lumley Vw. LS4: Leeds	.2B 30
Lumley Wlk. LS4: Leeds	.2B 30

Lunan Pl. LS8: Leeds	.1B 32
Lunan Ter. LS8: Leeds	.1B 32
Lupton Av. LS9: Leeds	.5C 32
Lupton Flats LS6: Leeds	.6B 20
Lupton's Bldgs. LS12: Leeds	.6H 29
Lupton St. LS10: Leeds	.4A 42
Luther St. LS13: Leeds	.6G 17
Luttrell Cl. LS16: Leeds	.1G 19
Luttrell Cres. LS16: Leeds	.1G 19
Luttrell Gdns. LS16: Leeds	.1G 19
Luttrell Pl. LS16: Leeds	.1G 19
Luttrell Rd. LS16: Leeds	.1G 19
Luxor Av. LS8: Leeds	.1B 32
Luxor Rd. LS8: Leeds	.1B 32
Luxor St. LS8: Leeds	.1B 32
Luxor Vw. LS8: Leeds	.1B 32
Lyddon Ter. LS2: Leeds	.1A 4 (3E 31)
Lydgate LS9: Leeds	.4B 32
Lydgate Pl. LS28: Pud	.4C 16
Lydgate St. LS28: Pud	.4C 16
Lyme Chase LS14: Leeds	.3H 33
Lymington Dr. BD4: B'frd	.3A 36
Lyndhurst Cl. LS15: Scho	.4F 25
Lyndhurst Cres. LS15: Scho	.4F 25
Lyndhurst Rd. LS15: Scho	.5F 25
Lyndhurst Vw. LS15: Scho	.5F 25
Lynfield Gdns. LS15: Scho	.5F 25
Lynton Av. WF3: Leeds	.1A 58
Lynwood Av. LS12: Leeds	.2A 40
LS26: Rothw	.3D 54
Lynwood Cl. BD11: B'frd	.5D 46
Lynwood Cres. LS12: Leeds	.2A 40
LS26: Rothw	.3D 54
Lynwood Gdns. LS28: Pud	.6E 27
Lynwood Gth. LS12: Leeds	.2A 40
Lynwood Gro. LS12: Leeds	.2A 40
Lynwood M. BD4: B'frd	.5B 36
Lynwood Mt. LS12: Leeds	.2A 40
Lynwood Ri. LS12: Leeds	.2A 40
Lynwood Vw. LS12: Leeds	.2A 40
Lytham Gro. LS12: Leeds	.3G 39
Lytham Pl. LS12: Leeds	.3G 39
Lytton St. LS10: Leeds	.4H 41

M

M1 Ind. Est. LS10: Leeds	.4H 41
MABGATE	.2G 5 (4H 31)
Mabgate LS9: Leeds	.3H 5 (5H 31)
Mabgate Grn. LS9: Leeds	.3H 5 (5H 31)
Mabgate Mills Ind. & Commercial Cen.	
LS9: Leeds	.2H 5 (4A 32)
Macaulay St. LS9: Leeds	.3H 5 (4A 32)
McClintock Ho. LS10: Leeds	.1H 41
(off The Boulevard)	
McClure Ho. LS10: Leeds	.1H 41
(off The Boulevard)	
Mackenzie Ho. LS10: Leeds	.6G 5
McLaren Flds. LS13: Leeds	.3D 28
Madison Av. BD4: B'frd	.6A 36
Mafeking Av. LS11: Leeds	.6E 41
Mafeking Gro. LS11: Leeds	.6E 41
Mafeking Mt. LS11: Leeds	.6E 41
Magdalene Cl. LS16: Leeds	.6G 11
Magdalin Dr. LS28: Pud	.3A 28
Magellan Ho. LS10: Leeds	.6G 5 (1H 41)
Magpie La. LS27: Morl	.6H 49
Mail Cl. LS15: Leeds	.2E 35
Main St. LS15: Scho	.5F 25
LS17: Leeds	.4F 15
LS20: Guis	.5A 6
LS29: Men	.1B 6
WF3: E Ard	.4H 57
WF3: Rothw	.6F 53
Maitland Pl. LS11: Leeds	.3E 41
Malden Rd. LS6: Leeds	.2D 20
Malham Cl. LS14: Leeds	.1A 34
MALHAM HOUSE DAY HOSPITAL	2A 4 (4E 31)
Mallard Cl. LS10: Leeds	.2B 52
Mallard Way LS27: Morl	.5B 50
Malmesbury Cl. BD4: B'frd	.6A 36
LS12: Leeds	.1A 40
Malmesbury Gro. LS12: Leeds	.1A 40
Malmesbury Pl. LS12: Leeds	.1A 40
Malmesbury Ter. LS12: Leeds	.1A 40
Maltby Ct. LS15: Leeds	.6D 34
Malting Cl. WF3: Rothw	.6D 52
Malting Ri. WF3: Rothw	.6D 52
Maltings, The LS6: Leeds	.3C 30
(off Alexandra Rd.)	
WF3: Rothw	.6D 52

Maltings Ct. LS11: Leeds	.3G 41
(off Moorside Maltings)	
Maltings Rd. LS11: Leeds	.4G 41
Malvern Gro. LS11: Leeds	.3E 41
Malvern Ri. LS11: Leeds	.3E 41
Malvern Rd. LS11: Leeds	.3E 41
Malvern St. LS11: Leeds	.3E 41
Malvern Vw. LS11: Leeds	.3E 41
Mandarin Way LS10: Leeds	.2B 52
Mandela Ct. LS7: Leeds	.6H 21
Mandela Ho. LS7: Leeds	.2H 31
Manderston Chase LS12: Leeds	.3F 29
Manitoba Pl. LS7: Leeds	.5A 22
Manor, The LS8: Leeds	.5E 23
(off Ladywood Rd.)	
Manor Av. LS6: Leeds	.1C 30
Manor Cl. BD11: B'frd	.2G 47
LS19: Yead	.2D 8
LS26: Rothw	.3G 53
Manor Ct. LS11: Leeds	.6C 40
LS17: Leeds	.5H 15
Manor Cres. LS26: Rothw	.3F 53
Manor Cft. LS15: Leeds	.6C 34
Manor Dr. LS6: Leeds	.2C 30
(not continuous)	
Mnr. Farm Cl. LS10: Leeds	.3H 51
Mnr. Farm Ct. BD4: B'frd	.2A 46
LS20: Guis	.4G 7
Mnr. Farm Cres. LS27: Morl	.1A 50
Mnr. Farm Dr. LS10: Leeds	.3G 51
LS27: Morl	.1A 50
Mnr. Farm Gdns. LS10: Leeds	.3G 51
Mnr. Farm Grn. LS10: Leeds	.3G 51
Mnr. Farm Gro. LS10: Leeds	.3G 51
Mnr. Farm Ri. LS10: Leeds	.3H 51
Mnr. Farm Rd. LS10: Leeds	.3G 51
Mnr. Farm Wlk. LS10: Leeds	.3H 51
Mnr. Farm Way LS10: Leeds	.4G 51
Manorfield LS11: Leeds	.4D 40
Manor Fold LS18: H'fth	.3A 18
Manor Gth. LS15: Leeds	.6C 34
Manor Gro. LS7: Leeds	.5H 21
Manor Ho. Cft. LS16: Leeds	.6B 12
Manor Ho. La. LS17: Leeds	.2B 14
Manor Ho. St. LS28: Pud	.6G 27
Manor La. LS26: Rothw	.4C 54
(off Aberford Rd.)	
Mnr. Mill La. LS11: Leeds	.6C 40
Manor Mills LS11: Leeds	.6C 40
Manor Pk. Gdns. BD19: B'frd	.6D 46
Manor Rd. LS11: Leeds	.1F 41
LS12: Leeds	.2A 40
LS18: H'fth	.3A 18
LS26: Rothw	.3F 53
LS27: Morl	.1A 50
Manor Sq. LS19: Yead	.2D 8
Manor St. LS7: Leeds	.3H 31
Manor St. Ind. Est. LS7: Leeds	.3A 32
(not continuous)	
Manor Ter. LS6: Leeds	.1C 30
LS19: Yead	.2D 8
Manor Vw. LS6: Leeds	.1C 30
LS28: Pud	.6G 27
Mansel M. BD4: B'frd	.6A 36
Mansfield Pl. LS6: Leeds	.5B 20
Mansion Ga. LS7: Leeds	.5A 22
Mansion Ga. Dr. LS7: Leeds	.5A 22
Mansion Ga. M. LS7: Leeds	.5A 22
Mansion Ga. Sq. LS7: Leeds	.5A 22
Mansion La. LS8: Leeds	.2D 22
MANSTON	.2D 34
Manston App. LS15: Leeds	.2C 34
Manston Av. LS15: Leeds	.2C 34
Manston Cres. LS15: Leeds	.2C 34
Manston Dr. LS15: Leeds	.2C 34
Manston Gdns. LS15: Leeds	.2D 34
Manston Gro. LS15: Leeds	.3C 34
Manston La. LS15: Leeds	.3D 34
Manston Ri. LS15: Leeds	.2C 34
Manston Ter. LS15: Leeds	.2D 34
Manston Way LS15: Leeds	.2C 34
Maple Av. BD3: B'frd	.5A 26
Maple Ct. LS11: Leeds	.5D 40
Maple Cft. LS12: Leeds	.2D 38
LS17: Leeds	.6A 14
Maple Dr. LS12: Leeds	.2D 38
Maple Fold LS12: Leeds	.2D 38
Maple Gro. LS12: Leeds	.2E 39
Maple Ri. LS26: Rothw	.5G 53
Maple Vw. LS19: Yead	.6H 7
Maple Way LS14: Leeds	.3C 24
Marchant Way LS27: Morl	.6A 40
Mardale Cres. LS14: Leeds	.2A 34

Margaret Cl.—Middleton District Cen.

Margaret Cl. LS27: Morl 4A **50**
Margate LS26: Rothw 3C **54**
Margetson Rd. BD11: B'frd 4A **48**
Marian Gro. LS11: Leeds 4F **41**
Marian Rd. LS6: Leeds 2F **31**
Marian Ter. LS6: Leeds 2F **31**
Marina Cres. LS27: Morl 6F **49**
Market Bldgs. LS2: Leeds 4G **5** (5H **31**)
Market Hall *LS27: Morl 5G 49*
(off Hope St.)
Market Pl. LS28: Pud 6G **27**
Market Sq. *LS27: Morl 5G 49*
(off Queen St.)
Market St. Arc. LS1: Leeds 5F **5** (6G **31**)
Markham Av. LS8: Leeds 1B **32**
LS19: Yead 4E **9**
Markham Cres. LS19: Yead 4E **9**
Markham Cft. LS19: Yead 4E **9**
Markington M. LS10: Leeds 6G **51**
Markington Pl. LS10: Leeds 6G **51**
Mark La. LS2: Leeds 3E **5** (5G **31**)
Marlborough Cotts. *LS29: Men 1D 6*
(off Marlborough Ct.)
Marlborough Ct. LS29: Men 1D **6**
Marlborough Gdns. *LS2: Leeds 3F 31*
(off Bk. Blenheim Ter.)
Marlborough Grange LS1: Leeds 3A **4**
Marlborough Gro. *LS2: Leeds 3F 31*
(off Bk. Blenheim Ter.)
Marlborough St. LS1: Leeds 4A **4** (5E **31**)
Marlborough Towers LS1: Leeds 3A **4** (5E **31**)
Marlborough Vs. LS29: Men 1D **6**
Marley Gro. LS11: Leeds 4D **40**
Marley Pl. LS11: Leeds 4D **40**
Marley St. LS11: Leeds 4D **40**
Marley Ter. LS11: Leeds 4D **40**
Marley Vw. LS11: Leeds 4D **40**
Marlowe Cl. LS28: Pud 2H **37**
Marlowe Ct. *LS20: Guis 4F 7*
(off Renton Dr.)
Marsden Av. LS11: Leeds 5E **41**
Marsden Ct. *LS28: Pud 2F 27*
(off Water La.)
Marsden Gro. LS11: Leeds 5E **41**
Marsden Memorial Homes
LS28: Pud 3F 27
(off Parkside Rd.)
Marsden Mt. LS11: Leeds 5E **41**
Marsden Pl. LS11: Leeds 5E **41**
Marsden Vw. LS11: Leeds 5E **41**
Marsett Way LS14: Leeds 3B **24**
Marsh LS28: Pud 6E **27**
Marsh, The BD4: B'frd 2B **46**
Marshall Av. LS15: Leeds 3D **34**
Marshall Cl. *LS27: Morl 5G 49*
(off Commercial St.)
Marshall Ct. LS11: Leeds 1E **41**
LS19: Yead 2D **8**
Marshall Mills LS11: Leeds 1E **41**
Marshall St. LS11: Leeds 1F **41**
LS15: Leeds 3C **34**
LS19: Yead 2D **8**
LS27: Morl 5G **49**
WF3: Wake 6H **59**
Marshall Ter. LS15: Leeds 3C **34**
Marsh Ct. LS28: Pud 6E **27**
Marsh La. BD11: B'frd 4C **46**
LS9: Leeds 5H **5** (6H **31**)
(not continuous)
Marsh Ri. LS28: Pud 6E **27**
Marsh St. LS6: Leeds 2E **31**
LS26: Rothw 5G **53**
Marsh Ter. LS28: Pud 6E **27**
Marsh Va. LS6: Leeds 2E **31**
Marston Av. LS27: Morl 6G **49**
Marston Mt. *LS9: Leeds 4A 32*
(off Cherry Pl.)
Martin Cl. LS27: Morl 5A **50**
Martin Ct. LS15: Leeds 5D **34**
Martindale Cl. BD2: B'frd 2A **26**
Martindale Dr. LS13: Leeds 4E **29**
Martingale Dr. LS10: Leeds 6G **51**
Martin Ter. LS4: Leeds 3A **30**
Marton Ct. BD3: B'frd 6A **26**
Marwood Rd. LS13: Leeds 6E **29**
Maryfield Av. LS15: Leeds 3A **34**
Maryfield Cl. LS15: Leeds 3A **34**
Maryfield Ct. LS15: Leeds 3B **34**
Maryfield Cres. LS15: Leeds 3B **34**
Maryfield Gdns. LS15: Leeds 3A **34**
Maryfield Grn. LS15: Leeds 3A **34**
Maryfield M. LS15: Leeds 3A **34**
Maryfield Va. LS15: Leeds 3A **34**
Mary St. LS28: Pud 1G **27**
WF3: E Ard 3A **58**
Mary Sunley Ho. *LS8: Leeds 2B 32*
(off Banstead St. W.)
Masefield St. LS20: Guis 5H **7**
Masham Ct. LS6: Leeds 5B **20**
Masham Gro. LS12: Leeds 6B **30**
Masham St. LS12: Leeds 6B **30**
Matrix Ct. LS11: Leeds 5F **41**
Matty La. LS26: Rothw 5D **52**
Maud Av. LS11: Leeds 5F **41**
Maude St. LS2: Leeds 5G **5** (6H **31**)
Maud Pl. LS11: Leeds 5F **41**
Mavis Av. LS16: Leeds 3E **11**
Mavis Gro. LS16: Leeds 4E **11**
Mavis La. LS16: Leeds 3E **11**
Mawcroft Cl. LS19: Yead 4C **8**
Mawcroft Grange Dr. LS19: Yead 4C **8**
Mawcroft M. LS19: Yead 4D **8**
May Av. LS27: Leeds, Morl 1A **50**
Maybrook Ind. Pk. LS12: Leeds 5C **30**
May Ct. LS27: Morl 6A **40**
Mayfield Ct. LS18: H'fth 2C **18**
Mayfield Rd. LS15: Leeds 5B **34**
Mayflower Ho. LS10: Leeds 5C **42**
Mayo Cl. LS8: Leeds 5F **23**
May Ter. LS9: Leeds 1B **42**
Mayville Av. LS6: Leeds 2C **30**
Mayville Pl. LS6: Leeds 2C **30**
Mayville Rd. LS6: Leeds 2C **30**
Mayville St. LS6: Leeds 2C **30**
Mayville Ter. LS6: Leeds 2C **30**
Mead Cl. LS15: Leeds 1E **45**
Mead Gro. LS15: Leeds 1E **45**
Meadowbrook Ct. LS27: Morl 6E **49**
Meadow Cl. WF1: Wake 6F **59**
Meadow Cft. BD11: B'frd 3F **47**
LS11: Leeds 2F **41**
WF1: Wake 6E **59**
Meadowcroft LS29: Men 2C **6**
Meadowcroft Cl. WF1: Wake 6F **59**
Meadowcroft Ct. WF1: Wake 6F **59**
Meadowcroft M. LS9: Leeds 6A **32**
Meadowcroft Rd. WF1: Wake 6F **59**
Meadow Gth. WF1: Wake 6E **59**
Meadowgate Cft. WF3: Rothw 1D **58**
Meadowgate Dr. WF3: Rothw 1D **58**
Meadowgate Va. WF3: Rothw 2D **58**
Meadowhurst Gdns. LS28: Pud 6F **27**
Meadow La. LS11: Leeds 6E **5** (1G **41**)
Meadow Pk. Cres. LS28: Pud 3D **26**
Meadow Pk. Dr. LS28: Pud 3D **26**
Meadow Rd. BD10: B'frd 3A **16**
LS11: Leeds 1F **41**
Meadows, The LS16: Leeds 6A **12**
Meadow Side Rd. WF3: E Ard 2A **58**
Meadow Va. WF1: Wake 6E **59**
Meadow Valley LS17: Leeds 4F **13**
Meadow Vw. LS6: Leeds 2C **30**
Meadow Wlk. LS7: Leeds 5A **22**
Meadow Way LS17: Leeds 4E **13**
WF3: E Ard 4B **56**
Mead Rd. LS15: Leeds 1E **45**
Mead Vw. BD4: B'frd 4A **36**
Mead Way LS15: Leeds 1E **45**
MEANWOOD 4D **20**
Meanwood Cl. LS7: Leeds 1F **31**
MEANWOOD GROVE 2C **20**
Meanwood Gro. LS6: Leeds 2C **20**
Meanwood Rd. LS6: Leeds 5D **20**
LS7: Leeds 1F **31**
Meanwood Towers LS6: Leeds 3E **21**
Meanwood Valley Cl. LS7: Leeds 5D **20**
Meanwood Valley Dr. LS7: Leeds 5D **20**
Meanwood Valley Grn. LS7: Leeds 5D **20**
Meanwood Valley Gro. LS7: Leeds 5D **20**
Meanwood Valley Mt. LS7: Leeds 5D **20**
Meanwood Valley Urban Farm 6F **21**
Meanwood Valley Wlk. LS7: Leeds 5D **20**
Mecca Bingo
Cross Gates 3C **34**
Hunslet 4H **41**
Leeds 5G **5**
Medeway LS28: Pud 3E **27**
Melbourne Gro. BD3: B'frd 5A **26**
LS13: Leeds 3C **28**
Melbourne Mills *LS27: Morl 5H 49*
(off Melbourne St.)
Melbourne Mill Yd. *LS27: Morl 5H 49*
(off Middleton Rd.)
Melbourne St. LS2: Leeds 2G **5** (4H **31**)
LS13: Leeds 3C **28**
LS27: Morl 5H **49**
Melbourne St. LS28: Pud 3F **27**
Melcombe Wlk. BD4: B'frd 3A **36**
Melrose Gro. LS18: H'fth 3E **19**
Melrose Ho. *BD4: B'frd 3A 36*
(off Ned La.)
Melrose Pl. LS18: H'fth 3D **18**
LS28: Pud 1F **37**
Melrose Ter. LS18: H'fth 3D **18**
Melrose Vs. *LS18: H'fth 3D 18*
(off Broadgate La.)
Melrose Wlk. LS18: H'fth 3D **18**
Melton Av. LS10: Leeds 5B **52**
Melton Cl. LS10: Leeds 5B **52**
Melton Gth. LS10: Leeds 5B **52**
Melton Ter. BD10: B'frd 1A **26**
Melville Cl. LS6: Leeds 2F **31**
Melville Gdns. LS6: Leeds 1F **31**
Melville Pl. LS6: Leeds 1F **31**
Melville Rd. LS6: Leeds 2F **31**
Memorial Cotts. *LS12: Leeds 4D 38*
(off Lawn La.)
Memorial Dr. LS6: Leeds 4D **20**
MENSTON 1B **6**
Menston Dr. LS29: Men 2C **6**
Menston Hall LS29: Men 1D **6**
Menston Station (Rail) 1C **6**
Merchants Quay LS9: Leeds 6H **5** (6H **31**)
Mercia Way LS15: Leeds 2E **35**
Merlin Cl. LS27: Morl 6A **50**
Merlyn-Rees Av. LS27: Morl 5G **49**
Merrion Cen. LS2: Leeds 2E **5** (4G **31**)
Merrion Pl. LS1: Leeds 3F **5** (5G **31**)
(not continuous)
LS2: Leeds 5G **31**
Merrion St. LS1: Leeds 3F **5** (5G **31**)
LS2: Leeds 3E **5** (5G **31**)
(not continuous)
Merrion Way LS2: Leeds 2E **5** (4G **31**)
Merriville LS18: H'fth 4D **18**
Merton Av. LS28: Pud 3F **27**
Merton Dr. LS28: Pud 3E **27**
Merton Gdns. LS28: Pud 3E **27**
METHLEY 6H **55**
Methley Dr. LS7: Leeds 5G **21**
Methley Gro. LS7: Leeds 5G **21**
Methley La. LS7: Leeds 5H **21**
LS26: Rothw 5C **54**
Methley Mt. LS7: Leeds 5H **21**
METHLEY PARK CLASSIC HOSPITAL 6G **55**
Methley Pl. LS7: Leeds 5G **21**
Methley Ter. LS7: Leeds 5H **21**
Methley Vw. LS7: Leeds 5H **21**
Mexborough Av. LS7: Leeds 1H **31**
Mexborough Dr. LS7: Leeds 1H **31**
Mexborough Gro. LS7: Leeds 1H **31**
Mexborough Pl. LS7: Leeds 2H **31**
Mexborough Rd. LS7: Leeds 2H **31**
Mexborough St. LS7: Leeds 1H **31**
Meynell App. LS11: Leeds 2E **41**
Meynell Av. LS26: Rothw 4G **53**
Meynell Ct. LS15: Leeds 6D **34**
Meynell Fold LS15: Leeds 1D **44**
Meynell Hgts. LS11: Leeds 2E **41**
Meynell La. LS15: Leeds 1D **44**
Meynell Mt. LS26: Rothw 4H **53**
Meynell Rd. LS15: Leeds 6D **34**
Meynell Sq. LS11: Leeds 2E **41**
Meynell Wlk. LS11: Leeds 2E **41**
Michael Av. WF3: Wake 6G **59**
Micklefield Ct. LS19: Yead 5D **8**
Micklefield La. LS19: Yead 5C **8**
Micklefield Rd. LS19: Yead 5D **8**
Mickley St. LS12: Leeds 6B **30**
Middlecroft Cl. LS10: Leeds 1B **52**
Middlecroft Rd. LS10: Leeds 1B **52**
Middle Cross St. LS12: Leeds 6B **30**
(not continuous)
Middle Fold LS9: Leeds 3H **5** (5H **31**)
Middleham Ct. BD4: B'frd 4A **36**
Middleham Moor LS10: Leeds 6H **51**
Middlemoor LS14: Leeds 3B **24**
Middle Rd. LS9: Leeds 5F **43**
Middlethorne Cl. LS17: Leeds 4D **14**
Middlethorne Ct. LS17: Leeds 4C **14**
Middlethorne M. LS17: Leeds 4D **14**
Middlethorne Ri. LS17: Leeds 4C **14**
MIDDLETON 4F **51**
Middleton Av. LS9: Leeds 4B **32**
LS26: Rothw 4C **52**
Middleton Cl. LS27: Morl 5H **49**
Middleton Cres. LS11: Leeds 5F **41**
Middleton District Cen.
LS10: Leeds 4H **51**

90 A-Z Leeds

Moor La. BD11: B'frd 5E **47**	Moseley Wood Gdns. LS16: Leeds 4D **10**	Naburn Gdns. LS14: Leeds 4B **24**
BD19: Cleck 6E **47**	Moseley Wood Grn. LS16: Leeds 4D **10**	Naburn Grn. LS14: Leeds 4B **24**
LS20: Guis 2G **7**	Moseley Wood Gro. LS16: Leeds 4D **10**	Naburn Pl. LS14: Leeds 3B **24**
LS29: Men 1A **6**	Moseley Wood La. LS16: Leeds 4E **11**	Naburn Rd. LS14: Leeds 4B **24**
Moor Pk. Av. LS6: Leeds 5B **20**	Moseley Wood Ri. LS16: Leeds 4D **10**	Naburn Vw. LS14: Leeds 4C **24**
Moor Pk. Dr. LS6: Leeds 5B **20**	Moseley Wood Vw. LS16: Leeds 3E **11**	Naburn Wlk. LS14: Leeds 4B **24**
Moor Pk. Mt. LS6: Leeds 5B **20**	Moseley Wood Wlk. LS16: Leeds 4D **10**	Nancroft Cres. LS12: Leeds 6A **30**
Moor Pk. Vs. LS6: Leeds 5C **20**	Moseley Wood Way LS16: Leeds 3D **10**	Nancroft Mt. LS12: Leeds 6A **30**
Moor Rd. LS6: Leeds 5B **20**	Moss Bri. Rd. LS13: Leeds 6H **17**	Nancroft Ter. LS12: Leeds 6A **30**
LS11: Leeds 3G **41**	Moss Gdns. LS17: Leeds 4E **13**	Nansen Av. LS13: Leeds 3B **28**
(not continuous)	Mosslea LS27: Morl 2H **49**	Nansen Gro. LS13: Leeds 3B **28**
LS16: B'hpe 1D **10**	Moss Ri. LS17: Leeds 4E **13**	Nansen Mt. LS13: Leeds 3B **28**
WF3: Wake 5G **59**	Moss Valley LS17: Leeds 4E **13**	Nansen Pl. LS13: Leeds 3B **28**
Moor Road Station	Motley La. LS20: Guis 3G **7**	Nansen St. LS13: Leeds 3A **28**
Middleton Railway 4H **41**	Motley Row LS20: Guis 3G **7**	Nansen Ter. LS13: Leeds 3B **28**
MOORSIDE	(off Motley La.)	Nansen Vw. LS13: Leeds 3B **28**
Bradford 4H **47**	Mount, The LS15: Leeds 4B **34**	Napier St. BD3: B'frd 6A **26**
Leeds 1C **28**	LS17: Leeds 3F **13**	Narrowboat Wharf LS13: Leeds 6H **17**
Moorside App. BD11: B'frd 4H **47**	LS19: Yead 6F **9**	Naseby Gdns. LS9: Leeds 5A **32**
Moorside Av. BD11: B'frd 2C **46**	LS26: Rothw 2H **53**	Naseby Gth. LS9: Leeds 4A **32**
(Moorlands Rd.)	LS27: Morl 2H **49**	Naseby Grange LS9: Leeds 5A **32**
BD11: B'frd 4H **47**	(off Elland Rd.)	(off Naseby Gdns.)
(Moorside Dr.)	Mountbatten Av. WF1: Wake 6E **59**	Naseby Ho. BD4: B'frd 6B **36**
Moorside Cl. BD11: B'frd 4H **47**	Mountbatten Cres. WF1: Wake 6E **59**	Naseby Pl. LS9: Leeds 5A **32**
Moorside Cres. BD11: B'frd 4G **47**	Mountbatten Gro. WF1: Wake 6F **59**	Naseby Ter. LS9: Leeds 5A **32**
Moorside Dr. BD11: B'frd 4H **47**	Mt. Cliffe Vw. LS27: Morl 2H **49**	Naseby Vw. LS9: Leeds 5A **32**
LS13: Leeds 1C **28**	Mount Dr. LS17: Leeds 3F **13**	Naseby Wlk. LS9: Leeds 5A **32**
Moorside Gdns. BD11: B'frd 4H **47**	Mountfields LS2: Leeds 1A **4**	Nassau Pl. LS7: Leeds 2A **32**
Moorside Grn. BD11: B'frd 3H **47**	Mount Gdns. LS17: Leeds 3F **13**	Nateby Ri. WF3: Rothw 6F **53**
Moorside Maltings LS11: Leeds 3G **41**	Mt. Pleasant LS10: Leeds 4G **51**	National Pk. LS10: Leeds 3A **42**
Moorside Mt. BD11: B'frd 4G **47**	LS13: Leeds 1B **28**	National Rd. LS10: Leeds 2A **42**
Moorside Pde. BD11: B'frd 4H **47**	LS18: H'fth 3D **18**	Navigation Ct. LS13: Leeds 5G **17**
Moorside Rd. BD11: B'frd 4G **47**	(off Broadgate La.)	Navigation Dr. BD10: B'frd 3A **16**
Moorside St. LS13: Leeds 1C **28**	LS20: Guis 3G **7**	Navigation Wlk. LS10: Leeds 6F **5** (6G **31**)
Moorside Ter. BD11: B'frd 4H **47**	LS28: Pud 4F **27**	Naylor Gth. LS6: Leeds 6D **20**
LS13: Leeds 1C **28**	(off Westbourne Pl.)	Naylor Pl. LS11: Leeds 3F **41**
Moorside Va. BD11: B'frd 3H **47**	Mt. Pleasant Av. LS8: Leeds 6B **22**	Neath Gdns. LS9: Leeds 2F **33**
Moorside Vw. BD11: B'frd 4H **47**	Mt. Pleasant Ct. LS28: Pud 5G **27**	Ned La. BD4: B'frd 3A **36**
Moorside Wlk. BD11: B'frd 4H **47**	Mt. Pleasant Gdns. LS8: Leeds 6B **22**	Needless Inn La. LS26: Rothw 2C **54**
MOOR TOP 6H **29**	(off Sycamore Av.)	Nelson Pl. LS27: Morl 4G **49**
Moor Top BD11: B'frd 3F **47**	Mt. Pleasant Rd. LS28: Pud 5G **27**	(off Sth. Nelson St.)
(not continuous)	Mt. Pleasant St. LS28: Pud 5H **27**	Nepshaw La. LS27: Morl 4F **49**
LS12: Leeds 5C **38**	Mt. Preston St. LS2: Leeds 1A **4** (4E **31**)	(Farm Hill Rd.)
LS20: Guis 1F **7**	Mount Ri. LS17: Leeds 3F **13**	LS27: Morl 5D **48**
LS29: Guis, Otley 1F **7**	Mount Rd. WF3: Wake 5H **59**	(Wakefield Rd.)
MOORTOWN 6H **13**	Mount Royal LS18: H'fth 3B **18**	Nepshaw La. Nth. LS27: Morl 4E **49**
Moortown Cnr. LS17: Leeds 1H **21**	Mt. Tabor St. LS28: Pud 6E **27**	Nepshaw La. Sth. LS27: Morl 4E **49**
Moor Vw. BD4: B'frd 2C **46**	Mt. Vernon Rd. LS19: Yead 5E **9**	Neptune St. LS9: Leeds 6H **5** (6H **31**)
LS6: Leeds 2D **30**	Mount Vw. LS27: Morl 2H **49**	Nesfield Cl. LS10: Leeds 3B **52**
(off Hyde Pk. Rd.)	Mowbray Chase LS26: Rothw 2B **54**	Nesfield Cres. LS10: Leeds 3B **52**
LS11: Leeds 2E **41**	Mowbray Ct. LS14: Leeds 2A **34**	Nesfield Gdns. LS10: Leeds 3A **52**
LS12: Leeds 6H **29**	Mowbray Cres. LS14: Leeds 2A **34**	Nesfield Gth. LS10: Leeds 3A **52**
LS19: Yead 2F **9**	Moxon St. WF1: Wake 6E **59**	Nesfield Grn. LS10: Leeds 3A **52**
Moorview Cft. LS29: Men 1B **6**	Moxon Way WF1: Wake 6E **59**	Nesfield Rd. LS10: Leeds 3A **52**
Moorville Cl. LS11: Leeds 3F **41**	Moynihan Cl. LS8: Leeds 1D **32**	Nesfield Vw. LS10: Leeds 3A **52**
Moorville Ct. LS11: Leeds 3F **41**	Mozart Way LS27: Morl 1A **50**	Nesfield Wlk. LS10: Leeds 3A **52**
Moorville Dr. BD11: B'frd 2C **46**	Muir Ct. LS6: Leeds 1B **30**	Nethercliffe Cres. LS20: Guis 3F **7**
Moorville Gro. LS11: Leeds 3E **41**	(off St Michael's Gro.)	Nethercliffe Rd. LS20: Guis 3F **7**
Moorville Rd. LS11: Leeds 3F **41**	Muirhead Ct. BD4: B'frd 5A **36**	Netherfield Cl. LS19: Yead 2D **8**
Moorway LS20: Guis 4D **6**	Muirhead Dr. BD4: B'frd 5A **36**	Netherfield Ct. LS20: Guis 4F **7**
Moravia Bank LS28: Pud 2G **37**	Muirhead Fold BD4: B'frd 5A **36**	(off Netherfield Rd.)
(off Fartown)	Mulberry Av. LS16: Leeds 5B **12**	Netherfield Dr. LS20: Guis 3F **7**
Moresdale La. LS14: Leeds 2H **33**	Mulberry Gdns. LS26: Mick 6H **55**	Netherfield Pl. LS20: Guis 4F **7**
MORLEY 4G **49**	Mulberry Gth. LS16: Leeds 6C **12**	Netherfield Rd. LS20: Guis 3F **7**
Morley Av. BD3: B'frd 4A **26**	Mulberry Ri. LS16: Leeds 5B **12**	Netherfield Ter. LS19: Yead 2D **8**
Morley Bottoms LS27: Morl 4G **49**	Mulberry St. LS28: Pud 6G **27**	LS20: Guis 4F **7**
MORLEY HOLE 4F **49**	Mulberry Vw. LS16: Leeds 6B **12**	(off Netherfield Rd.)
Morley Leisure Cen. 5G **49**	Mullins Ct. LS9: Leeds 6B **32**	Nether St. LS28: Pud 2F **27**
Morley Mkt. LS27: Morl 5G **49**	Murchants Ho. LS2: Leeds 2G **5**	NETHERTOWN 2A **48**
(off Queen St.)	Murray St. LS18: H'fth 3E **19**	NETHER YEADON 5D **8**
Morley Station (Rail) 4A **50**	Murton Cl. LS14: Leeds 1A **34**	Nettleton Cl. BD4: B'frd 5G **37**
Morpeth Pl. LS9: Leeds 6A **32**	Museum St. LS9: Leeds 4B **32**	Nettleton Ct. LS15: Leeds 5D **34**
Morris Av. LS5: Leeds 6G **19**	Musgrave Bank LS13: Leeds 3E **29**	Neville App. LS9: Leeds 1E **43**
Morris Gro. LS5: Leeds 1G **29**	Musgrave Bldgs. LS28: Pud 5H **27**	Neville Av. LS9: Leeds 1E **43**
Morris La. LS5: Leeds 6G **19**	Musgrave Ct. LS28: Pud 6G **27**	Neville Cl. LS9: Leeds 1E **43**
Morris Mt. LS5: Leeds 1G **29**	Musgrave Mt. LS13: Leeds 3E **29**	Neville Cres. LS9: Leeds 5F **33**
Morris Pl. LS27: Morl 4F **49**	Musgrave Ri. LS13: Leeds 3E **29**	Neville Gth. LS9: Leeds 6E **33**
Morris Vw. LS5: Leeds 1G **29**	Musgrave Vw. LS13: Leeds 3E **29**	Neville Gro. LS9: Leeds 6E **33**
Morritt Av. LS15: Leeds 4B **34**	Musgrove Ho. LS5: Leeds 1F **29**	LS26: Swil 5G **45**
Morritt Dr. LS15: Leeds 5H **33**	(off Broad La.)	Neville Mt. LS9: Leeds 1E **43**
Morritt Gro. LS15: Leeds 5H **33**	Mushroom St. LS9: Leeds 1H **5** (4H **31**)	Neville Pde. LS9: Leeds 6E **33**
Mortec Pk. LS15: Scho 4E **25**		Neville Pl. LS9: Leeds 6F **33**
Morton Ter. LS20: Guis 4F **7**		Neville Rd. LS9: Leeds 6F **33**
Morwick Gro. LS15: Scho 5F **25**	**N**	LS15: Leeds 5F **33**
Morwick Ter. LS14: T'ner 3E **25**		Neville Row LS9: Leeds 1E **43**
Moseley Pl. LS6: Leeds 2F **31**	Nab La. WF17: Bat 6A **48**	Neville Sq. LS9: Leeds 6F **33**
Moseley Wood App. LS16: Leeds 5D **10**	(not continuous)	Neville St. LS1: Leeds 6D **4** (1F **41**)
Moseley Wood Av. LS16: Leeds 3D **10**	Naburn App. LS14: Leeds 2B **24**	LS11: Leeds 6D **4** (6F **31**)
Moseley Wood Bank LS16: Leeds 4D **10**	Naburn Chase LS14: Leeds 4C **24**	Neville Ter. LS9: Leeds 6E **33**
Moseley Wood Cl. LS16: Leeds 5D **10**	Naburn Cl. LS14: Leeds 4B **24**	Neville Vw. LS9: Leeds 6E **33**
Moseley Wood Cres. LS16: Leeds 4D **10**	Naburn Ct. LS14: Leeds 3B **24**	Neville Wlk. LS9: Leeds 6E **33**
Moseley Wood Cft. LS16: Leeds 5C **10**	Naburn Dr. LS14: Leeds 4B **24**	New Adel Av. LS16: Leeds 6G **11**
Moseley Wood Dr. LS16: Leeds 4D **10**	Naburn Fold LS14: Leeds 4C **24**	New Adel Gdns. LS16: Leeds 6G **11**

Noster Hill—Oriental St.

Noster Hill LS11: Leeds 4D 40
Noster Pl. LS11: Leeds 4D 40
Noster Rd. LS11: Leeds 4D 40
Noster St. LS11: Leeds 4D 40
Noster Ter. LS11: Leeds 4D 40
Noster Vw. LS11: Leeds 4D 40
Nottingham Cl. WF3: Rothw 6C 52
Nottingham St. BD3: B'frd 6A 26
Nova La. WF17: Bat 6F 47
Nowell App. LS9: Leeds 4D 32
Nowell Av. LS9: Leeds 4D 32
Nowell Cl. LS9: Leeds 4D 32
Nowell Ct. LS9: Leeds 4D 32
Nowell Cres. LS9: Leeds 4D 32
Nowell End Row LS9: Leeds 4D 32
Nowell Gdns. LS9: Leeds 4D 32
Nowell Gro. LS9: Leeds 4D 32
Nowell La. LS9: Leeds 4D 32
Nowell Mt. LS9: Leeds 4D 32
Nowell Pde. LS9: Leeds 4D 32
Nowell Pl. LS9: Leeds 4D 32
Nowell St. LS9: Leeds 4D 32
Nowell Ter. LS9: Leeds 4D 32
Nowell Vw. LS9: Leeds 4D 32
Nowell Wlk. LS9: Leeds 4D 32
Nunington Av. LS12: Leeds 5A 30
Nunington St. LS12: Leeds 5A 30
Nunington Ter. LS12: Leeds 5A 30
Nunington Vw. LS12: Leeds 4A 30
Nunroyd Av. LS17: Leeds 2H 21
LS20: Guis 5H 7
Nunroyd Gro. LS17: Leeds 2H 21
Nunroyd Lawn LS17: Leeds 2H 21
Nunroyd Rd. LS17: Leeds 2H 21
Nunroyd St. LS17: Leeds 2H 21
Nunroyd Ter. LS17: Leeds 2H 21
Nunthorpe Rd. LS13: Leeds 6H 17
Nursery Cl. LS17: Leeds 5G 13
Nursery Gro. LS17: Leeds 5E 13
Nursery La. LS17: Leeds 5E 13
Nursery Mt. LS10: Leeds 6A 42
Nursery Mt. Rd. LS10: Leeds 5A 42
Nursery Rd. LS20: Guis 2F 7
Nussey Av. WF17: Bat 6G 47
Nutter La. WF17: Bat 6F 47
Nutting Gro. Ter. LS12: Leeds 2E 39

O

Oak Av. LS27: Morl 6H 49
WF3: Wake 6H 59
Oak Cres. LS15: Leeds 6H 33
Oakdale Cl. BD10: B'frd 2A 26
WF3: Wake 5D 58
Oakdale Dr. BD10: B'frd 2A 26
Oakdale Gth. LS14: Leeds 2B 24
Oakdale Mdw. LS14: Leeds 2B 24
Oakdene LS26: Rothw 2D 54
Oakdene Cl. LS28: Pud 2H 37
Oakdene Ct. LS17: Leeds 5C 14
Oakdene Dr. LS17: Leeds 5C 14
Oakdene Gdns. LS17: Leeds 5C 14
Oakdene Va. LS17: Leeds 5C 14
Oakdene Way LS17: Leeds 5C 14
Oak Dr. LS16: Leeds 1H 19
Oakfield LS6: Leeds 1C 30
Oakfield Av. LS26: Rothw 3G 53
Oakfield Ter. LS18: H'fth 3E 19
(off Low La.)
Oakford Ter. LS18: H'fth 2E 19
Oak Gro. LS27: Morl 6H 49
Oakham M. LS9: Leeds 6D 32
Oakhampton Ct. LS8: Leeds 3E 23
Oakham Way LS9: Leeds 6D 32
Oak Ho. LS5: Leeds 1F 29
LS7: Leeds 4H 21
(off Allerton Pk.)
LS15: Leeds 1G 43
Oakhurst LS6: Leeds 1C 30
Oakhurst Av. LS11: Leeds 6E 41
Oakhurst Gro. LS11: Leeds 6D 40
Oakhurst Mt. LS11: Leeds 6D 40
Oakhurst Rd. LS11: Leeds 6D 40
Oakhurst St. LS11: Leeds 6E 41
Oaklands WF3: Rothw 6C 52
Oaklands Av. LS13: Leeds 6G 17
LS16: Leeds 6B 12
Oaklands Cl. LS16: Leeds 6B 12
Oaklands Dr. LS16: Leeds 1B 20
Oaklands Fold LS16: Leeds 6B 12
Oaklands Gro. LS13: Leeds 6G 17
LS16: Leeds 6B 12
Oaklands Rd. LS13: Leeds 6G 17
Oaklands Rd. Trad. Est. LS13: Leeds 6G 17
Oaklea Gdns. LS16: Leeds 1B 20
Oaklea Hall Cl. LS16: Leeds 1B 20
Oaklea Rd. LS15: Scho 5F 25
Oakley Gro. LS11: Leeds 4G 41
Oakley St. WF3: E Ard 2A 58
Oakley Ter. LS11: Leeds 5G 41
Oakley Vw. LS11: Leeds 5G 41
Oakridge Av. LS29: Men 1D 6
Oak Rd. LS7: Leeds 6H 21
LS12: Leeds 6C 30
LS15: Leeds 6H 33
LS27: Morl 6F 49
Oakroyd LS26: Rothw 5H 53
Oakroyd Cl. BD11: B'frd 4C 46
Oakroyd Dr. BD11: B'frd 5C 46
Oakroyd Fold LS27: Morl 1A 50
Oakroyd Mt. LS28: Pud 5G 27
Oakroyd Ter. LS27: Morl 1A 50
LS28: Pud 5G 27
Oaks, The LS20: Guis 3G 7
LS27: Morl 2H 49
Oak St. LS27: Morl 2H 49
LS28: Pud 5E 27
Oak Ter. LS15: Leeds 2D 34
(off Church La.)
Oak Tree Bus. Pk. LS14: Leeds 4A 24
Oak Tree Cl. LS9: Leeds 2E 33
Oak Tree Ct. LS9: Leeds 2E 33
(off Oak Tree Pl.)
Oak Tree Cres. LS9: Leeds 2E 33
Oak Tree Dr. LS8: Leeds 2E 33
Oak Tree Gro. LS9: Leeds 2E 33
Oak Tree Mt. LS9: Leeds 2E 33
Oak Tree Pl. LS9: Leeds 2E 33
Oak Tree Wlk. LS9: Leeds 2E 33
Oakway BD11: B'frd 5D 46
OAKWELL 6F 47
Oakwell Av. LS8: Leeds 5C 22
Oakwell Cl. BD11: B'frd 4A 48
Oakwell Ct. LS13: Leeds 2B 28
LS28: Pud 2F 27
(off Water La.)
WF17: Bat 6A 48
(not continuous)
Oakwell Cres. LS8: Leeds 5C 22
Oakwell Dr. LS8: Leeds 5C 22
Oakwell Gdns. LS8: Leeds 5C 22
Oakwell Gro. LS13: Leeds 2C 28
Oakwell Hall 6F 47
Oakwell Hall Country Pk. 6E 47
Oakwell Hall Farm Vis. Cen. 6F 47
Oakwell Ind. Est. WF17: Bat 6A 48
Oakwell Ind. Pk. WF17: Bat 6H 47
Oakwell Mt. LS8: Leeds 5C 22
Oakwell Oval LS8: Leeds 5C 22
Oakwell Rd. BD11: B'frd 4A 48
Oakwell Ter. LS28: Pud 2F 27
Oakwell Way WF17: Bat 6A 48
OAKWOOD 5E 23
Oakwood Av. BD11: B'frd 5C 46
LS8: Leeds 5D 22
Oakwood Boundary Rd. LS8: Leeds 5D 22
Oakwood Ct. LS8: Leeds 5E 23
Oakwood Dr. LS8: Leeds 5D 22
LS26: Rothw 2F 53
Oakwood Fitness Cen. 6E 23
Oakwood Gdns. LS8: Leeds 5D 22
LS28: Pud 1G 37
Oakwood Gth. LS8: Leeds 5E 23
Oakwood Grange LS8: Leeds 5E 23
Oakwood Grange La. LS8: Leeds 5E 23
Oakwood Grn. LS8: Leeds 5E 23
Oakwood Gro. LS8: Leeds 5D 22
Oakwood Ho. LS13: Leeds 5F 17
(off Rodley La.)
Oakwood La. LS8: Leeds 5D 22
LS9: Leeds 2F 33
Oakwood Mt. LS8: Leeds 5D 22
Oakwood Nook LS8: Leeds 5D 22
Oakwood Pk. LS8: Leeds 6E 23
Oakwood Pl. LS8: Leeds 5D 22
Oakwood Ri. LS8: Leeds 5E 23
Oakwood Ter. LS28: Pud 1G 37
Oakwood Vw. LS8: Leeds 5E 23
Oakwood Wlk. LS8: Leeds 5E 23
Oasby Cft. BD4: B'frd 6A 36
Oast Ho. Cft. WF3: Rothw 6D 52
Oastler Rd. LS28: Pud 5D 16
Oatland Cl. LS7: Leeds 3G 31
Oatland Ct. LS7: Leeds 1F 5 (3G 31)
Oatland Dr. LS7: Leeds 3G 31
Oatland Gdns. LS7: Leeds 3G 31
Oatland Grn. LS7: Leeds 3G 31
Oatland Hgts. LS7: Leeds 1G 5
Oatland La. LS7: Leeds 3G 31
Oatland Pl. LS7: Leeds 2G 31
Oatland Rd. LS7: Leeds 3G 31
Oatland Towers LS7: Leeds 1F 5 (3G 31)
Oban Cl. WF3: E Ard 2B 56
Oban Pl. LS12: Leeds 5G 29
Oban St. LS12: Leeds 5H 29
Oban Ter. LS12: Leeds 5H 29
WF3: E Ard 2B 56
Occupation La. LS28: Pud 1E 37
Odda La. LS20: Guis 4A 6
Oddfellow St. LS27: Morl 5G 49
Oddy Pl. LS6: Leeds 5B 20
Oddy's Fold LS6: Leeds 3C 20
Oddy St. BD4: B'frd 6A 36
Odeon Cinema
Bradford 5B 26
Ogden Ho. BD4: B'frd 3B 36
Ogilby Ct. LS26: Rothw 2B 54
Ogilby M. LS26: Rothw 2B 54
O'Grady Sq. LS9: Leeds 6B 32
Old Barn Cl. LS17: Leeds 4E 13
Old Brandon La. LS17: Leeds 5G 15
Old Cl. LS11: Leeds 1B 50
Old Farm App. LS16: Leeds 3F 19
Old Farm Cl. LS16: Leeds 3G 19
Old Farm Cross LS16: Leeds 3G 19
Old Farm Dr. LS16: Leeds 3F 19
Old Farm Gth. LS16: Leeds 3G 19
Old Farm Pde. LS16: Leeds 3G 19
Old Farm Wlk. LS16: Leeds 3F 19
Oldfield Av. LS12: Leeds 1A 40
Oldfield Ct. LS7: Leeds 5A 22
Oldfield La. LS12: Leeds 1A 40
Oldfield St. LS12: Leeds 1A 40
Old Fold LS28: Pud 2F 27
Old Hall Rd. WF3: E Ard 3D 56
Old Haworth La. LS19: Yead 2D 8
Old Hollins Hill BD17: B'frd, Guis 6E 7
LS20: Guis 6E 7
Old La. BD11: B'frd 2H 47
(Lumb Bottom)
BD11: B'frd 3C 46
(Station La.)
LS11: Leeds 5D 40
LS20: Guis 5A 6
Old Marsh LS28: Pud 6E 27
Old Mill Bus. Pk. LS10: Leeds 3B 42
Old Mill La. LS10: Leeds 3A 42
Old Oak Cl. LS16: Leeds 4G 19
Old Oak Dr. LS16: Leeds 4G 19
Old Oak Gth. LS16: Leeds 4F 19
Old Oak Lawn LS16: Leeds 4G 19
Old Orchard, The LS29: Men 1D 6
(off Station Rd.)
Old Pk. Rd. LS8: Leeds 3C 22
(not continuous)
Old Rd. LS27: Morl 1A 50
LS28: Pud 4E 27
Oldroyd Cres. LS11: Leeds 5C 40
Old Run Rd. LS10: Leeds 5H 41
Old Run Vw. LS10: Leeds 1H 51
Old School Lofts LS12: Leeds 6G 29
Old School M. LS27: Morl 1A 50
Old Whack Ho. La. LS19: Yead 3B 8
Olive Lodge LS18: H'fth 2C 18
(off Broadgate La.)
Oliver Ct. BD11: B'frd 4F 47
Oliver Hill LS18: H'fth 4C 18
Olrika Ct. LS7: Leeds 1H 31
Ontario Pl. LS7: Leeds 5H 21
Open University 5E 5
Orange Tree Gro. WF3: E Ard 4G 57
Orchard Av. WF3: Wake 6H 59
Orchard Cl. WF3: E Ard 5H 57
Orchard Ct. LS16: Leeds 4B 20
(off St Chads Rd.)
LS20: Guis 4G 7
(off Orchard La.)
Orchard Cft. LS15: Leeds 3B 34
Orchard Gro. LS29: Men 1D 6
Orchard La. LS20: Guis 4G 7
Orchard Mt. LS15: Leeds 3C 34
Orchard Rd. LS15: Leeds 3B 34
Orchards, The LS15: Leeds 3B 34
Orchard Sq. LS15: Leeds 3B 34
Orchard Way LS20: Guis 4G 7
LS26: Rothw 3G 53
Orchid Ct. WF3: Rothw 1D 58
Oriental St. LS12: Leeds 6A 30

94 A-Z Leeds

Park Vw. Ter.—Portland St.

Park Vw. Ter. *LS15: Leeds* *5A* ***34***
(off Park St.)
LS19: Yead 5D **8**
Park Villa Ct. LS8: Leeds 2C **22**
PARK VILLAS 1C 22
Park Vs. LS8: Leeds 2C **22**
Parkville Pl. LS13: Leeds 1C **28**
Parkville Rd. LS13: Leeds 2C **28**
Park Way LS29: Men 1C **6**
Parkway LS27: Morl 3C **48**
Parkway Cl. LS14: Leeds 1G **33**
Parkway Ct. LS14: Leeds 2G **33**
Parkway Grange LS14: Leeds 2G **33**
Parkways LS26: Rothw 3B **54**
Parkways Av. LS26: Rothw 4B **54**
Parkways Cl. LS26: Rothw 3B **54**
Parkways Ct. LS26: Rothw 3B **54**
Parkways Dr. LS26: Rothw 3B **54**
Parkways Gth. LS26: Rothw 4B **54**
Parkways Gro. LS26: Rothw 3B **54**
Parkway Towers LS14: Leeds 1G **33**
Parkway Va. LS14: Leeds 2G **33**
(not continuous)
Park W. LS26: Rothw 4G **53**
Park Wood Av. LS11: Leeds 1D **50**
Parkwood Av. LS8: Leeds 4C **22**
Park Wood Cl. LS11: Leeds 2D **50**
Parkwood Ct. LS8: Leeds 3C **22**
Park Wood Cres. LS11: Leeds 2D **50**
Park Wood Dr. LS11: Leeds 1D **50**
Parkwood Gdns. LS8: Leeds 4C **22**
LS28: Pud 5C **16**
Parkwood M. LS8: Leeds 4C **22**
Park Wood Rd. LS11: Leeds 2D **50**
Parkwood Rd. LS28: Pud 5D **16**
Parkwood Vw. LS8: Leeds 4C **22**
Parkwood Way LS8: Leeds 4C **22**
Parliament Pl. LS12: Leeds 5B **30**
Parliament Rd. LS12: Leeds 6B **30**
Parnaby Av. LS10: Leeds 6B **42**
Parnaby Rd. LS10: Leeds 6B **42**
Parnaby St. LS10: Leeds 6B **42**
Parnaby Ter. LS10: Leeds 6B **42**
Parsley M. LS26: Mick 6H **55**
Partons Pl. WF3: Wake 5E **59**
Partridge Cl. LS27: Morl 5B **50**
Pasture Av. LS7: Leeds 4H **21**
Pasture Cres. LS7: Leeds 4H **21**
Pasture Gro. LS7: Leeds 4H **21**
Pasture La. LS7: Leeds 4H **21**
Pasture Mt. LS12: Leeds 5H **29**
Pasture Pde. LS7: Leeds 4H **21**
Pasture Pl. LS7: Leeds 4H **21**
Pasture Rd. LS8: Leeds 1A **32**
Pasture St. LS7: Leeds 4H **21**
Pasture Ter. LS7: Leeds 4H **21**
Pasture Vw. LS12: Leeds 5H **29**
Pasture Vw. Rd. LS26: Rothw 4G **53**
Patrick Grn. LS26: Wake 3H **59**
Pavilion Bus. Pk. LS12: Leeds 4A **40**
Pavilion Cl. LS28: Pud 3G **27**
Pavilion Gdns. LS26: Rothw 3C **54**
LS28: Pud 3G **27**
Pavilion M. LS6: Leeds 2B **30**
Pavilion Way LS28: Pud 6F **27**
Pawson St. LS27: Morl 6F **49**
WF3: E Ard 3A **58**
WF3: Rothw 1D **58**
Paxton Ct. LS12: Leeds 3F **29**
Peacock Grn. LS27: Morl 6A **50**
Pearson Av. LS6: Leeds 2C **30**
Pearson Gro. LS6: Leeds 2C **30**
Pearson St. LS10: Leeds 2H **41**
LS28: Pud 4D **16**
Pearson Ter. LS6: Leeds 2C **30**
Peasehill Cl. LS19: Yead 5E **9**
Peasehill Pk. LS19: Yead 5E **9**
Peckover Dr. LS28: Pud 4B **26**
Peel Cl. BD4: B'frd 1A **36**
Peel Mills Bus. Cen. LS27: Morl 5H **49**
Peel Sq. LS5: Leeds 1G **29**
Peel St. LS27: Morl 5H **49**
Pelham Ct. LS10: Leeds 6H **51**
Pelham Pl. LS7: Leeds 4G **21**
Pelican Walks LS26: Rothw 2D **52**
Pembroke Cl. LS27: Morl 4F **49**
Pembroke Dr. LS27: Morl 4F **49**
LS28: Pud 5G **27**
Pembroke Grange LS9: Leeds 3F **33**
Pembroke Ho. *BD4: B'frd* *5A* ***36***
(off Launceston Dr.)
Pembroke Rd. LS28: Pud 5G **27**
Pembroke Towers LS9: Leeds 2F **33**
Pembury Mt. LS15: Leeds 2F **35**
Penarth Rd. LS15: Leeds 3B **34**
Pendas Dr. LS15: Leeds 3D **34**
PENDAS FIELDS 2F 35
Pendas Gro. LS15: Leeds 2D **34**
Pendas Wlk. LS15: Leeds 3D **34**
Pendas Way LS15: Leeds 3D **34**
Pendil Cl. LS15: Leeds 5C **34**
Pendragon Ter. LS20: Guis 4F **7**
Penfield Rd. BD11: B'frd 3H **47**
Penlands Cres. LS15: Leeds 6D **34**
Penlands Lawn LS15: Leeds 6D **34**
Penlands Wlk. LS15: Leeds 6D **34**
Pennine Ind. Est. LS12: Leeds 6H **29**
Pennine Vw. WF17: Bat 6A **48**
Pennington Ct. LS6: Leeds 2E **31**
Pennington Gro. LS6: Leeds 1E **31**
Pennington Pl. LS6: Leeds 2E **31**
Pennington St. LS6: Leeds 2E **31**
Pennington Ter. LS6: Leeds 1E **31**
Pennwell Cft. *LS14: Leeds* *6D* ***24***
(off Whinmoor Way)
Pennwell Dean LS14: Leeds 6D **24**
Pennwell Fld. LS14: Leeds 6E **25**
Pennwell Gth. LS14: Leeds 6D **24**
Pennwell Ga. LS14: Leeds 6D **24**
Pennwell Grn. LS14: Leeds 6D **24**
Pennwell Lawn LS14: Leeds 6D **24**
Pennyfield Cl. LS6: Leeds 2D **20**
Penny Hill Cen., The LS10: Leeds 3A **42**
Penny La. Way LS10: Leeds 3H **41**
Pennythorne Ct. LS19: Yead 4C **8**
Pennythorne Dr. LS19: Yead 4C **8**
Penraevon 1 Light Ind. Est. LS7: Leeds 2G **31**
Penraevon Av. LS7: Leeds 2G **31**
Penraevon Ind. Est. *LS7: Leeds* *2G* ***31***
(off Education Rd.)
Penrith Gro. LS12: Leeds 1A **40**
Pentland Way LS27: Morl 6G **49**
Pepper Gdns. LS13: Leeds 1E **29**
Pepper Hills LS17: Leeds 5H **13**
Pepper La. LS10: Leeds 4B **42**
LS13: Leeds 1D **28**
Pepper Rd. LS10: Leeds 5B **42**
Percival St. LS2: Leeds 2D **4** (4F **31**)
Percy St. LS12: Leeds 1B **40**
Peregrine Av. LS27: Morl 5B **50**
Perseverance St. LS28: Pud 6E **27**
Perseverance Ter. LS26: Rothw 5G **53**
Perth Dr. WF3: E Ard 3D **56**
Perth Mt. LS18: H'fth 5B **10**
Peter La. LS27: Morl 4B **50**
Peter Laylock Ind. Est. LS7: Leeds 2G **31**
Petersfield Av. LS10: Leeds 2A **52**
Petrel Way LS27: Morl 6A **50**
Petrie Cres. LS13: Leeds 6F **17**
Petrie Gro. BD3: B'frd 6A **26**
Petrie Rd. BD3: B'frd 6A **26**
Petrie St. LS13: Leeds 6F **17**
Peverell Cl. BD4: B'frd 4A **36**
Pheasant Dr. WF17: Bat 6A **48**
Philip Gth. WF1: Wake 6D **58**
Philippa Way LS12: Leeds 4A **40**
Philip's Gro. WF3: Wake 5E **59**
Phil May Ct. *LS12: Leeds* *1C* ***40***
(off Green La.)
Phoenix Cl. LS14: Leeds 2A **34**
Phoenix Way BD4: Pud 1A **36**
Pickard Bank LS6: Leeds 6D **20**
Pickard Ct. LS15: Leeds 5C **34**
Pickering Mt. LS12: Leeds 5B **30**
Pickering St. LS12: Leeds 5B **30**
Pickpocket La. LS26: Rothw 2A **54**
Pickup Bus. Pk. LS28: Pud 3H **27**
Piece Wood Rd. LS16: Leeds 6D **10**
Pigeon Cote Cl. LS14: Leeds 5A **24**
Pigeon Cote Rd. LS14: Leeds 5A **24**
Pilden La. WF3: E Ard 5G **57**
Pilgrim Way LS28: Pud 3A **28**
Pilot St. LS9: Leeds 1H **5** (4A **32**)
Pinder Av. LS12: Leeds 3F **39**
Pinder Gro. LS12: Leeds 3F **39**
Pinder St. LS12: Leeds 3F **39**
Pinder Vw. LS12: Leeds 3F **39**
Pine Ct. LS2: Leeds 5G **5** (6H **31**)
Pinfold Ct. LS15: Leeds 5B **34**
Pinfold Gro. LS15: Leeds 5A **34**
Pinfold Hill LS15: Leeds 5B **34**
Pinfold La. LS12: Leeds 6H **29**
LS15: Leeds 5A **34**
LS16: Leeds 3E **11**
Pinfold Mt. LS15: Leeds 6B **34**
Pinfold Rd. LS15: Leeds 6B **34**
Pinfold Sq. LS15: Leeds 5A **34**
Pipe & Nook La. LS12: Leeds 6F **29**
Pipit Mdw. LS27: Morl 6A **50**
Pitchstone Ct. LS12: Leeds 6D **28**
Pitfall St. LS1: Leeds 6F **5** (6G **31**)
Pit Fld. Rd. WF3: Rothw 1F **59**
Pitt Row LS1: Leeds 6E **5** (6G **31**)
Place's Rd. LS9: Leeds 6A **32**
Plaid Row LS9: Leeds 5A **32**
Plane Tree Av. LS17: Leeds 5B **14**
Plane Tree Cl. LS17: Leeds 5B **14**
Plane Tree Cft. LS17: Leeds 5B **14**
Plane Tree Gdns. LS17: Leeds 5B **14**
Plane Tree Gro. LS19: Yead 3F **9**
Plane Tree Ri. LS17: Leeds 5B **14**
Plane Trees Cl. BD19: Cleck 6A **46**
Plane Tree Vw. LS17: Leeds 5B **14**
Plantation Av. LS15: Leeds 6H **33**
LS17: Leeds 4C **14**
Plantation Gdns. LS17: Leeds 4C **14**
Playfair Rd. LS10: Leeds 5H **41**
Playground LS12: Leeds 4D **38**
Plaza, The LS2: Leeds 1E **5**
Pleasance, The LS26: Swil 6G **45**
Pleasant Ct. *LS6: Leeds* *2E* ***31***
(off Rampart Rd.)
Pleasant M. LS11: Leeds 2E **41**
Pleasant Pl. LS11: Leeds 2E **41**
Pleasant St. LS11: Leeds 2E **41**
Pleasant Ter. LS11: Leeds 2E **41**
Pleasant Vw. WF3: Wake 4B **58**
Pleasant Vw. Ter. *LS26: Rothw* *5D* ***52***
(off Copley La.)
Plevna St. LS10: Leeds 5C **42**
Plover Way LS27: Morl 6A **50**
Plowmans Wlk. LS19: Yead 3B **8**
Poets Pl. LS18: H'fth 1C **18**
Pogson's Cotts. *LS14: Leeds* *6B* ***24***
(off York Rd.)
Point, The *LS12: Leeds* *1D* ***40***
(off Whitehall Pl.)
Pollard La. LS13: Leeds 5B **18**
Pollard St. WF3: Wake 5E **59**
Ponderosa Cl. LS8: Leeds 2B **32**
Pontefract Av. LS9: Leeds 6B **32**
Pontefract La. LS9: Leeds, Swil 5B **32**
(not continuous)
LS15: Swil 4A **44**
Pontefract La. Cl. LS9: Leeds 6B **32**
Pontefract Rd. LS10: Leeds 5C **42**
LS26: Rothw 1F **53**
Pontefract St. LS9: Leeds 6B **32**
Poole Cres. LS15: Leeds 3B **34**
Poole Mt. LS15: Leeds 4B **34**
Poole Rd. LS15: Leeds 3B **34**
Poole Sq. LS15: Leeds 4B **34**
Poplar Av. LS15: Leeds 3D **34**
Poplar Cl. LS13: Leeds 5F **29**
Poplar Ct. LS13: Leeds 5E **29**
Poplar Cres. WF3: Morl 2A **56**
Poplar Cft. LS13: Leeds 5E **29**
Poplar Dr. LS18: H'fth 3H **17**
Poplar Gdns. LS13: Leeds 5E **29**
Poplar Gth. LS13: Leeds 5E **29**
Poplar Ga. LS13: Leeds 5E **29**
Poplar Grn. LS13: Leeds 5E **29**
Poplar Mt. LS13: Leeds 5E **29**
Poplar Pl. LS28: Pud 6D **26**
Poplar Ri. LS13: Leeds 4E **29**
Poplars, The LS6: Leeds 1C **30**
LS20: Guis 3G **7**
WF3: Wake 3E **59**
Poplar Sq. LS28: Pud 3F **27**
Poplar St. WF3: Wake 5E **59**
Poplar Vw. LS12: Leeds 4G **39**
LS13: Leeds 5E **29**
Poplar Way LS13: Leeds 5E **29**
Poplarwood Gdns. BD10: B'frd 6A **16**
Poppleton Ct. WF3: E Ard 2C **56**
Poppleton Cft. WF3: E Ard 3C **56**
Poppleton Dr. WF3: E Ard 2C **56**
Poppleton Ri. WF3: E Ard 3C **56**
Poppleton Rd. WF3: E Ard 2C **56**
Poppleton Way WF3: E Ard 2C **56**
Poppy La. WF3: E Ard 3A **58**
Portage Av. LS15: Leeds 6H **33**
Portage Cres. LS15: Leeds 6G **33**
Portland Cres. LS1: Leeds 2D **4** (4F **31**)
Portland Ga. LS1: Leeds 2D **4** (4F **31**)
(not continuous)
LS2: Leeds 2D **4** (4F **31**)
Portland Rd. LS12: Leeds 1A **40**
Portland St. LS1: Leeds 3C **4** (5F **31**)

96 A-Z Leeds

Railway Ter. WF1: Wake 6D 58	Recreation Av. LS11: Leeds 3E 41	Rein M. WF3: E Ard .3A 56
WF3: E Ard 2G 57	Recreation Cres. LS11: Leeds 3D 40	Rein Rd. LS18: H'fth 4B 18
Raincliffe Gro. LS9: Leeds 5C 32	Recreation Gro. LS11: Leeds 3D 40	LS27: Morl 2A 56
Raincliffe Mt. LS9: Leeds 6C 32	Recreation Mt. LS11: Leeds 3D 40	WF3: Morl 2A 56
Raincliffe Rd. LS9: Leeds 5C 32	Recreation Pl. LS11: Leeds 3D 40	Rein St. LS27: Morl 2A 56
Raincliffe St. LS9: Leeds 5C 32	Recreation Rd. LS11: Leeds 5D 40	Reinwood Av. LS8: Leeds 6F 23
Raincliffe Ter. LS9: Leeds 6C 32	Recreation Row LS11: Leeds 3D 40	Rembrandt Av. WF3: E Ard 3D 56
Rakehill Rd. LS15: Bar E, Scho 4F 25	Recreation St. LS11: Leeds 3D 40	Renaissance Ct. LS27: Morl 1A 50
Rampart Rd. LS6: Leeds 2E 31	Recreation Ter. LS11: Leeds 3D 40	Renaissance Dr. LS27: Morl 1A 50
Ramsgate WF3: Rothw 2D 58	Recreation Vw. LS11: Leeds 3D 40	Renton Av. LS20: Guis 4F 7
Ramsgate Cres. WF3: Rothw 2D 58	Rectory St. LS9: Leeds 4A 32	Renton Dr. LS20: Guis 5F 7
Ramshead App. LS14: Leeds 5A 24	Redbarn Cl. LS10: Leeds 1G 57	Renton Lea LS20: Guis 5F 7
Ramshead Cl. LS14: Leeds 4A 24	Redbarn Cl. LS10: Leeds 1G 57	Restmore Av. LS20: Guis 3F 7
Ramshead Cres. LS14: Leeds 4H 23	Redbeck Cotts. LS18: Yead 3G 17	Revie Rd. LS11: Leeds 4D 40
Ramshead Dr. LS14: Leeds 4H 23	Redcar Rd. BD10: B'frd 5A 16	Revie Rd. Ind. Est. LS11: Leeds 4D 40
Ramshead Gdns. LS14: Leeds 4H 23	Redcote La. LS4: Leeds 4A 30	Reyden M. LS12: Leeds 1A 40
Ramshead Gro. LS14: Leeds 5A 24	LS12: Leeds 5H 29	Rhodes Gdns. WF3: Wake 5E 59
Ramshead Hgts. LS14: Leeds 6A 24	Redesdale Gdns. LS16: Leeds 6G 11	Rhodes Ter. LS12: Leeds 1C 40
(Bailey's La.)	Red Hall App. LS14: Leeds 2H 23	Riccall Nook BD10: B'frd 5A 16
LS14: Leeds 5A 24	Red Hall Av. LS17: Leeds 2H 23	Richardshaw Dr. LS28: Pud 4G 27
(Eastdean Rd.)	Red Hall Chase LS14: Leeds 2A 24	Richardshaw La. LS28: Pud 4G 27
Ramshead Hill LS14: Leeds 5A 24	Redhall Cl. LS11: Leeds 6C 40	Richardshaw Rd. LS28: Pud 4G 27
Ramshead Pl. LS14: Leeds 5A 24	Red Hall Ct. LS14: Leeds 2A 24	Richardson Cres. LS9: Leeds 6D 32
Ramshead Vw. LS14: Leeds 5A 24	Redhall Cres. LS11: Leeds 6C 40	Richardson Rd. LS9: Leeds 6D 32
Randolph St. BD3: B'frd 5A 26	Red Hall Cft. LS14: Leeds 2A 24	Richmond Av. LS6: Leeds 1C 30
LS13: Leeds 3A 28	Red Hall Dr. LS14: Leeds 2A 24	Richmond Cl. LS13: Leeds 3A 28
Ranelagh Av. BD10: B'frd 6A 16	Red Hall Gdns. LS17: Leeds 2H 23	LS26: Rothw 3H 53
Rathmell Rd. LS15: Leeds 6G 33	Red Hall Gth. LS14: Leeds 2A 24	LS27: Morl 6G 49
Raven Rd. LS6: Leeds 1C 30	Redhall Ga. LS11: Leeds 6C 40	Richmond Ct. LS9: Leeds 6B 32
Ravenscar Av. LS8: Leeds 5C 22	Red Hall Grn. LS14: Leeds 2H 23	LS26: Rothw 3H 53
Ravenscar Mt. LS8: Leeds 5C 22	Red Hall La. LS14: Leeds 2A 24	Richmond Cft. LS9: Leeds 6B 32
Ravenscar Ter. LS8: Leeds 5C 22	LS17: Leeds 2H 23	Richmond Gdns. LS28: Pud 6A 28
Ravenscar Vw. LS8: Leeds 5C 22	Red Hall Va. LS14: Leeds 3A 24	Richmond Gro. BD19: Cleck 6D 46
Ravenscar Wlk. LS8: Leeds 5C 22	Red Hall Vw. LS14: Leeds 2A 24	RICHMOND HILL 6B 32
RAVENSCLIFFE 1A 26	Red Hall Wlk. LS14: Leeds 2A 24	Richmond Hill App. LS9: Leeds 6A 32
Ravenscliffe Av. BD10: B'frd 6A 16	Red Hall Way LS14: Leeds 2A 24	Richmond Hill Cl. LS9: Leeds 6A 32
Ravenscliffe Rd. LS28: Pud 5B 16	Redhill Av. WF3: E Ard 6C 56	Richmond Hill Sports & Recreation Cen. . . .5B 32
Ravens Mt. LS28: Pud 6H 27	WF3: E Ard 6C 56	Richmond Ho. LS8: Leeds 1D 22
Ravensworth Cl. LS15: Leeds 2F 35	Redhill Cl. BD4: B'frd 1C 46	(off Street La.)
Ravensworth Way LS15: Leeds 2F 35	WF3: E Ard 6C 56	Richmond Mt. LS6: Leeds 1C 30
RAWDON 6F 9	Redhill Cres. WF3: E Ard 6C 56	Richmond Rd. LS6: Leeds 1C 30
Rawdon Crematorium LS19: Yead 2G 17	Redhill Dr. WF3: E Ard 6C 56	LS28: Pud 3E 27
Rawdon Dr. LS19: Yead 6D 8	Redhouse La. LS29: Men 2C 6	Richmond St. LS9: Leeds 6H 5 (6A 32)
Rawdon Hall Dr. LS19: Yead 6D 8	Red La. LS28: Pud 2E 27	Richmond Ter. LS20: Guis 4F 7
Rawdon Pk. LS19: Yead 4D 8	Red Lodge Cl. LS8: Leeds 1F 33	LS28: Pud 6A 28
Rawdon Rd. LS18: H'fth, Yead 1G 17	Redmire Ct. LS14: Leeds 1A 34	Rickard St. LS12: Leeds 1D 40
Rawfolds Av. WF17: Bat 6H 47	Redmire Dr. LS14: Leeds 1A 34	Rider Rd. LS6: Leeds 1F 31
Rawling Way LS6: Leeds 6E 21	Redmire St. BD3: B'frd 6A 26	Rider St. LS9: Leeds 5A 32
Rawson Av. BD3: B'frd 5A 26	Redmire Vw. LS14: Leeds 1A 34	Ridge Cl. LS20: Guis 6E 21
Rawson Pl. LS11: Leeds 4G 41	Redshaw Rd. LS12: Leeds 1A 40	Ridge Gro. LS7: Leeds 6E 21
Rawson Ter. LS11: Leeds 4G 41	Red Va. BD19: Cleck 6D 46	Ridge Mt. LS6: Leeds 1E 31
Raygill Cl. LS17: Leeds 4D 14	Redvers Cl. LS16: Leeds 2G 19	Ridge Rd. LS7: Leeds 1F 31
Raylands Cl. LS10: Leeds 3B 52	Redwald Dr. LS20: Guis 4F 7	Ridge Ter. LS6: Leeds 6C 20
Raylands Ct. LS10: Leeds 3B 52	Redwood Av. WF3: E Ard 3E 57	Ridge Vw. LS13: Leeds 5C 28
Raylands Fold LS10: Leeds 3B 52	Redwood Cl. LS19: Yead 6H 7	Ridge Way LS8: Leeds 5B 22
Raylands Gth. LS10: Leeds 3B 52	LS26: Rothw 3E 55	Ridge Way Cl. LS8: Leeds 5B 22
Raylands La. LS10: Leeds 3B 52	Redwood Gro. LS19: Yead 6H 7	Ridgeway LS20: Guis 5D 6
Raylands Pl. LS10: Leeds 3B 52	Redwood Way LS19: Yead 6H 7	Ridgeway Ter. LS6: Leeds 1E 31
Raylands Rd. LS10: Leeds 3B 52	Reedling Dr. LS27: Morl 6A 50	(off Delph La.)
Raylands Way LS10: Leeds 4A 52	Reed Rd. LS12: Leeds 1B 40	Ridings Cl. WF3: Wake 5D 58
Raynel App. LS16: Leeds 6G 11	Reedsdale Av. LS27: Morl 2C 48	Ridings Ct. WF3: Wake 5D 58
Raynel Cl. LS16: Leeds 5F 11	Reedsdale Dr. LS27: Morl 2C 48	Ridings Gdns. WF3: Wake 5D 58
Raynel Dr. LS16: Leeds 6G 11	Reedsdale Gdns. LS27: Morl 2C 48	Ridings La. WF3: Wake 5D 58
Raynel Gdns. LS16: Leeds 5G 11	Regal Pde. LS15: Leeds 3B 34	Ridings M. WF3: Wake 5D 58
Raynel Grn. LS16: Leeds 6G 11	Regency Ct. LS6: Leeds 1C 30	Ridings Way WF3: Wake 5D 58
Raynel Mt. LS16: Leeds 5G 11	Regency Gdns. WF3: E Ard 3E 57	Rigton App. LS9: Leeds 5A 32
Raynel Way LS16: Leeds 5F 11	Regency Pk. Gro. LS28: Pud 2G 37	Rigton Cl. LS9: Leeds 5B 32
Raynor Ter. LS28: Pud 5H 27	Regency Pk. Rd. LS28: Pud 2G 37	Rigton Dr. LS9: Leeds 5A 32
Raynville App. LS13: Leeds 3E 29	Regent Av. LS18: H'fth 4C 18	Rigton Grn. LS9: Leeds 5A 32
Raynville Av. LS13: Leeds 2E 29	Regent Cl. LS18: H'fth 4C 18	Rigton Lawn LS9: Leeds 5A 32
Raynville Cl. LS13: Leeds 2E 29	Regent Ct. LS1: Leeds 5F 5	Rigton M. LS9: Leeds 5A 32
Raynville Ct. LS12: Leeds 3F 29	LS18: H'fth 4C 18	Rillbank La. LS3: Leeds 4D 30
LS13: Leeds 3E 29	Regent Cres. LS18: H'fth 4B 18	Rillbank St. LS3: Leeds 4D 30
Raynville Cres. LS13: Leeds 3F 29	Regent Pk. Av. LS6: Leeds 1D 30	(off Rillbank La.)
Raynville Dene LS12: Leeds 2F 29	Regent Pk. Cross Av. LS6: Leeds 1D 30	Rillington Mead BD10: B'frd 5A 16
Raynville Dr. LS13: Leeds 2E 29	(off Regent Pk. Av.)	Rimswell Holt BD10: B'frd 5A 16
Raynville Gdns. LS12: Leeds 3F 29	Regent Pk. Ter. LS6: Leeds 1D 30	Ring Hay Rd. BD4: B'frd 6C 36
Raynville Gth. LS12: Leeds 3F 29	Regent Rd. LS18: H'fth 4B 18	Ring Rd. Adel LS16: Leeds 1B 20
Raynville Grange LS13: Leeds 3E 29	Regent St. LS2: Leeds 3H 5 (5H 31)	Ring Rd. Beeston LS12: Leeds 3A 40
(off Raynville Rd.)	LS7: Leeds 3H 5 (4H 21)	Ring Rd. Beeston Pk. LS10: Leeds 1D 50
Raynville Grn. LS13: Leeds 3E 29	Regent Ter. LS6: Leeds 3D 30	LS11: Leeds 1E 51
Raynville Gro. LS13: Leeds 2E 29	LS7: Leeds 4H 21	Ring Rd. Bramley LS13: Leeds 5D 28
Raynville Mt. LS13: Leeds 3E 29	Regina Dr. LS7: Leeds 5H 21	Ring Rd. Cross Gates LS15: Leeds 2C 34
Raynville Pl. LS13: Leeds 3E 29	Regina Ho. LS13: Leeds 5D 28	Ring Rd. Farnley LS12: Leeds 5D 28
Raynville Ri. LS13: Leeds 3E 29	Reginald Mt. LS7: Leeds 1H 31	Ring Rd. Farsley LS13: Leeds, Pud 3D 26
Raynville Rd. LS12: Leeds 2E 29	Reginald Pl. LS7: Leeds 1H 31	LS28: Pud 3D 26
LS13: Leeds 2D 28	Reginald Row LS7: Leeds 1H 31	Ring Rd. Halton LS15: Leeds 4C 34
Raynville St. LS13: Leeds 2E 29	Reginald St. LS7: Leeds 1H 31	Ring Rd. Horsforth LS16: Leeds 3E 19
Raynville Ter. LS13: Leeds 2E 29	Reginald Ter. LS7: Leeds 1H 31	LS18: H'fth, Leeds 3E 19
Raynville Wlk. LS13: Leeds 3E 29	Reginald Vw. LS7: Leeds 1H 31	Ring Rd. Lwr. Wortley LS12: Leeds 1F 39
Raynville Way LS12: Leeds 3F 29	Reighton Cft. BD10: B'frd 5A 16	Ring Rd. Meanwood LS6: Leeds 1C 20
Raywood Cl. LS19: Yead 1C 8	Rein, The LS14: Leeds 5H 23	LS16: Leeds 1C 20
	Rein Gdns. WF3: E Ard 3A 56	LS17: Leeds 1C 20

Ring Rd. Middleton—Royds Gro.

Ring Rd. Middleton LS10: Leeds .4H 51
Ring Rd. Moortown LS6: Leeds .1E 21
LS17: Leeds .1E 21
Ring Rd. Seacroft LS14: Leeds .3H 23
Ring Rd. Shadwell LS17: Leeds .6E 15
Ring Rd. Weetwood LS16: Leeds .2H 19
Ring Rd. W. Pk. LS16: Leeds .2F 19
Ringwood Av. LS14: Leeds .3H 23
Ringwood Ct. WF1: Wake .6F 59
Ringwood Cres. LS14: Leeds .2A 24
Ringwood Dr. LS14: Leeds .3A 24
Ringwood Gdns. LS14: Leeds .3A 24
Ringwood Mt. LS14: Leeds .3A 24
Ripley La. LS20: Guis .2G 7
Ripon Ho. LS28: Pud .2F 27
Rise, The LS5: Leeds .6G 19
Riverside Ct. LS1: Leeds .6F 5 (6G 31)
Riverside Way LS1: Leeds .6B 4 (6E 31)
River Vw. LS18: H'fth .2B 18
Riviera Gdns. LS7: Leeds .5G 21
Roans Brae BD10: B'frd .5A 16
Robb Av. LS11: Leeds .6E 41
Robb St. LS11: Leeds .6E 41
Robert Ho. *LS27: Morl .4H 49*
(off Pullman Ct.)
Roberts Av. LS9: Leeds .3D 32
Roberts Ct. LS9: Leeds .3D 32
Robertsgate WF3: Rothw .2D 58
Robertsgate Sq. *WF3: Rothw .2D 58*
(off Robertsgate)
Roberts Pl. LS9: Leeds .4D 32
Roberts St. LS26: Rothw .3C 54
Roberts Wharf LS9: Leeds .6H 5 (1A 42)
Robin Chase LS28: Pud .6H 27
ROBIN HOOD .6D 52
Robin La. LS28: Pud .6G 27
Robin's Gro. LS26: Rothw .4H 53
Robinwood Ct. LS8: Leeds .2C 22
Rocheford Cl. LS10: Leeds .4B 42
Rocheford Ct. LS10: Leeds .4B 42
Rocheford Gdns. LS10: Leeds .4B 42
Rocheford Gro. LS10: Leeds .4B 42
Rocheford Wlk. LS10: Leeds .4B 42
Rochester Gdns. LS13: Leeds .1H 27
Rochester Rd. WF17: Bat .6G 47
Rochester Ter. LS6: Leeds .1B 30
Rochester Wynd LS17: Leeds .5C 14
Rock Ct. LS27: Morl .4H 49
Rockery Cft. LS18: H'fth .1C 18
Rockery Rd. LS18: H'fth .1C 18
Rockfield *LS19: Yead .2E 9*
(off Rockfield Ter.)
Rockfield Ter. LS19: Yead .2E 9
Rockingham Cl. LS15: Leeds .2F 35
Rockingham Rd. LS15: Leeds .2F 35
Rockingham Way LS15: Leeds .2F 35
Rock La. LS13: Leeds .1B 28
Rockley Hall Yd. LS1: Leeds .4F 5
Rock Ter. LS15: Leeds .5H 33
LS27: Morl .4H 49
WF12: Dew .5A 56
Rockville Ter. *LS19: Yead .3E 9*
(off South Vw. Ter.)
Rockwood Cres. LS28: Pud .3C 26
Rockwood Gro. LS28: Pud .2D 26
Rockwood Hill Ct. LS28: Pud .3C 26
Rockwood Rd. LS28: Pud .3C 26
Roderick St. LS12: Leeds .6H 29
RODLEY .6G 17
Rodley La. LS13: Leeds .1A 28
(Airedale Quay)
LS13: Leeds .5E 17
(Brookfield Av.)
LS28: Leeds, Pud .5E 17
Rods Vw. LS27: Morl .6H 49
Rogers Ct. WF3: Wake .5H 59
Rogers Pl. LS28: Pud .5H 27
Rokeby Gdns. BD10: B'frd .5A 16
LS6: Leeds .6A 20
Roker La. LS28: Pud .2H 37
ROKER LANE BOTTOM .3A 38
Roman Av. LS8: Leeds .1C 22
Romanby Shaw BD10: B'frd .5A 16
Roman Ct. LS8: Leeds .1D 22
Roman Cres. LS8: Leeds .1D 22
Roman Dr. LS8: Leeds .1D 22
Roman Gdns. LS8: Leeds .1C 22
Roman Gro. LS8: Leeds .1C 22
Roman Mt. LS8: Leeds .1D 22
Roman Pl. LS8: Leeds .1D 22
Roman Ter. LS8: Leeds .1C 22
Roman Vw. LS8: Leeds .1D 22
Rombalds Av. LS12: Leeds .5A 30
Rombalds Ct. LS29: Men .1B 6
Rombalds Cres. LS12: Leeds .4A 30
Rombalds Cft. LS19: Yead .2D 8
Rombalds Gro. LS12: Leeds .5A 30
Rombalds Pl. LS12: Leeds .4A 30
Rombalds St. LS12: Leeds .4A 30
Rombalds Ter. LS12: Leeds .5A 30
Rombalds Vw. LS12: Leeds .4A 30
Romford Av. LS27: Morl .6G 49
Romney Mt. LS28: Pud .2A 38
Romsey Gdns. BD4: B'frd .4A 36
Romsey M. BD4: B'frd .4A 36
Rona Cft. LS26: Rothw .4A 54
Rook's Nest Rd. WF1: Wake .6F 59
WF3: Wake .6F 59
Rookwith Pde. BD10: B'frd .5A 16
Rookwood Av. LS9: Leeds .5E 33
Rookwood Cres. LS9: Leeds .5E 33
Rookwood Cft. LS9: Leeds .6E 33
Rookwood Gdns. LS9: Leeds .5E 33
Rookwood Hill LS9: Leeds .5E 33
Rookwood Mt. LS9: Leeds .5E 33
Rookwood Pde. LS9: Leeds .5F 33
Rookwood Pl. LS9: Leeds .5E 33
Rookwood Rd. LS9: Leeds .5E 33
Rookwood Sq. LS9: Leeds .5F 33
Rookwood St. LS9: Leeds .6E 33
Rookwood Ter. LS9: Leeds .5E 33
Rookwood Va. LS9: Leeds .6E 33
Rookwood Vw. LS9: Leeds .5E 33
Rookwood Wlk. LS9: Leeds .5E 33
ROOMS .1F 49
Rooms Fold LS27: Morl .3G 49
Rooms La. LS27: Morl .1F 49
Rooms Way LS27: Morl .2F 49
Roper Av. LS8: Leeds .3B 22
Roper Gro. LS8: Leeds .3B 22
Roscoe St. LS7: Leeds .3H 31
Roscoe Ter. LS12: Leeds .6H 29
Roseate Grn. LS27: Morl .6A 50
Rose Av. LS18: H'fth .4B 18
Rosebank Cres. LS3: Leeds .3D 30
Rosebank Gdns. LS3: Leeds .4D 30
Rosebank Ho. LS3: Leeds .3D 30
Rosebank Rd. LS3: Leeds .4D 30
Rosebank Row LS3: Leeds .4D 30
Rosebery St. LS28: Pud .5E 27
Rosebery Ter. LS28: Pud .3H 27
Rosebud Wlk. LS8: Leeds .3A 32
Rosecliffe Mt. LS13: Leeds .2B 28
Rosecliffe Ter. LS13: Leeds .3C 28
Rosedale LS26: Rothw .3H 53
Rosedale Bank LS10: Leeds .6H 41
Rosedale Ct. BD4: B'frd .2A 46
WF3: E Ard .5C 56
Rosedale Dr. WF3: E Ard .5C 56
Rosedale Gdns. LS10: Leeds .6H 41
(not continuous)
WF3: E Ard .3F 57
Rosedale Grn. LS10: Leeds .6H 41
Rosedale Wlk. LS10: Leeds .6H 41
Rose Gro. LS26: Rothw .3F 53
Rosemary Av. *LS12: Leeds .6B 30*
(off Armley Gro. Pl.)
Rosemont Av. LS13: Leeds .3C 28
LS28: Pud .5H 27
Rosemont Dr. LS28: Pud .5H 27
Rosemont Gro. LS13: Leeds .3B 28
Rosemont Pl. LS13: Leeds .3C 28
Rosemont Rd. LS13: Leeds .3C 28
Rosemont St. LS13: Leeds .3C 28
LS28: Pud .5H 27
Rosemont Ter. LS13: Leeds .3C 28
LS28: Pud .5H 27
Rosemont Vw. LS13: Leeds .3B 28
Rosemont Vs. LS28: Pud .5H 27
Rosemont Wlk. LS13: Leeds .3C 28
Rose Mt. BD4: B'frd .1C 46
Rosemount *LS7: Leeds .5G 21*
(off Henconner La.)
Rose Mt. Pl. LS12: Leeds .1B 40
Roseneath Pl. LS12: Leeds .1B 40
Roseneath St. LS12: Leeds .1B 40
Roseneath Ter. LS12: Leeds .1B 40
Rose St. LS18: H'fth .3B 18
Rose Ter. LS18: H'fth .3A 18
Roseville Rd. LS8: Leeds .1H 5 (3A 32)
Roseville St. LS8: Leeds .3A 32
Roseville Ter. *LS15: Leeds .2D 34*
(off Church La.)
Roseville Way LS8: Leeds .3A 32
Rosewood Ct. *LS17: Leeds .6E 13*
(off Cranmer Cl.)
Rosewood Ct. LS26: Rothw .2H 53
Rosgill Dr. LS14: Leeds .6H 23
Rosgill Grn. LS14: Leeds .6A 24
Rosgill Wlk. LS14: Leeds .6H 23
Rossall Rd. LS8: Leeds .1B 32
Rossefield App. LS13: Leeds .4D 28
Rossefield Av. LS13: Leeds .3D 28
Rossefield Chase LS13: Leeds .3D 28
Rossefield Cl. LS13: Leeds .3D 28
Rossefield Dr. LS13: Leeds .3D 28
Rossefield Gdns. LS13: Leeds .3D 28
Rossefield Gth. LS13: Leeds .3D 28
Rossefield Grn. *LS13: Leeds .3D 28*
(off Rossefield Dr.)
Rossefield Gro. LS13: Leeds .3D 28
Rossefield Lawn LS13: Leeds .3D 28
Rossefield Pde. *LS13: Leeds .3D 28*
(off Rossefield Gro.)
Rossefield Pl. LS13: Leeds .3D 28
Rossefield Ter. LS13: Leeds .3D 28
Rossefield Vw. LS13: Leeds .3D 28
Rossefield Wlk. LS13: Leeds .3D 28
Rossefield Way LS13: Leeds .3D 28
Rossett Bus. Pk. LS13: Leeds .1B 28
Ross Gro. LS13: Leeds .1A 28
Rossington Gro. LS8: Leeds .1A 32
Rossington Pl. LS8: Leeds .1A 32
Rossington Rd. LS8: Leeds .6C 22
Rossington St. LS2: Leeds .3D 4 (5F 31)
Ross Ter. LS13: Leeds .1A 28
Rothbury Gdns. LS16: Leeds .6H 11
ROTHWELL .4G 53
ROTHWELL HAIGH .3F 53
Rothwell La. LS26: Rothw .3A 54
Rothwell Sports Cen. .5C 54
ROUNDHAY .2C 22
Roundhay Av. LS8: Leeds .6B 22
Roundhay Cres. LS8: Leeds .6B 22
Roundhay Gdns. LS8: Leeds .6B 22
Roundhay Gro. LS8: Leeds .6B 22
Roundhay Mt. LS8: Leeds .6B 22
Roundhay Pk. Cvn. & Camping Site
LS8: Leeds .3F 23
Roundhay Pk. La. LS17: Leeds .4D 14
Roundhay Pl. LS8: Leeds .6B 22
Roundhay Rd. LS7: Leeds .3H 31
LS8: Leeds .1C 32
Roundhay Vw. LS8: Leeds .6B 22
Roundhead Fold BD10: B'frd .3A 16
Roundhouse Bus. Pk. LS12: Leeds .6A 4 (6D 30)
Roundway, The LS27: Morl .5E 49
Roundwood Av. BD10: B'frd .6A 16
Roundwood Glen BD10: B'frd .4A 16
Roundwood Vw. BD10: B'frd .5A 16
Row, The LS19: Yead .5C 8
Rowan Av. BD3: B'frd .6A 26
Rowan Ct. LS19: Yead .4D 8
LS26: Rothw .3E 55
Rowans, The LS13: Leeds .2H 27
Rowanwood Gdns. BD10: B'frd .6A 16
Rowland Pl. LS11: Leeds .4F 41
Rowland Rd. LS11: Leeds .4F 41
Rowland Ter. LS11: Leeds .4F 41
Rowlestone Ri. BD10: B'frd .5A 16
Rowton Thorpe BD10: B'frd .5A 16
Roxby Cl. LS9: Leeds .4A 32
Roxholme Av. LS7: Leeds .6A 22
Roxholme Gro. LS7: Leeds .6A 22
Roxholme Pl. LS7: Leeds .6A 22
Roxholme Rd. LS7: Leeds .6A 22
Roxholme Ter. LS7: Leeds .6A 22
Royal Armouries Mus., The .6H 5 (1H 41)
Royal Cl. LS10: Leeds .5H 41
Royal Ct. LS10: Leeds .5H 41
Royal Dr. LS10: Leeds .5H 41
Royal Gdns. LS10: Leeds .5H 41
Royal Gro. LS10: Leeds .5H 41
Royal London Ind. Est., The LS11: Leeds .6D 40
Royal Pk. Av. LS6: Leeds .3D 30
Royal Pk. Gro. LS6: Leeds .2D 30
Royal Pk. Mt. LS6: Leeds .2D 30
Royal Pk. Rd. LS6: Leeds .3C 30
Royal Pk. Ter. LS6: Leeds .3D 30
Royal Pk. Vw. LS6: Leeds .2D 30
Royal Pl. LS10: Leeds .5H 41
Royd Moor Rd. BD4: B'frd .6B 36
Royds Av. BD11: B'frd .4D 46
Royds Cl. LS12: Leeds .3A 40
Royds Ct. *LS26: Rothw .4H 53*
(off Marsh St.)
Royds Farm Rd. LS12: Leeds .5A 40
ROYDS GREEN .6B 54
Royds Gro. WF1: Wake .6E 59

A-Z Leeds 99

Royds Hall Rd. LS12: Leeds	.3A **40**
Royds La. LS12: Leeds	.3A **40**
LS26: Rothw	.5H **53**
Royds Pk. LS12: Leeds	.3A **40**
Roydstone Rd. BD3: B'frd	.5A **26**
Royd Vw. LS28: Pud	.1E **37**
Royd Well BD11: B'frd	.4D **46**
Royston Cl. WF3: E Ard	.5H **57**
Royston Hill WF3: E Ard	.5H **57**
Ruby St. LS9: Leeds	.1H **5** (4A **32**)
Rufford Av. LS19: Yead	.3D **8**
Rufford Bank LS19: Yead	.3E **9**
Rufford Cl. LS19: Yead	.3E **9**
Rufford Cres. LS19: Yead	.3E **9**
Rufford Dr. LS19: Yead	.3E **9**
Rufford Gdns. LS19: Yead	.3D **8**
RUFFORD PARK	.3D **8**
Rufford Ridge LS19: Yead	.3E **9**
Rufford Ri. LS19: Yead	.3D **8**
Rugby League Hall of Fame	.5C **54**
Rugby Training Cen.	.2G **29**
Runswick Av. LS11: Leeds	.2D **40**
Runswick Pl. LS11: Leeds	.2D **40**
Runswick St. LS11: Leeds	.2D **40**
Runswick Ter. LS11: Leeds	.2E **41**
Rushmoor Rd. BD4: B'frd	.5A **26**
Rusholme Dr. LS28: Pud	.2E **27**
Rushton Av. BD3: B'frd	.5A **26**
Rushton Rd. BD3: B'frd	.5A **26**
Rushton St. LS28: Pud	.5D **16**
Rushton Ter. BD3: B'frd	.6A **26**
Rushworth Cl. WF3: Wake	.6G **59**
Ruskin Cres. LS20: Guis	.5H **7**
Ruskin St. LS28: Pud	.4E **27**
Russell Gro. BD11: B'frd	.4D **46**
LS8: Leeds	.1B **32**
Russell St. LS1: Leeds	.4D **4** (5F **31**)
Ruswarp Cres.	
BD10: B'frd	.5A **16**
Ruthven Vw. LS8: Leeds	.2C **32**
Rutland Cl. LS26: Rothw	.3D **54**
Rutland Ct. LS28: Pud	.5G **27**
(off Richardshaw La.)	
Rutland Mt. LS3: Leeds	.3A **4** (5D **30**)
Rutland St. LS3: Leeds	.3A **4** (5E **31**)
Rutland Ter. LS3: Leeds	.3A **4** (5D **30**)
Ryan Pl. LS8: Leeds	.1C **32**
Rycroft Av. LS13: Leeds	.4A **28**
Rycroft Cl. LS13: Leeds	.4B **28**
Rycroft Ct. LS13: Leeds	.4B **28**
Rycroft Dr. LS13: Leeds	.4B **28**
Rycroft Pl. LS13: Leeds	.4B **28**
Rycroft Grn. LS13: Leeds	.4B **28**
Rycroft Sq. LS13: Leeds	.4A **28**
Rycroft Towers LS13: Leeds	.4A **28**
Rydal Cres. LS27: Morl	.4B **50**
Rydal Dr. LS27: Morl	.4B **50**
Rydall Pl. LS11: Leeds	.2D **40**
Rydall St. LS11: Leeds	.2D **40**
Rydall Ter. LS11: Leeds	.2D **40**
Ryder Gdns. LS8: Leeds	.4C **22**
Ryecroft Cl. WF1: Wake	.6E **59**
Ryedale Av. LS12: Leeds	.3H **39**
Ryedale Ct. LS14: Leeds	.6H **23**
Ryedale Holt LS12: Leeds	.2A **40**
Ryedale Way WF3: E Ard	.3C **56**
Rye Pl. LS14: Leeds	.4H **33**
Ryton Dale BD10: B'frd	.5A **16**

S

Sackville App. LS7: Leeds	.2G **31**
Sackville St. LS7: Leeds	.1G **31**
Sadler Cl. LS16: Leeds	.5A **12**
Sadler Copse LS16: Leeds	.5A **12**
Sadler Way LS16: Leeds	.5A **12**
Sagar Pl. LS6: Leeds	.1B **30**
St Alban App. LS9: Leeds	.4E **33**
St Alban Cl. LS9: Leeds	.4E **33**
St Alban Ct. LS9: Leeds	.4E **33**
St Alban Cres. LS9: Leeds	.4E **33**
St Alban Gro. LS9: Leeds	.4E **33**
St Alban Mt. LS9: Leeds	.4E **33**
St Alban Rd. LS9: Leeds	.4E **33**
St Alban's Pl. LS2: Leeds	.2F **5** (4G **31**)
St Alban Vw. LS9: Leeds	.4E **33**
St Andrews Av. LS27: Morl	.6E **49**
St Andrews Cl. LS13: Leeds	.6G **17**
LS19: Yead	.1E **9**
LS27: Morl	.6E **49**
St Andrew's Ct. LS3: Leeds	.5D **30**
(off Cavendish St.)	

St Andrew's Ct. LS19: Yead	.1D **8**
(off St Andrew's Rd.)	
St Andrew's Cft. LS17: Leeds	.5F **13**
St Andrew's Dr. LS17: Leeds	.5G **13**
St Andrews Gro. LS27: Morl	.6F **49**
St Andrews Pl. LS3: Leeds	.5D **30**
St Andrew's Rd. LS19: Yead	.2E **9**
St Andrew's St. LS3: Leeds	.5D **30**
St Andrews Ter. LS27: Morl	.6F **49**
St Andrew's Wlk. LS17: Leeds	.5G **13**
St Annes Ct. LS5: Leeds	.1A **30**
St Anne's Dr. LS4: Leeds	.1A **30**
St Annes Pl. LS5: Leeds	.1H **29**
St Anne's Rd. LS6: Leeds	.6A **20**
St Anne's Roman Catholic Cathedral	
	.3D **4** (5F **31**)
St Anne's St. LS2: Leeds	.3D **4** (5F **31**)
St Ann's Av. LS4: Leeds	.3B **30**
St Ann's Cl. LS4: Leeds	.2A **30**
St Ann's Gdns. LS4: Leeds	.2A **30**
St Ann's Grn. LS4: Leeds	.1A **30**
St Ann's La. LS4: Leeds	.1A **30**
St Ann's Mt. LS4: Leeds	.2B **30**
St Ann's Ri. LS4: Leeds	.2H **29**
St Ann's Sq. LS4: Leeds	.2A **30**
LS9: Leeds	.5A **32**
(off Shannon St.)	
St Ann's Way LS4: Leeds	.2A **30**
St Anthony's Dr. LS11: Leeds	.5D **40**
St Anthony's Rd. LS11: Leeds	.5C **40**
St Anthony's Ter. LS11: Leeds	.6C **40**
St Augustines Ct. LS8: Leeds	.2B **32**
(off Harehills Pl.)	
St Barnabas Rd. LS11: Leeds	.1F **41**
St Bartholomews Cl. LS12: Leeds	.6A **30**
St Benedicts Chase LS13: Leeds	.6D **18**
St Benedicts Dr. LS13: Leeds	.6E **19**
St Benedicts Gdns. LS13: Leeds	.6E **19**
St Catherine's Bus. Complex	
LS13: Leeds	.1D **28**
(off Broad La.)	
St Catherines Cres. LS13: Leeds	.1D **28**
St Catherine's Dr. LS13: Leeds	.1D **28**
St Catherines Grn. LS13: Leeds	.1D **28**
St Catherine's Hill LS13: Leeds	.1D **28**
St Catherines Wlk. LS8: Leeds	.5C **22**
St Cecilia St. LS2: Leeds	.4H **5** (5H **31**)
St Chad's Av. LS6: Leeds	.5A **20**
St Chad's Dr. LS6: Leeds	.5A **20**
St Chad's Gro. LS6: Leeds	.5A **20**
St Chads Pde. LS16: Leeds	.5B **20**
St Chad's Ri. LS6: Leeds	.5A **20**
St Chads Rd. LS16: Leeds	.5B **20**
St Chad's Vw. LS6: Leeds	.6A **20**
St Christopher's Av. LS26: Rothw	.4H **53**
St Clements Av. LS26: Rothw	.5G **53**
St Clements Cl. LS26: Rothw	.5F **53**
St Clements Ri. LS26: Rothw	.4F **53**
St Cyprian's Gdns. LS9: Leeds	.3D **32**
St Davids Cl. WF3: Rothw	.1D **58**
St Davids Gth. WF3: Rothw	.1D **58**
St Davids Rd. WF3: Rothw	.1D **58**
St Edmunds Cl. LS8: Leeds	.1C **22**
St Elmo Gro. LS9: Leeds	.5C **32**
St Francis Pl. LS11: Leeds	.1F **41**
St Gabriels Ct. LS18: H'fth	.5B **10**
ST GEMMA'S HOSPICE	.1H **21**
St George's Av. LS26: Rothw	.2E **53**
St George's Cres. LS26: Rothw	.2E **53**
St Georges Rd. LS1: Leeds	.2C **4** (4F **31**)
LS10: Leeds	.4H **51**
St Helenas Cvn. Pk. LS18: H'fth	.1C **10**
St Helens Av. LS16: Leeds	.6B **12**
St Helens Cl. LS16: Leeds	.6B **12**
(not continuous)	
St Helens Cft. LS16: Leeds	.6A **12**
St Helens Gdns. LS16: Leeds	.6A **12**
St Helens Gro. LS16: Leeds	.6A **12**
St Helens La. LS16: Leeds	.6H **11**
St Helen's St. LS10: Leeds	.2H **41**
St Helens Way LS16: Leeds	.6B **12**
St Hilda's Av. LS9: Leeds	.1B **42**
St Hilda's Cres. LS9: Leeds	.1B **42**
St Hilda's Gro. LS9: Leeds	.1B **42**
St Hilda's Mt. LS9: Leeds	.1B **42**
St Hilda's Pl. LS9: Leeds	.1B **42**
St Hilda's Rd. LS9: Leeds	.1B **42**
St Hilda's Ter. BD3: B'frd	.5A **26**
St Hughes Lodge LS12: Leeds	.5A **30**
(off Armley Lodge Rd.)	
St Ives Gro. LS12: Leeds	.5G **29**
St Ives Mt. LS12: Leeds	.5G **29**
St James App. LS14: Leeds	.1A **34**

St James Av. LS18: H'fth	.2C **18**
St James Cl. LS12: Leeds	.5F **29**
St James Cres. LS28: Pud	.6D **26**
St James Dr. LS18: H'fth	.2D **18**
St James M. LS12: Leeds	.2D **18**
LS15: Leeds	.2D **34**
St James's Ct. LS9: Leeds	.3A **32**
ST JAMES'S UNIVERSITY HOSPITAL	.3B **32**
St James Ter. LS18: H'fth	.2D **18**
St James Wlk. LS18: H'fth	.2D **18**
St John's Av. LS6: Leeds	.3D **30**
LS28: Pud	.3F **27**
St John's Cen. LS2: Leeds	.3E **5** (5G **31**)
St John's Cl. LS6: Leeds	.3D **30**
St John's Ct. LS7: Leeds	.1H **31**
LS19: Yead	.3C **8**
St John's Dr. LS19: Yead	.3C **8**
St John's Gro. LS6: Leeds	.3D **30**
St John's Pk. LS29: Men	.1B **6**
St John's Pl. BD11: B'frd	.3C **46**
LS5: Leeds	.1H **29**
(off Kirkstall La.)	
St John's Rd. LS3: Leeds	.2A **4** (4D **30**)
LS19: Yead	.3C **8**
St John's St. LS26: Rothw	.4C **54**
St John's Ter. LS3: Leeds	.3D **30**
St Johns Wlk. LS26: Swil	.6H **45**
St John's Way LS19: Yead	.3C **8**
St John's Yd. LS26: Rothw	.4C **54**
St Joseph's Ct. LS19: Yead	.1D **16**
St Lawrence Cl. LS28: Pud	.6F **27**
St Lawrence St. LS7: Leeds	.5H **21**
St Lawrence Ter. LS28: Pud	.6G **27**
St Luke's Cres. LS11: Leeds	.3E **41**
St Luke's Grn. LS11: Leeds	.3E **41**
St Luke's Rd. LS11: Leeds	.3E **41**
St Luke's St. LS11: Leeds	.3E **41**
St Luke's Vw. LS11: Leeds	.3E **41**
St Margaret's Av. LS8: Leeds	.5C **22**
LS18: H'fth	.2B **18**
St Margaret's Cl. LS18: H'fth	.1B **18**
St Margaret's Dr. LS8: Leeds	.5C **22**
LS18: H'fth	.1B **18**
St Margaret's Gro. LS8: Leeds	.5C **22**
St Margaret's Rd. LS18: H'fth	.1B **18**
St Margaret's Vw. LS8: Leeds	.5C **22**
St Mark's Av. LS2: Leeds	.3E **31**
St Mark's Flats LS2: Leeds	.2E **31**
(off Low Cl. St.)	
St Mark's Ho. LS2: Leeds	.2F **31**
St Mark's Rd. LS2: Leeds	.3F **31**
LS6: Leeds	.2E **31**
(not continuous)	
St Mark's St. LS2: Leeds	.3E **31**
St Martin's Av. LS7: Leeds	.6G **21**
St Martins Ct. WF3: Rothw	.1D **58**
St Martin's Cres. LS7: Leeds	.6H **21**
St Martin's Dr. LS7: Leeds	.5H **21**
St Martins Fold WF3: Rothw	.1D **58**
St Martin's Gdns. LS7: Leeds	.6G **21**
St Martin's Gro. LS7: Leeds	.6H **21**
St Martin's Rd. LS7: Leeds	.6H **21**
St Martin's Ter. LS7: Leeds	.6H **21**
St Martin's Vw. LS7: Leeds	.6H **21**
St Mary's Av. LS26: Swil	.6G **45**
St Mary's Cl. LS7: Leeds	.6H **21**
LS12: Leeds	.1B **40**
WF3: E Ard	.4A **56**
St Mary's Ct. LS7: Leeds	.6H **21**
ST MARY'S HOSPITAL	.5F **29**
St Mary's Pk. App. LS12: Leeds	.5F **29**
St Mary's Pk. Cl. LS12: Leeds	.5F **29**
St Mary's Pk. Cres.	
LS12: Leeds	.5F **29**
St Mary's Pk. Grn. LS12: Leeds	.5F **29**
St Mary's Rd. LS7: Leeds	.6H **21**
St Mary's Sq. LS27: Morl	.5A **49**
St Mary's St. LS9: Leeds	.3H **5** (5H **31**)
St Matthew's St. LS11: Leeds	.2E **41**
St Matthews Wlk. LS7: Leeds	.3G **21**
St Matthias Cl. LS4: Leeds	.3B **30**
St Matthias Gro. LS4: Leeds	.3B **30**
St Matthias St. LS4: Leeds	.4B **30**
(not continuous)	
St Matthias Ter. LS4: Leeds	.3B **30**
St Michael Ct. LS13: Leeds	.2C **28**
St Michael's Ct. LS6: Leeds	.6B **20**
St Michael's Cres. LS6: Leeds	.1B **30**
St Michael's Gro. LS6: Leeds	.1B **30**
St Michael's La. LS4: Leeds	.2A **30**
LS6: Leeds	.1B **30**
St Michael's Rd. LS6: Leeds	.1B **30**
St Michael's Ter. LS6: Leeds	.1B **30**

St Michael's Vs.—Seventh Av.

St Michael's Vs. *LS6: Leeds* *1B* **30**
(off St Michael's Cres.)
St Oswald's Gth. LS20: Guis 4H **7**
St Oswald's Ter. LS20: Guis 4G **7**
St Paul's Av. BD11: B'frd 4D **46**
St Paul's Pl. LS1: Leeds 4C **4** (5F **31**)
St Paul's Rd. BD11: B'frd 4D **46**
St Paul's St. LS1: Leeds 4B **4** (5E **31**)
LS27: Morl 6H **49**
St Peter's Av. LS26: Rothw 4H **53**
St Peter's Bldgs. LS9: Leeds 4H **5** (6H **31**)
St Peter's Ct. LS11: Leeds 3G **41**
LS13: Leeds 2D **28**
St Peter's Cres. LS27: Morl 3G **49**
St Peter's Gdns. LS13: Leeds 2C **28**
St Peter's Mt. LS13: Leeds 3D **28**
St Peter's Pl. LS9: Leeds 4H **5** (5H **31**)
St Peter's Sq. LS9: Leeds 4H **5** (5H **31**)
St Peter's St. LS2: Leeds 4G **5** (5H **31**)
St Peter's Way LS29: Men 1B **6**
St Philip's Av. LS10: Leeds 4F **51**
St Philip's Cl. LS10: Leeds 4F **51**
St Stephen's Ct. LS9: Leeds 5B **32**
St Stephen's Rd. LS9: Leeds 5B **32**
LS28: Pud 4C **16**
St Thomas Row LS2: Leeds 2G **5** (4H **31**)
St Vincent Rd. LS28: Pud 1G **37**
St Wilfrid's Av. LS8: Leeds 1C **32**
(not continuous)
St Wilfrid's Cir. LS8: Leeds 2D **32**
St Wilfrid's Cres. LS8: Leeds 1D **32**
St Wilfrid's Dr. LS8: Leeds 1C **32**
St Wilfrid's Gth. LS8: Leeds 2D **32**
St Wilfrid's Gro. LS8: Leeds 1C **32**
St Wilfrid's St. LS28: Pud 4D **16**
Salcombe Pl. BD4: B'frd 5A **36**
Salem Pl. LS10: Leeds 6F **5** (1G **41**)
Salisbury Av. LS12: Leeds 5A **30**
Salisbury Ct. LS18: H'fth 2D **18**
Salisbury Gro. LS12: Leeds 5A **30**
Salisbury M. LS18: H'fth 2D **18**
WF3: E Ard 2B **56**
Salisbury Pl. LS28: Pud 5C **16**
Salisbury Rd. LS12: Leeds 5A **30**
Salisbury St. LS19: Yead 5D **8**
LS28: Pud 5C **16**
Salisbury Ter. LS12: Leeds 5A **30**
Salisbury Vw. LS12: Leeds 5A **30**
LS18: H'fth 2D **18**
Salmon Cres. LS18: H'fth 2C **18**
Salters Gdn. *LS28: Pud* *6G* **27**
(off Crawshaw Rd.)
Samuel Dr. WF3: Wake 6G **59**
Sandacre Cl. BD10: B'frd 2A **26**
Sandbed Ct. LS15: Leeds 2D **34**
Sandbed La. LS15: Leeds 2D **34**
Sandbed Lawns LS15: Leeds 2D **34**
Sanderling Gth. LS10: Leeds 4H **51**
Sanderling Way LS10: Leeds 4H **51**
Sandfield Av. LS6: Leeds 5C **20**
Sandfield Gth. LS6: Leeds 5C **20**
Sandfield Vw. *LS6: Leeds* *5C* **20**
(off Sandfield Av.)
SANDFORD **1E 29**
Sandford Pl. LS5: Leeds 1G **29**
Sandford Rd. LS5: Leeds 2H **29**
Sandgate Wlk. BD4: B'frd 5B **36**
Sandhill Ct. LS17: Leeds 6H **13**
Sandhill Cres. LS17: Leeds 5A **14**
Sandhill Dr. LS17: Leeds 5H **13**
Sandhill Gro. LS17: Leeds 4A **14**
Sand Hill La. LS17: Leeds 6H **13**
Sandhill Lawns LS17: Leeds 6H **13**
Sandhill Mt. LS17: Leeds 4A **14**
Sandhill Oval LS17: Leeds 4A **14**
Sandhurst Av. LS8: Leeds 2C **32**
Sandhurst Gro. LS8: Leeds 2C **32**
Sandhurst Mt. LS8: Leeds 1C **32**
Sandhurst Pl. LS8: Leeds 2C **32**
Sandhurst Rd. LS8: Leeds 2C **32**
Sandhurst St. LS28: Pud 4C **16**
Sandhurst Ter. LS8: Leeds 2C **32**
Sandiford Cl. LS15: Leeds 2D **34**
Sandiford Ter. LS15: Leeds 2D **34**
Sandleas Way LS15: Leeds 3F **35**
Sandlewood Cl. LS11: Leeds 2E **41**
Sandlewood Ct. LS6: Leeds 2D **20**
Sandlewood Cres. LS6: Leeds 2D **20**
Sandlewood Grn. LS11: Leeds 2F **41**
Sandmead Cl. BD4: B'frd 4A **36**
LS27: Morl 3G **49**
Sandmead Cft. LS27: Morl 3G **49**
Sandmead Way LS27: Morl 3G **49**
Sandmoor Av. LS17: Leeds 3H **13**
Sandmoor Chase LS17: Leeds 4H **13**
Sandmoor Cl. LS17: Leeds 4H **13**
Sandmoor Ct. LS17: Leeds 4H **13**
Sandmoor Dr. LS17: Leeds 3H **13**
Sandmoor Grn. LS17: Leeds 3G **13**
Sandmoor La. LS17: Leeds 3H **13**
Sandmoor M. LS17: Leeds 4H **13**
Sandon Gro. LS10: Leeds 5A **42**
Sandon Mt. LS10: Leeds 5A **42**
Sandon Pl. LS10: Leeds 5A **42**
Sandpiper App. LS27: Morl 6A **50**
Sandringham App. LS17: Leeds 6A **14**
Sandringham Av. LS28: Pud 1G **37**
Sandringham Cl. LS27: Morl 4A **50**
Sandringham Ct. LS17: Leeds 5H **13**
Sandringham Cres. LS17: Leeds 6H **13**
Sandringham Dr. LS17: Leeds 6H **13**
Sandringham Fold LS27: Morl 4A **50**
Sandringham Gdns. LS17: Leeds 6H **13**
Sandringham Grn. LS17: Leeds 5A **14**
Sandringham Mt. LS17: Leeds 6A **14**
Sandringham Way LS17: Leeds 6H **13**
Sandstone Dr. LS12: Leeds 6C **28**
Sandway LS15: Leeds 3B **34**
Sandway Gdns. LS15: Leeds 3B **34**
Sandway Gro. LS15: Leeds 3B **34**
Sandyacres LS26: Rothw 3H **53**
Sandyacres Cres. LS26: Rothw 3H **53**
Sandyacres Dr. LS26: Rothw 3H **53**
Sandy Bank Av. LS26: Rothw 3H **53**
Sandy Gro. LS26: Rothw 3H **53**
Sandy Way LS19: Yead 2D **8**
Sandywood Ct. LS18: H'fth 4C **18**
Santorini LS12: Leeds 5A **4** (6E **31**)
Sarah St. WF3: E Ard 3H **57**
Sardinia St. LS10: Leeds 2H **41**
Savannah Way LS26: Leeds 1D **52**
Savile Av. LS7: Leeds 2H **31**
Savile Dr. LS7: Leeds 1H **31**
Savile Mt. LS7: Leeds 2H **31**
Savile Pk. Rd. BD19: Cleck 6A **46**
Savile Pl. LS7: Leeds 2H **31**
Savile Rd. LS7: Leeds 2H **31**
Saville Cl. WF3: Rothw 2E **59**
Saville Grn. LS9: Leeds 5B **32**
Saville's Sq. *LS27: Morl* *5G* **49**
(off Queen St.)
Savins Mill Way LS5: Leeds 1G **29**
Savoy Ct. LS28: Pud 4F **27**
Saw Mill Yd. LS11: Leeds 1F **41**
Saxon Ct. LS17: Leeds 6F **13**
Saxon Ga. LS17: Leeds 1F **21**
Saxon Grn. LS17: Leeds 1E **21**
Saxon Gro. LS17: Leeds 6E **13**
Saxon Mt. LS17: Leeds 6F **13**
Saxon Rd. LS17: Leeds 1E **21**
Saxstead Ri. LS12: Leeds 1A **40**
Saxton Gdns. *LS9: Leeds* *6A* **32**
(off The Drive, not continuous)
Saxton Ho. LS19: Yead 3D **8**
Saxton La. LS9: Leeds 5H **5** (6A **32**)
Sayers Cl. LS5: Leeds 1H **29**
Sayner La. LS10: Leeds 1H **41**
Sayner Rd. LS10: Leeds 1H **41**
Scala Ct. LS10: Leeds 2H **41**
Scarborough Junc. LS13: Leeds 4C **28**
Scarborough La. WF3: E Ard 2B **56**
Scarborough St. WF3: E Ard 2B **56**
Scarcroft Vw. LS17: S'cft 3H **15**
Scargill Bldgs. LS27: Morl 5B **50**
Scargill Cl. LS9: Leeds 4B **32**
Scargill Grange LS9: Leeds 5B **32**
Scarth Av. LS9: Leeds 3C **32**
Scatcherd La. LS27: Morl 6F **49**
Scatcherd Pk. Av. LS27: Morl 4G **49**
Scatcherd's Bldgs.
LS27: Morl 3H **49**
Schofield Ct. *LS27: Morl* *5G* **49**
(off Queensway)
Scholars Way LS15: Leeds 1E **45**
SCHOLEBROOK **4E 37**
Scholebrook Ct. *BD4: B'frd* *6A* **36**
(off Broadfield Cl.)
Scholebrook La. BD4: B'frd 4E **37**
SCHOLES **4F 25**
Scholes La. LS15: Scho 3E **25**
School Cl. LS12: Leeds 4D **38**
School Cft. LS26: Rothw 3G **53**
School La. LS6: Leeds 5C **20**
LS7: Leeds 5G **21**
LS15: Leeds 1E **45**
(Colton Rd. E.)
School La. LS15: Leeds 5A **34**
(Pinfold Gro.)
LS17: Leeds 1D **14**
School M. LS12: Leeds 6A **30**
School St. LS27: Morl 1A **50**
(Old Rd.)
LS27: Morl 5H **49**
(South Pde.)
LS28: Pud 2F **27**
(Back La.)
LS28: Pud 1F **37**
(Greenside, not continuous)
WF3: E Ard 6B **56**
School Vw. LS6: Leeds 2C **30**
Scotch Pk. Trad. Est. LS12: Leeds 5B **30**
SCOTLAND **4B 10**
Scotland Cl. LS18: H'fth 6B **10**
Scotland La. LS18: H'fth 1A **10**
Scotland Mill La. LS6: Leeds 1D **20**
LS17: Leeds 1D **20**
Scotland Way LS18: H'fth 5A **10**
Scotland Wood Rd. LS17: Leeds 1D **20**
Scott Bldgs. *LS6: Leeds* *5B* **20**
(off Oddy Pl.)
Scott Cl. LS26: Swil 6G **45**
SCOTT GREEN **2B 48**
Scott Grn. LS27: Morl 1B **48**
Scott Grn. Cres. LS27: Morl 1B **48**
Scott Grn. Dr. LS27: Morl 1B **48**
Scott Grn. Gro. LS27: Morl 1C **48**
Scott Grn. Mt. LS27: Morl 1B **48**
Scott Grn. Vw. LS27: Morl 1C **48**
SCOTT HALL **6G 21**
Scott Hall Av. LS7: Leeds 6G **21**
Scott Hall Cres. LS7: Leeds 5F **21**
Scott Hall Dr. LS7: Leeds 1G **31**
Scott Hall Grn. LS7: Leeds 6G **21**
Scott Hall Gro. LS7: Leeds 6G **21**
Scott Hall Pl. LS7: Leeds 6G **21**
Scott Hall Rd. LS7: Leeds 4F **21**
LS17: Leeds 4F **21**
Scott Hall Row LS7: Leeds 1H **31**
Scott Hall Sports Cen. **5G 21**
Scott Hall Sq. LS7: Leeds 6G **21**
Scott Hall St. LS7: Leeds 1G **31**
Scott Hall Ter. LS7: Leeds 6G **21**
Scott Hall Wlk. LS7: Leeds 1G **31**
Scott Hall Way LS7: Leeds 5G **21**
Scott La. LS27: Morl 6D **48**
Scotts Almshouse's LS10: Leeds 6A **42**
Scott St. LS28: Pud 1H **37**
Scott Wood La. LS7: Leeds 1G **31**
(Buslingthorpe La.)
LS7: Leeds 6F **21**
(Potternewton Cres.)
Scratcherd Gro. LS27: Morl 5F **49**
SEACROFT **6A 24**
Seacroft Av. LS14: Leeds 6B **24**
Seacroft Cres. LS14: Leeds 6B **24**
Seacroft Family Activity Cen. **2A 34**
Seacroft Ga. LS14: Leeds 6B **24**
(not continuous)
SEACROFT HOSPITAL **4A 34**
Seacroft Ind. Est. LS14: Leeds 3B **24**
(Coal Rd., not continuous)
LS14: Leeds 4A **24**
(Limewood Rd.)
Seaforth Av. LS9: Leeds 2C **32**
Seaforth Gro. LS9: Leeds 2C **32**
Seaforth Mt. LS9: Leeds 2C **32**
Seaforth Pl. LS9: Leeds 2C **32**
Seaforth Rd. LS9: Leeds 2C **32**
Seaforth Ter. LS9: Leeds 2C **32**
Second Av. LS12: Leeds 6C **30**
LS19: Yead 4E **9**
LS26: Rothw 2H **53**
Sedburgh Cl. LS15: Leeds 6F **33**
Sefton Av. LS11: Leeds 4E **41**
Sefton Ct. LS6: Leeds 5B **20**
Sefton St. LS11: Leeds 4F **41**
Sefton Ter. LS11: Leeds 4E **41**
Selby Av. LS9: Leeds 5G **33**
Selby Rd. LS9: Leeds 5G **33**
LS15: Leeds, Swil 6A **34**
LS25: Gar 1G **45**
Seminary St. LS2: Leeds 1B **4** (4E **31**)
Servia Dr. LS7: Leeds 2G **31**
Servia Gdns. LS7: Leeds 2G **31**
Servia Hill LS6: Leeds 2F **31**
LS7: Leeds 2F **31**
Servia Rd. LS7: Leeds 2F **31**
Service Rd. LS9: Leeds 5E **43**
Seventh Av. LS26: Rothw 3A **54**

A-Z Leeds 101

Stainburn Pde.—Sunbeam Ter.

Stainburn Pde. LS17: Leeds 2H **21**
Stainburn Rd. LS17: Leeds 3H **21**
Stainburn Ter. LS17: Leeds 3H **21**
Stainburn Vw. LS17: Leeds 2A **22**
Stainmore Cl. LS14: Leeds 2A **34**
Stainmore Pl. LS14: Leeds 2A **34**
Stainton La. WF3: Rothw 5F **53**
Stairfoot Cl. LS16: Leeds 4B **12**
Stair Foot La. LS16: Leeds 4B **12**
LS17: Leeds 4B **12**
Stairfoot Vw. LS16: Leeds 4B **12**
Stairfoot Wlk. LS16: Leeds 4B **12**
Staithe Av. LS10: Leeds 4H **51**
Staithe Cl. LS10: Leeds 4H **51**
Staithe Gdns. LS10: Leeds 4H **51**
Stanbeck Ct. LS7: Leeds 3G **21**
Standale Av. LS28: Pud 5F **27**
Standale Cres. LS28: Pud 5F **27**
Standale Ri. LS28: Pud 5F **27**
Standard Vs. LS12: Leeds 3H **39**
Stanhall Av. LS28: Pud 4F **27**
Stanhope Av. LS18: H'fth 1C **18**
Stanhope Cl. LS18: H'fth 1C **18**
Stanhope Dr. LS18: H'fth 3B **18**
Stanhope Gdns. WF3: E Ard 2A **58**
Stanhope Rd. WF3: E Ard 2A **58**
STANKS **6D 24**
Stanks App. LS14: Leeds 1D **34**
Stanks Av. LS14: Leeds 1D **34**
Stanks Cl. LS14: Leeds 1E **35**
Stanks Cross LS14: Leeds 1E **35**
Stanks Dr. LS14: Leeds 5C **24**
Stanks Gdns. LS14: Leeds 6D **24**
Stanks Gth. LS14: Leeds 1E **35**
Stanks Grn. LS14: Leeds 1E **35**
Stanks Gro. LS14: Leeds 1D **34**
Stanks La. Nth. LS14: Leeds 5C **24**
Stanks La. Sth. LS14: Leeds 1D **34**
Stanks Pde. LS14: Leeds 1D **34**
Stanks Ri. LS14: Leeds 1E **35**
Stanks Rd. LS14: Leeds 1D **34**
Stanks Way LS14: Leeds 1D **34**
STANLEY **6H 59**
Stanley Av. LS9: Leeds 3B **32**
Stanley Dr. LS8: Leeds 1D **22**
Stanley Gro. LS20: Guis 5G **7**
Stanley Ho. LS10: Leeds 1H **41**
Stanley Pl. LS9: Leeds 3C **32**
Stanley Rd. LS7: Leeds 2H **31**
LS9: Leeds 3B **32**
Stanley St. BD10: B'frd 4A **16**
Stanley Ter. LS9: Leeds 3C **32**
(not continuous)
LS12: Leeds 6A **30**
Stanley Vw. LS12: Leeds 6A **30**
Stanmoor Dr. WF3: Wake 5G **59**
Stanmore Av. LS4: Leeds 2A **30**
Stanmore Cres. LS4: Leeds 2A **30**
Stanmore Gro. LS4: Leeds 2A **30**
Stanmore Hill LS4: Leeds 2B **30**
Stanmore Mt. LS4: Leeds 2A **30**
Stanmore Pl. LS4: Leeds 2A **30**
Stanmore Rd. LS4: Leeds 2A **30**
Stanmore St. LS4: Leeds 2A **30**
Stanmore Ter. LS4: Leeds 2A **30**
Stanmore Vw. LS4: Leeds 2A **30**
STANNINGLEY **3H 27**
Stanningley By-Pass LS13: Leeds 4A **28**
LS28: Pud 4E **27**
Stanningley Fld. Cl. LS13: Leeds 4A **28**
Stanningley Ind. Est. LS28: Pud 4F **27**
Stanningley Rd. LS12: Leeds 4E **29**
LS13: Leeds 4E **29**
LS28: Pud 3H **27**
Stansfield Fold *LS18: H'fth* *1C* ***18***
(off Rockery Rd.)
Star Health & Fitness Club *5C* ***32***
(off Glenthorpe Cres.)
Station Apartments *LS15: Leeds* *3C* ***34***
(off Station Rd.)
Station Av. LS13: Leeds 3B **28**
Station Ct. LS15: Leeds 4C **34**
Station Cres. LS12: Leeds 6H **29**
Station La. BD11: B'frd 3C **46**
LS26: Rothw 2D **54**
WF3: E Ard 2H **57**
(Bidder Dr.)
WF3: E Ard 2C **56**
(Thorpe La.)
WF3: Leeds 1C **56**
Station Mt. LS13: Leeds 3B **28**
Station Pde. LS5: Leeds 1H **29**
Station Pl. LS13: Leeds 3C **28**
Station Rd. BD11: B'frd 4G **47**
LS12: Leeds 6H **29**
LS15: Leeds 3C **34**
LS15: Scho 4F **25**
LS18: H'fth 1C **18**
LS20: Guis 4F **7**
LS26: Mick 6H **55**
LS27: Morl 4G **49**
LS29: Men 1D **6**
Station St. LS28: Pud 1F **37**
Station Ter. LS13: Leeds 3C **28**
Station Vw. LS15: Leeds 4C **34**
Station Wlk. LS27: Morl 4H **49**
Station Way LS12: Leeds 6H **29**
Stead Rd. BD4: B'frd 1A **46**
Steads Yd. LS18: H'fth 1C **18**
Steander LS9: Leeds 6H **5** (6H **31**)
Steel Grn. LS12: Leeds 4G **39**
Steel Ter. *LS26: Rothw* *4H* ***53***
(off Blackburn Ct.)
Stephenson Dr. LS12: Leeds 4D **38**
Stephenson Ho. *LS27: Morl* *4H* ***49***
(off Pullman Ct.)
Stephenson Way LS12: Leeds 4D **38**
WF2: Wake 6B **58**
Ster Century Cinema
Leeds **3E 5 (5F 31)**
Sterling Ct. WF3: Morl 1C **56**
Sterling Way WF3: Morl 1B **56**
Stewart Cl. LS15: Leeds 6C **34**
Stile Hill Way LS15: Leeds 6F **35**
Stirling Cres. BD4: B'frd 4A **36**
LS18: H'fth 5A **10**
Stockheld La. LS15: Scho 2F **25**
Stocks App. LS14: Leeds 1B **34**
Stocks Hill LS11: Leeds 2E **41**
LS12: Leeds 5A **30**
LS29: Men 1B **6**
Stocks Hill Gth. *LS29: Men* *1B* ***6***
(off Stocks Hill)
Stocks Ri. LS14: Leeds 1B **34**
Stocks Rd. LS14: Leeds 1C **34**
Stocks St. LS7: Leeds 2G **31**
Stonebridge App. LS12: Leeds 1E **39**
Stonebridge Av. LS12: Leeds 1F **39**
Stone Bri. Ct. *LS12: Leeds* *1E* ***39***
(off Farnley Cres.)
Stonebridge Gro. LS12: Leeds 1E **39**
Stonebridge La. LS12: Leeds 2E **39**
Stone Bridge Lea *LS12: Leeds* *1E* ***39***
(off Farnley Cres.)
Stone Brig Grn. LS26: Rothw 5F **53**
Stone Brig La. LS26: Rothw 5F **53**
Stonechat Ri. LS27: Morl 5A **50**
Stonecliffe Bank LS12: Leeds 1E **39**
Stonecliffe Cl. LS12: Leeds 1E **39**
Stonecliffe Cres. LS12: Leeds 1E **39**
Stonecliffe Dr. LS12: Leeds 1E **39**
Stonecliffe Gdns. LS12: Leeds 1E **39**
Stonecliffe Gth. LS12: Leeds 1E **39**
Stonecliffe Grn. LS12: Leeds 1E **39**
Stonecliffe Gro. LS12: Leeds 1E **39**
Stonecliffe Lawn LS12: Leeds 1E **39**
Stonecliffe Mt. LS12: Leeds 1E **39**
Stonecliffe Pl. *LS12: Leeds* *1E* ***39***
(off Stonecliffe Way)
Stonecliffe Ter. LS12: Leeds 1E **39**
Stonecliffe Vw. LS12: Leeds 1E **39**
Stonecliffe Wlk. LS12: Leeds 2E **39**
Stonecliffe Way LS12: Leeds 1E **39**
Stonecroft WF3: Wake 6G **59**
Stone Cft. Ct. LS26: Rothw 4C **54**
Stonedene LS6: Leeds 3D **20**
Stonefield Ter. LS27: Morl 1A **50**
Stonegate LS7: Leeds 2G **31**
(not continuous)
Stonegate App. LS7: Leeds 5D **20**
Stonegate Chase LS7: Leeds 4D **20**
Stonegate Cl. LS17: Leeds 6H **13**
Stonegate Cres. LS7: Leeds 4E **21**
Stonegate Dr. LS7: Leeds 4E **21**
Stonegate Edge LS7: Leeds 4E **21**
Stonegate Farm Cl. LS7: Leeds 4D **20**
Stonegate Gdns. LS7: Leeds 4D **20**
Stonegate Grn. LS7: Leeds 5D **20**
Stonegate Gro. LS7: Leeds 4E **21**
Stonegate La. LS7: Leeds 4D **20**
Stonegate M. LS7: Leeds 5D **20**
Stonegate Pl. LS7: Leeds 5D **20**
Stonegate Rd. LS6: Leeds 4D **20**
Stonegate Vw. LS7: Leeds 4D **20**
Stonegate Wlk. LS7: Leeds 5E **21**
Stonehurst LS14: Leeds 1D **34**
Stonelea BD4: B'frd 1C **46**
Stonelea Ct. LS6: Leeds 6B **20**
LS7: Leeds 4E **21**
Stoneleigh Av. LS17: Leeds 5B **14**
Stoneleigh Cl. LS17: Leeds 5B **14**
Stoneleigh Ct. LS17: Leeds 5B **14**
Stoneleigh Gth. LS17: Leeds 6B **14**
Stoneleigh La. LS17: Leeds 6B **14**
Stoneleigh Way LS17: Leeds 6B **14**
Stone Mill App. LS6: Leeds 4C **20**
Stone Mill Ct. LS6: Leeds 4C **20**
Stone Mill Way LS6: Leeds 4C **20**
Stone Pits La. LS27: Morl 3D **48**
Stone Vs. LS6: Leeds 5B **20**
Stoneycroft LS18: H'fth 3B **18**
LS19: Yead *5E* ***9***
(off Batter La.)
Stoneyhurst Sq. BD4: B'frd 4A **36**
Stoneyhurst Way BD4: B'frd 4A **36**
Stoney La. LS18: H'fth 3B **18**
WF2: Wake 6H **57**
WF3: E Ard 6G **57**
Stoney Ri. LS18: H'fth 3B **18**
Stoney Rock Ct. LS9: Leeds 4B **32**
Stoney Rock Gro. LS9: Leeds 4B **32**
Stoney Rock La. LS9: Leeds 4B **32**
Stoneythorpe LS18: H'fth 3B **18**
Stony Royd LS28: Pud 2E **27**
Storey Pl. LS14: Leeds 4G **33**
Stott Rd. LS6: Leeds 2C **30**
Stott St. LS12: Leeds 6B **30**
STOURTON **6D 42**
Stowe Gro. LS9: Leeds 5E **33**
Stradbroke Way LS12: Leeds 1A **40**
Strafford Way BD10: B'frd 3A **16**
Stratford Av. LS11: Leeds 4E **41**
Stratford Ct. LS7: Leeds 5G **21**
Stratford St. LS11: Leeds 5F **41**
Stratford Ter. LS11: Leeds 4F **41**
Strathmore Av. LS9: Leeds 3C **32**
Strathmore Dr. LS9: Leeds 2C **32**
Strathmore St. LS9: Leeds 3D **32**
Strathmore Ter. LS9: Leeds 3C **32**
Strathmore Vw. LS9: Leeds 3C **32**
Stratton Vw. BD4: B'frd 3A **36**
Strawberry La. LS12: Leeds 6A **30**
(not continuous)
Strawberry Rd. LS12: Leeds 6A **30**
Streamside LS6: Leeds 5C **20**
Street La. LS8: Leeds 1C **22**
LS17: Leeds 1G **21**
LS27: Morl 4C **48**
Stretton Av. LS6: Leeds 2C **20**
Strickland Av. LS17: Leeds 5H **15**
Strickland Cl. LS17: Leeds 5H **15**
Strickland Cres. LS17: Leeds 5H **15**
Strone, The BD10: B'frd 2B **16**
Stubbs La. WF3: E Ard 4A **58**
Studfold Vw. LS14: Leeds 3A **34**
Studio Rd. LS3: Leeds 4C **30**
Studley Ter. LS28: Pud 5G **27**
Styebank La. LS26: Rothw 3H **53**
Suffield Cl. LS27: Morl 1B **48**
Suffield Cres. LS27: Morl 1B **48**
Suffield Dr. LS27: Morl 1B **48**
Suffield Rd. LS27: Morl 1B **48**
Suffolk Ct. LS19: Yead 2D **8**
Sugar Hill Cl. LS26: Rothw 6C **54**
Sugar Well App. LS7: Leeds 6E **21**
Sugar Well Ct. LS7: Leeds 1F **31**
Sugar Well Mt. LS7: Leeds 6E **21**
Sugar Well Rd. LS7: Leeds 6E **21**
Sulby Gro. BD10: B'frd 4A **16**
Summerbank Cl. BD11: B'frd 2H **47**
Summerdale BD19: Cleck 6D **46**
Summerfield Av. LS13: Leeds 2A **28**
Summerfield Dr. LS13: Leeds 2A **28**
Summerfield Gdns. LS13: Leeds 2A **28**
Summerfield Grn. LS13: Leeds 2A **28**
Summerfield Pl. LS13: Leeds 2A **28**
LS28: Pud *5G* ***27***
(off Richardshaw La.)
Summerfield Rd. LS13: Leeds 2A **28**
Summerfield Wlk. LS13: Leeds 2A **28**
Summerhill Gdns. LS8: Leeds 1D **22**
Summerhill Pl. LS8: Leeds 1D **22**
Summerseat LS19: Yead 6F **9**
Summersgill Sq. LS18: H'fth 3B **18**
Summerville Rd. LS28: Pud 4E **27**
Sunbeam Av. LS11: Leeds 4F **41**
Sunbeam Gro. LS11: Leeds 4F **41**
Sunbeam Pl. LS11: Leeds 4F **41**
Sunbeam Ter. LS11: Leeds 4F **41**

104 A-Z Leeds

Victoria Gdns.—Wellington Rd.

Victoria Gdns. LS18: H'fth 4B **18**
LS28: Pud 6E **27**
Victoria Grange Dr. LS27: Morl 4G **49**
Victoria Grange Way LS27: Morl 4G **49**
Victoria Gro. LS9: Leeds 5D **32**
LS18: H'fth 5A **18**
LS28: Pud 6E **27**
Victoria Ind. Pk. LS14: Leeds 4B **24**
Victoria M. LS18: H'fth 4A **18**
LS27: Morl 4G **49**
Victoria Mt. LS18: H'fth 3A **18**
Victoria Pk. Av. LS13: Leeds 2E **29**
Victoria Pk. Gro. LS5: Leeds 2F **29**
LS13: Leeds .2E **29**
Victoria Pl. LS11: Leeds 1F **41**
LS19: Yead 2C **8**
Victoria Quarter LS1: Leeds 4F **5** (5G **31**)
Victoria Ri. LS28: Pud 6E **27**
Victoria Rd. LS5: Leeds 1G **29**
LS6: Leeds 2C **30**
LS11: Leeds 1F **41**
LS14: Leeds 4B **24**
LS20: Guis 5F **7**
LS26: Rothw 3F **53**
LS27: Morl 4G **49**
LS28: Pud 3F **27**
(Northcote St.)
LS28: Pud 6E **27**
(Uppermoor)
Victoria Sq. LS1: Leeds 3C **4** (5F **31**)
Victoria St. LS3: Leeds 2A **4** (4D **30**)
LS7: Leeds 4H **21**
LS27: Morl 2A **50**
(Back Grn.)
LS27: Morl 4F **49**
(Kingsmill Cl.)
LS28: Pud 5C **16**
Victoria Ter. LS3: Leeds 2A **4** (4D **30**)
LS5: Leeds 1G **29**
LS6: Leeds 5B **20**
LS19: Yead 2E **9**
LS20: Guis 4G 7
(off Lands La.)
LS28: Pud 3H **27**
Victoria Vs. LS28: Pud 4G **27**
Victoria Wlk. *LS1: Leeds 4E 5*
(in The Headrow Cen.)
LS18: H'fth 4A **18**
Victor St. BD3: B'frd 6A **26**
Vienna Ct. LS27: Morl 1A **50**
View, The LS8: Leeds 3B **22**
LS17: Leeds 3D **12**
Viewlands Cres. LS29: Men 1F **7**
Viewlands Mt. LS29: Men 1F **7**
Viewlands Ri. LS29: Men 1F **7**
Village Av. LS4: Leeds 3B **30**
Village Gdns. LS15: Leeds 1D **44**
(not continuous)
Village Hotel & Leisure Club 3A **20**
Village Pl. LS4: Leeds 3B **30**
Village St., The LS4: Leeds 3B **30**
Village Ter. LS4: Leeds 2B **30**
Vine Ct. LS20: Guis 5G **7**
Vinery Av. LS9: Leeds 5C **32**
Vinery Gro. LS9: Leeds 5C **32**
Vinery Mt. LS9: Leeds 6C **32**
Vinery Pl. LS9: Leeds 6C **32**
Vinery Rd. LS4: Leeds 3B **30**
Vinery St. LS9: Leeds 5C **32**
Vinery Ter. LS9: Leeds 6C **32**
Vinery Vw. LS9: Leeds 6C **32**
Virginia Cl. WF3: Wake 5C **58**
Virginia Ct. WF3: Wake 5C **58**
Virginia Dr. WF3: Wake 5C **58**
Virginia Gdns. WF3: Wake 5C **58**
Vollan's Ct. LS14: Leeds 6A **24**
Vue Cinema
Leeds 4B **30**
Vulcan St. BD4: B'frd 6A **36**

W

Wade La. LS2: Leeds 3E **5** (5G **31**)
Wade St. LS28: Pud 2F **27**
Wadlands Cl. LS28: Pud 1F **27**
Wadlands Dr. LS28: Pud 2E **27**
Wadlands Gro. LS28: Pud 1E **27**
Wadlands Ri. LS28: Pud 2E **27**
Waincliffe Cres. LS11: Leeds 6D **40**
Waincliffe Dr. LS11: Leeds 1D **50**
Waincliffe Gth. LS11: Leeds 6D **40**
Waincliffe Mt. LS11: Leeds 6D **40**
Waincliffe Pl. LS11: Leeds 6D **40**
Waincliffe Sq. LS11: Leeds 6D **40**
Waincliffe Ter. LS11: Leeds 1D **50**
Wainfleet Ho. *BD3: B'frd 5A 26*
(off Rushton Rd.)
Wakefield 41 Ind. Pk. WF2: Wake 5B **58**
(Lingwell Ga. La.)
WF2: Wake 6B **58**
(Telford Way)
Wakefield Av. LS14: Leeds 4H **33**
Wakefield Rd. BD11: B'frd 3H **47**
(not continuous)
LS10: Leeds 5B **42**
LS26: Kip, Swil 1E **55**
LS26: Rothw 4D **52**
(Castlefields)
LS26: Rothw 6B **54**
(Sanderson La.)
LS27: Morl 4C **48**
Walesby Ct. LS16: Leeds 1E **19**
Walford Av. LS9: Leeds 5C **32**
Walford Gro. LS9: Leeds 5C **32**
Walford Mt. LS9: Leeds 5C **32**
Walford Rd. LS9: Leeds 5C **32**
Walford Ter. LS9: Leeds 5C **32**
Walk, The LS28: Pud 3E **27**
Walker Ho. LS5: Leeds 1F **29**
Walker Pl. LS27: Morl 2H **49**
Walker Rd. LS18: H'fth 2B **18**
LS29: Men 1B **6**
Walkers Bldgs. *LS28: Pud 5G 27*
(off Clifton Hill)
Walker's Grn. LS12: Leeds 3A **40**
Walker's La. LS12: Leeds 3A **40**
(not continuous)
Walkers Mt. LS6: Leeds 6D **20**
Walkers Row LS19: Yead 2C **8**
Wallace Gdns. WF3: Wake 5D **58**
Walmer Gro. LS28: Pud 2H **37**
Walmsley Rd. LS6: Leeds 2C **30**
Walnut Cl. LS14: Leeds 3C **24**
Walsh La. LS12: Leeds 5C **38**
Walter Cres. LS9: Leeds 6B **32**
Walter St. LS4: Leeds 4B **30**
Walton Cft. *LS28: Pud 2F 27*
(off Water La.)
Walton Dr. BD11: B'frd 3H **47**
Walton Gth. BD11: B'frd 4H **47**
Walton St. LS10: Leeds 3A **42**
LS11: Leeds 1F **41**
Wansford Cl. BD4: B'frd 5A **36**
Ward La. LS10: Leeds 6H **41**
Wareham Cnr. BD4: B'frd 5A **36**
Warehouse, The *LS5: Leeds 1F 29*
(off Broad La.)
Warings Bldgs. WF3: E Ard 4B **56**
Warley Vw. LS13: Leeds 1B **28**
Warm La. LS19: Yead 4C **8**
Warnford Gro. BD4: B'frd 4A **36**
Warrel's Av. LS13: Leeds 2C **28**
Warrel's Ct. LS13: Leeds 3C **28**
Warrel's Gro. LS13: Leeds 3C **28**
Warrel's Mt. LS13: Leeds 3C **28**
Warrel's Pl. LS13: Leeds 2C **28**
Warrel's Rd. LS13: Leeds 2C **28**
Warrel's Row LS13: Leeds 3C **28**
Warrel's St. LS13: Leeds 3C **28**
Warrel's Ter. LS13: Leeds 3C **28**
Warren Ho. La. LS19: Yead 1F **9**
Warrens La. BD11: B'frd 4G **47**
WF17: Bat, B'frd 6F **47**
Warwick Ct. LS18: H'fth 4C **18**
Washington Pl. LS13: Leeds 5A **28**
Washington St. LS3: Leeds 5C **30**
LS13: Leeds 5A **28**
Washington Ter. LS13: Leeds 5A **28**
Waterfront M. BD10: B'frd 3A **16**
Water Gdns. LS26: Rothw 2F **53**
Water Ho. Ct. LS18: H'fth 4B **18**
Waterhouse Ct. *LS10: Leeds 3H 41*
(off The Oval)
Waterhouse Dr. WF3: E Ard 4F **57**
Watering La. LS27: Morl 6B **50**
WF3: Morl 6B **50**
Watering Mdw. LS27: Morl 5B **50**
Water La. LS11: Leeds 6E **5** (6G **31**)
(Hunslet Rd.)
LS11: Leeds 6C **4** (1E **41**)
(Triumph Cl.)
LS12: Leeds 6D **28**
LS18: H'fth 2H **17**
LS28: Pud 2F **27**
Waterloo Apartments LS10: Leeds 6F **5**
Waterloo Cres. BD10: B'frd 3B **16**
LS13: Leeds 2D **28**
Waterloo Gro. LS28: Pud 6D **26**
Waterloo La. LS13: Leeds 2D **28**
Waterloo Mt. LS28: Pud 5D **26**
Waterloo Rd. LS10: Leeds 3A **42**
LS28: Pud 5D **26**
Waterloo St. LS10: Leeds 6F **5** (6G **31**)
Waterloo Way LS13: Leeds 2D **28**
Waterside Ct. LS13: Leeds 6H **17**
Waterside Ind. Pk. LS10: Leeds 4D **42**
Waterside Rd. LS10: Leeds 5D **42**
Waters Wlk. BD10: B'frd 3A **16**
Waterwood Cl. WF3: E Ard 4D **56**
Watson Rd. LS14: Leeds 4H **33**
Watson St. LS27: Morl 6F **49**
Watt St. BD4: B'frd 1A **36**
Waveney Rd. LS12: Leeds 1A **40**
Waverley Gth. LS11: Leeds 3F **41**
Wayland App. LS16: Leeds 5B **12**
Wayland Cl. LS16: Leeds 5B **12**
Wayland Ct. LS16: Leeds 5B **12**
Wayland Cft. LS16: Leeds 5B **12**
Wayland Dr. LS16: Leeds 5B **12**
Weaver Gdns. LS27: Morl 6B **50**
Weaver Grn. LS28: Pud 6G **27**
Weavers Ct. LS12: Leeds 6H **29**
LS28: Pud 2H **37**
Weavers Cft. LS28: Pud 1H **37**
Weavers Grange LS20: Guis 3G **7**
Weavers Row LS28: Pud 1H **37**
Weaver St. LS4: Leeds 4B **30**
Weaverthorpe Retail Pk. BD4: B'frd 6A **36**
Weaverthorpe Rd. BD4: B'frd 6A **36**
Webster Row LS12: Leeds 1H **39**
Webton Ct. LS7: Leeds 4H **21**
Wedgewood Ct. LS8: Leeds 2C **22**
Wedgewood Dr. LS8: Leeds 3C **22**
Wedgewood Gro. LS8: Leeds 3C **22**
WEETWOOD 4H **19**
Weetwood Av. LS16: Leeds 4B **20**
Weetwood Ct. LS16: Leeds 3A **20**
Weetwood Cres. LS16: Leeds 3B **20**
Weetwood Grange Gro. LS16: Leeds 3H **19**
Weetwood Ho. Ct. LS16: Leeds 3H **19**
Weetwood La. LS16: Leeds 2A **20**
Weetwood Mnr. LS16: Leeds 3A **20**
Weetwood Mill La. LS16: Leeds 3B **20**
Weetwood Pk. Dr. LS16: Leeds 3H **19**
Weetwood Rd. LS16: Leeds 3H **19**
Weetwood Ter. LS16: Leeds 3B **20**
Weetwood Wlk. LS16: Leeds 3A **20**
Welbeck Rd. LS9: Leeds 6C **32**
WF17: Bat 6H **47**
Welburn Av. LS16: Leeds 4H **19**
Welburn Dr. LS16: Leeds 4H **19**
Welburn Gro. LS16: Leeds 4H **19**
Weldon Ct. BD4: B'frd 3A **36**
Well Cl. LS19: Yead 6E **9**
Well Cl. Ri. LS7: Leeds 3G **31**
Wellcroft Gro. WF3: E Ard 4D **56**
Wellfield Pl. *LS6: Leeds 6B 20*
(off Chapel St.)
Wellfield Ter. LS27: Morl 2C **48**
Well Gth. LS15: Leeds 3C **34**
Well Gth. Bank LS13: Leeds 1B **28**
Well Gth. Mt. LS15: Leeds 3C **34**
Well Gth. Vw. LS13: Leeds 1C **28**
Well Grn. Ct. BD4: B'frd 2A **46**
Well Hill LS19: Yead 2D **8**
Well Hill Ct. *LS19: Yead 3D 8*
(off Well Hill)
Well Holme Mead LS12: Leeds 4E **39**
Well Ho. Av. LS8: Leeds 6C **22**
Well Ho. Ct. LS8: Leeds 6C **22**
Well Ho. Cres. LS8: Leeds 6C **22**
Well Ho. Dr. LS8: Leeds 6C **22**
Well Ho. Gdns. LS8: Leeds 6C **22**
Well Ho. Rd. LS8: Leeds 6C **22**
Wellington Bri. St. LS1: Leeds 5A **4** (6D **30**)
LS3: Leeds 4A **4** (5D **30**)
Wellington Ct. BD11: B'frd 3C **46**
Wellington Gdns.
LS13: Leeds 2D **28**
Wellington Gth. LS13: Leeds 1D **28**
Wellington Gro. LS13: Leeds 1D **28**
LS28: Pud 6E **27**
WELLINGTON HILL 3H **23**
Wellington Hill LS17: Leeds 1A **24**
Wellington Mt. LS13: Leeds 1D **28**
Wellington Pl. LS1: Leeds 5A **4** (6E **31**)
Wellington Rd. LS1: Leeds 5A **4** (6D **30**)
LS12: Leeds 1C **40**

108 A-Z Leeds

Windsor Cres.—Woodstock Cl.

Windsor Cres. LS26: Rothw 3G **53**
Windsor Mt. LS15: Leeds 5B **34**
Windsor Oval WF3: E Ard 6B **56**
Windsor Ter. LS27: Morl 2D **48**
Winfield Dr. BD4: B'frd 3A **46**
Winfield Gro. *LS2: Leeds 3F **31***
(off Blenheim Av.)
Winfield Pl. LS2: Leeds 3F **31**
Winfield Ter. *LS2: Leeds 3F **31***
(off Winfield Pl.)
Winnipeg Pl. LS7: Leeds 5H **21**
Winrose App. LS10: Leeds 2A **52**
Winrose Av. LS10: Leeds 1H **51**
Winrose Cres. LS10: Leeds 1H **51**
Winrose Dr. LS10: Leeds 1H **51**
Winrose Gth. LS10: Leeds 1A **52**
Winrose Gro. LS10: Leeds 1A **52**
Winrose Hill LS10: Leeds 6A **42**
Winslow Rd. BD10: B'frd 1A **26**
Winstanley Ter. *LS6: Leeds 2C **30***
(off Victoria Rd.)
Winston Gdns. LS6: Leeds 6A **20**
Winston Mt. LS6: Leeds 6A **20**
Winstons Health Club *5E **31***
(off West St.)
Winterbourne Av. LS27: Morl 3H **49**
Winthorpe Av. WF3: Leeds 1H **57**
Winthorpe Cres. WF3: Leeds 1H **57**
Winthorpe St. LS6: Leeds 5D **20**
Winthorpe Vw. WF3: Leeds 1A **58**
Wintoun St. LS7: Leeds 1G **5** (4H **31**)
Wira Ho. LS16: Leeds 2F **19**
WIRING FIELD 6A **30**
Withens Rd. WF17: Bat 6G **47**
Wolley Av. LS12: Leeds 4D **38**
Wolley Ct. LS12: Leeds 4D **38**
Wolley Dr. LS12: Leeds 4D **38**
Wolley Gdns. LS12: Leeds 4D **38**
Wolseley Rd. LS4: Leeds 4B **30**
(not continuous)
Wolston Cl. BD4: B'frd 5A **36**
Womersley Ct. *LS28: Pud 1F **37***
(off Womersley Pl.)
Womersley Pl. LS28: Pud 1F **37**
(Carlisle Rd.)
LS28: Pud 4D **26**
(Woodhall Pk. Gdns.)
Woodale Ho. LS29: Men 2D **6**
Woodbine Ter. LS6: Leeds 5C **20**
LS13: Leeds 2C **28**
*LS18: H'fth 4C **18***
(off Wood La.)
WOODBOTTOM 3F **17**
Wood Bottom LS19: Yead 3F **17**
Woodbourne LS8: Leeds 4E **23**
Woodbourne Av. LS17: Leeds 2G **21**
Woodbridge Cl. LS6: Leeds 6H **19**
Woodbridge Cres. LS6: Leeds 5G **19**
Woodbridge Fold LS6: Leeds 6G **19**
Woodbridge Gdns. LS6: Leeds 6G **19**
Woodbridge Gth. LS6: Leeds 6H **19**
Woodbridge Grn. LS6: Leeds 6H **19**
Woodbridge Lawn LS6: Leeds 6G **19**
Woodbridge Pl. LS6: Leeds 6G **19**
Woodbridge Rd. LS6: Leeds 6G **19**
Woodbridge Va. LS6: Leeds 6G **19**
Wood Cl. LS7: Leeds 4G **21**
LS26: Rothw 3F **53**
Wood Cres. LS26: Rothw 3F **53**
Woodcross LS27: Morl 3G **49**
Woodcross End LS27: Morl 2G **49**
Woodcross Fold LS27: Morl 3G **49**
Woodcross Gdns. LS27: Morl 3G **49**
Woodcross Gth. LS27: Morl 2G **49**
Wood Dr. LS26: Rothw 3E **53**
Woodeson Ct. LS13: Leeds 6H **17**
Woodeson Lea LS13: Leeds 6H **17**
Woodfield Ter. *LS28: Pud 1H **37***
(off Sheridan Way)
Woodgarth Gdns. BD4: B'frd 4B **36**
Wood Gro. LS12: Leeds 6D **28**
WOODHALL 3C **26**
Woodhall Av. BD3: B'frd 4A **26**
LS5: Leeds 5E **19**
Woodhall Cl. LS28: Pud 3C **26**
Woodhall Ct. LS15: Leeds 1D **44**
LS28: Pud 6C **16**
Woodhall Cft. LS28: Pud 3C **26**
Woodhall Dr. LS5: Leeds 5E **19**
WOODHALL HILLS 2C **26**
Woodhall Hills LS28: Pud 2B **26**
Woodhall La. LS28: Pud 2C **26**
WOODHALL PARK 3D **26**
Woodhall Pk. Av. LS28: Pud 3C **26**
Woodhall Pk. Cres. E. LS28: Pud 4D **26**
Woodhall Pk. Cres. W. LS28: Pud 4C **26**
Woodhall Pk. Dr. LS28: Pud 4C **26**
Woodhall Pk. Gdns. LS28: Pud 4D **26**
Woodhall Pk. Gro. LS28: Pud 4C **26**
Woodhall Pk. Mt. LS28: Pud 3C **26**
Woodhall Pl. BD3: B'frd 4A **26**
Woodhall Retail Cen., The BD3: B'frd 4A **26**
Woodhall Rd. BD3: B'frd 5A **26**
BD3: Pud 4A **26**
LS28: Pud 1C **26**
Woodhall Ter. BD3: B'frd 4A **26**
Woodhall Vw. BD3: B'frd 4B **26**
Woodhead La. LS27: Morl 2C **48**
Woodhead Rd. WF17: Bat 6B **48**
Wood Hill LS26: Rothw 3F **53**
Wood Hill Ct. LS16: Leeds 5D **10**
Wood Hill Cres. LS16: Leeds 6C **10**
Wood Hill Gdns. LS16: Leeds 5D **10**
Wood Hill Gth. LS16: Leeds 5D **10**
Wood Hill Gro. LS16: Leeds 6C **10**
Wood Hill Ri. LS16: Leeds 5D **10**
Woodhill Ri. BD10: B'frd 3A **16**
Wood Hill Rd. LS16: Leeds 6D **10**
WOODHOUSE 3F **31**
WOODHOUSE CARR 2F **31**
WOODHOUSE CLIFF 1E **31**
Woodhouse Cliff LS6: Leeds 1E **31**
Woodhouse Cl. WF3: E Ard 5F **57**
Woodhouse Flats *LS2: Leeds 2E **31***
(off St Mark's St.)
WOODHOUSE HILL 5H **41**
Woodhouse Hill Av. LS10: Leeds 5A **42**
Woodhouse Hill Gro.
LS10: Leeds 5A **42**
Woodhouse Hill Pl. LS10: Leeds 5A **42**
Woodhouse Hill Rd. LS10: Leeds 5A **42**
(not continuous)
Woodhouse La. LS1: Leeds 1D **4** (4F **31**)
LS2: Leeds 1C **4** (2E **31**)
WF3: E Ard 6F **57**
Woodhouse Sq. LS3: Leeds 3B **4** (5E **31**)
Woodhouse St. LS6: Leeds 2E **31**
WOODKIRK 4B **56**
Woodkirk Av. WF3: E Ard 3A **56**
Woodkirk Gro. WF3: E Ard 3B **56**
Woodland Av. LS26: Swil 6G **45**
Woodland Cl. LS15: Leeds 5C **34**
Woodland Ct. LS8: Leeds 6C **22**
Woodland Cres. LS26: Rothw 3F **53**
LS26: Swil 6G **45**
Woodland Cft. LS18: H'fth 1C **18**
Woodland Dr. LS7: Leeds 4H **21**
LS26: Swil 6F **45**
Woodland Gro. LS7: Leeds 1A **32**
LS26: Swil 6G **45**
Woodland Hill LS15: Leeds 5B **34**
Woodland La. LS7: Leeds 4H **21**
Woodland Mt. LS7: Leeds 1A **32**
Woodland Pk. LS26: Rothw 4C **54**
Woodland Pk. Rd. LS6: Leeds 6C **20**
Woodland Ri. LS15: Leeds 5C **34**
Woodland Rd. LS15: Leeds 5B **34**
Woodlands LS17: Leeds 1A **22**
WF3: E Ard 4G **57**
Woodlands, The *LS26: Rothw 4C **54***
(off Farrer La.)
Woodlands Av. LS28: Pud 4E **27**
Woodlands Cl. BD10: Yead 2B **16**
WF3: E Ard 4G **57**
Woodlands Ct. LS16: Leeds 2H **19**
LS28: Pud 2F **37**
Woodlands Dr. BD10: Yead 2B **16**
LS19: Yead 1C **16**
LS27: Morl 3F **49**
WF3: E Ard 4F **57**
Woodlands Fold BD11: B'frd 4D **46**
Woodlands Gro. LS28: Pud 4E **27**
Woodlands Pk. Gro. LS28: Pud 2F **37**
Woodlands Pk. Rd. LS28: Pud 2F **37**
Woodland Sq. LS12: Leeds 5F **29**
Woodlands Ter. LS28: Pud 4E **27**
Woodland Ter. LS7: Leeds 4E **21**
Woodland Vw. LS7: Leeds 4H **21**
LS28: Pud 4C **16**
WF3: E Ard 6B **56**
Wood Land Vs. LS14: Leeds 1D **34**
Wood La. LS6: Leeds 6B **20**
LS7: Leeds 4G **21**
(not continuous)
LS12: Leeds 5D **28**
(Ring Rd. Farnley)
Wood La. LS12: Leeds 5D **38**
(Wentworth Farm Res. Pk.)
LS13: Leeds 1C **28**
(Bellmount Pl.)
LS13: Leeds 5D **28**
(Ring Rd. Farnley)
LS15: Leeds, Scho 6E **25**
LS18: H'fth 4C **18**
LS26: Rothw 2D **52**
LS28: Pud 4D **16**
Wood La. Ct. LS6: Leeds 6C **20**
Woodlea App. LS6: Leeds 2D **20**
LS19: Yead 3B **8**
Woodlea Av. LS6: Leeds 2D **20**
Woodlea Chase LS6: Leeds 3D **20**
Woodlea Cl. LS19: Yead 4B **8**
Woodlea Ct. LS6: Leeds 3D **20**
LS17: Leeds 5D **14**
Woodlea Cft. LS6: Leeds 2D **20**
Woodlea Dr. LS6: Leeds 2D **20**
LS19: Yead 4B **8**
Woodlea Fold LS6: Leeds 2D **20**
Woodlea Gdns. LS6: Leeds 2D **20**
Woodlea Gth. LS6: Leeds 2D **20**
Woodlea Ga. LS6: Leeds 3D **20**
Woodlea Grn. LS6: Leeds 2D **20**
Woodlea Gro. LS6: Leeds 3D **20**
*LS11: Leeds 4D **40***
(off Woodlea St.)
LS19: Yead 3B **8**
Woodlea Holt LS6: Leeds 2D **20**
Woodlea La. LS6: Leeds 2D **20**
Woodlea Lawn LS6: Leeds 2D **20**
Woodlea Mt. LS11: Leeds 4D **40**
LS19: Yead 3B **8**
Woodlea Pk. LS6: Leeds 3D **20**
Woodlea Pl. LS6: Leeds 2D **20**
LS11: Leeds 4E **41**
Woodlea Rd. LS19: Yead 3B **8**
Woodlea Sq. LS6: Leeds 3D **20**
Woodlea St. LS11: Leeds 4D **40**
Woodlea Vw. LS6: Leeds 3D **20**
LS19: Yead 4B **8**
Woodleigh Hall M. LS19: Yead 2F **17**
Woodleigh Hall Vw.
LS19: Yead 2G **17**
WOODLESFORD 2C **54**
Woodlesford Station (Rail) 2D **54**
Woodliffe Ct. LS7: Leeds 4G **21**
Woodliffe Cres. LS7: Leeds 4G **21**
Woodliffe Dr. LS7: Leeds 4G **21**
Woodman St. LS15: Leeds 5A **34**
Woodman Yd. *LS16: Leeds 5B **20***
(off Otley Rd.)
Wood Moor Ct. LS17: Leeds 3A **14**
Wood Mt. LS26: Rothw 3E **53**
Woodnook Cl. LS16: Leeds 1D **18**
Woodnook Dr. LS16: Leeds 1D **18**
Woodnook Gth. LS16: Leeds 1D **18**
Woodnook Rd. LS16: Leeds 6D **10**
Wood Nook Ter. LS28: Pud 4E **27**
WOOD ROW 6H **55**
Wood Row LS26: Mick 6H **55**
Woodrow Cres. LS26: Mick 6G **55**
Woodside LS26: Mick 6G **55**
Woodside Av. LS4: Leeds 3A **30**
LS7: Leeds 4D **20**
Woodside Cl. LS27: Morl 3G **49**
Woodside Ct. LS16: Leeds 2F **19**
*LS18: H'fth 3E **19***
(off Broadgate La.)
LS18: H'fth 3E **19**
(Tanhouse Hill)
Woodside Dr. LS27: Morl 2G **49**
Woodside Gdns. LS27: Morl 2G **49**
Woodside Hill Cl.
LS18: H'fth 3E **19**
Woodside La. LS27: Morl 2G **49**
Woodside Lawn LS12: Leeds 6D **28**
Woodside M. LS7: Leeds 4D **20**
Woodside Pk. Av. LS18: H'fth 3D **18**
Woodside Pk. Dr. LS18: H'fth 3D **18**
Woodside Pl. LS4: Leeds 3A **30**
Woodside Ter. LS4: Leeds 3A **30**
Woodside Vw. LS4: Leeds 2A **30**
WF3: Wake 3D **58**
Woodsley Grn. LS6: Leeds 3D **30**
Woodsley Rd. LS2: Leeds 4C **30**
LS3: Leeds 4C **30**
LS6: Leeds 4C **30**
Woodsley Ter. LS2: Leeds 1A **4** (4E **31**)
Woods Row LS28: Pud 4G **27**
Woodstock Cl. LS16: Leeds 6B **12**

A-Z Leeds 111